RADCLIFFE BIOGRAPHY SERIES

Buying the Night Flight

The Autobiography of a Woman Foreign Correspondent

Georgie Anne Geyer

A Merloyd Lawrence Book
DELACORTE PRESS/SEYMOUR LAWRENCE

A MERLOYD LAWRENCE BOOK

Published by Delacorte Press/Seymour Lawrence
1 Dag Hammarskjold Plaza
New York, N.Y. 10017

Portions of this book were first published, in a different form, in *The Young Russians* by Georgie Anne Geyer (Copyright © 1975 by ETC Publications) and her article "Enemies" in *The Progressive*.

Manufactured in the United States of America

Designed by MaryJane DiMassi

Library of Congress Cataloging in Publication Data

Geyer, Georgie Anne, 1935–
  Buying the night flight.

  (Radcliffe biography series)
  "A Merloyd Lawrence book."
  Includes index.
    1. Geyer, Georgie Anne, 1935–   2. Foreign
correspondents—United States—Biography.   I. Title.
II. Series.
PN4874.G356A33   1983   070.4'33'0924[B]   82–14895
ISBN 0–440–00725–9
9 8 7 6 5 4 3

This book is dedicated, with the deepest love and gratitude, to the "old crowd" from Chicago and Northwestern. Without their faithful support, their affection, and their wonderful humor, I could never have wandered so far and so creatively:

Georgia and Dale Goetz, Joan and Howard Ritter, Winifred and James Reidy, Bertha Siegle and all the Siegles, the Lengeriches, the Beukes and the Biallises, Ann Moroff Borman and her family, Jody and Bruno Vovrich, Mary McDermott, Harriet Ellis, Trudi Blum, Don Purdy, Bill Evans, Aura Shaffer, Mary and Jack Shaffer, Louis Hanzelka, Alice Slusser, Phil Ryan, George Nett, Lynne and Don Basta, Carol and Gerald Petersen, Lucy and Kenneth Wiesner, Frieda and Charles Dettling, Hans and Rose Koops, Emery and Beth Biro, Clarice and Rolf Stetter, Marcia and Frances Wojtynek, Estelle Rejak, Robert Ludwig, Catherine Watgen, William Bromfield, John Bramson, and (last but by far not least) Gary Paulson.

ACKNOWLEDGMENTS

Above all I want to acknowledge and thank Deane Lord, director of the Harvard News Office, for it was her creative genius and vision that gave birth to the Radcliffe series on women, and it was her canny wit that kept my own project going. Without her it would certainly not have been possible.

I also want to thank my wonderful assistants, who helped me at the different stages of this book: Muriel Southerland, Cynthia Gallagher, Tam Mehuron, and Didi Schanche, all of whom typed and copied and carried things around with perseverance, grace, and good humor. Their advice on a "woman's" book was sound and valuable.

Foreword

      Radcliffe College is pleased and proud to sponsor the Radcliffe Biographies, a series of lives of extraordinary American women.

      Each volume of the Radcliffe Biographies serves to remind us of two of the values of biographical writing. A fine biography is first of all a work of scholarship, grounded in the virtues of diligent and scrupulous research, judicious evaluation of information, and a fresh vision of the connections between persons, places, and events.

      Beyond this, fine biographies give us both a glimpse of ourselves and a reflection of the human spirit. Biography illuminates history, inspires by example, and fires the imagination to life's possibilities. Good biography can create for us lifelong models. Reading about others' experiences encourages us to persist, to face hardship, and to feel less alone. Biography tells us about choice, steadfastness, and chance.

      The women whose lives are told in the Radcliffe Biographies have been teachers, adventurers, writers, scholars. The lives of some of them were hard pressed by poverty, cultural heritage, or physical handicap. Some of the women achieved fame; the victories and defeats of others have been unsung. Some of the women lived and died years ago; others are our contemporaries. We can learn from all of them something of ourselves. In sponsoring this series, Radcliffe College is responding to the renewed interest of our society in exploring and understanding the experience of women.

The Radcliffe Biographies project found its inspiration in the publication in 1971 of *Notable American Women,* a scholarly encyclopedia sponsored by Radcliffe's Schlesinger Library on the History of Women in America. We became convinced that some of the encyclopedia's essays should be expanded into full-length biographies, so that a wider audience could grasp the many contributions women have made to American life—an awareness of which is as yet by no means universal. It seemed appropriate that an institution dedicated to the higher education of women should initiate such a project, to hold a mirror up to the lives of particular women, to pay tribute to them, and so to deepen our understanding of them and of ourselves.

We have been joined in this project by two distinguished publishing houses and by a remarkable group of writers. I am grateful to them and to the editorial board—and particularly to Deane Lord, who first proposed the series, both in concept and in detail. Finally, I am happy to present this volume of the Radcliffe Biographies.

MATINA S. HORNER
President
Radcliffe College
Cambridge, Massachusetts

Contents

Introduction

You'd have to say the odds were enormous and discouraging. In 1960 a Chicago bookie might have given 1,000 to 1 against Georgie Anne Geyer—Gee Gee, as her friends call her—ever being in the position to write this dazzling book.

Consider what she was up against.

Her ambition was to be a foreign correspondent. Fine. Most newspaper reporters want, at one time or another, to be foreign correspondents. It's the ultimate reporting challenge, covering another country, a war, a revolution. It's always been the glamor job of newspapering.

The problem was (and still is) that only a relative handful of one thousand or so American daily newspapers had foreign reporters on their staff. The others picked up the news wires.

And those who had the foreign assignments dug in and kept them until death or retirement. A city-staff reporter could grow too old just waiting for an opening.

Beyond the lack of opportunity, though, there was the simple fact that most reporters—even the very good ones—weren't good enough. Foreign correspondents had to be outstanding reporters, exceptional writers, self-motivators, imaginative, determined, adventurous, able to cover a war or a fast-breaking revolution, and do a scholarly analysis of a country's history—but written so clearly that a subway commuter could understand it.

And add to that Gee Gee's most serious handicap—as an old rewrite man at the *Chicago Daily News* put it: "Her sexual persuasion."

She was a female when females on newspaper staffs were just about as common as snail darters.

I should correct that. There were women on newspapers. You could find them in the "women's pages" writing fluff about fashions and home furnishings and raising children. Women's work, the editors called it.

But out in the newsroom—and the *Chicago Daily News* was typical of major newspapers of that era—a woman was as rare as a teetotaler.

A woman would usually have the education beat. The editors' thinking was that since most teachers were women, and they dealt with children, covering them really wasn't a manly job.

And there would be one or two women on general assignment. But it was a specialized form of general assignment. A tragedy occurs? Send one of the women to do a three-handkerchief sob story. Political campaigns? Have a woman interview the candidates' wives. Ditto for the wives of ball players and other celebrities.

If necessity required that one of the females cover a major story, the headline usually began: "Our Gal at . . ."

This was the man's world into which Gee Gee somehow elbowed her way more than two decades ago, emerging from the women's pages a tough, determined, brilliant young reporter, cleverly concealed behind an irrepressible smile, apple cheeks, and honey-blond hair.

"She's nuts," we all laughed, in our basso voices, when Gee Gee made clear her intentions to become a foreign correspondent. The *Daily News* was fortunate to have a small but highly regarded foreign service in those days.

We were still chuckling when she managed to get herself assigned to South America.

But the laughter subsided when Gee Gee began trooping into the mountains for exclusive interviews with revolutionaries, when she demonstrated her uncanny ability to sense where the big story was going to break next, and when she began filing those sensitive, perceptive interviews that have become her trademark.

As Professor Henry Higgins might have exulted, for the wrong reasons, of course: "By God, she did it!"

And she did. After a while we began taking for granted the Geyer exclusive from this or that Latin American country. If someone was going to beard Fidel in his den, we knew it would be Gee Gee.

As the years passed Latin America wasn't big enough to hold her and she became one of those genuine, and rare, globe-hopping correspondents. The Middle East, Russia, Poland, Africa—wherever the dateline originated, the quality was unsurpassed. She had not only become a foreign correspondent, she had become a great one.

She made it look easy. So easy, in fact, that even her friends didn't know how tough a job she had: The long process of studying the countries, the developing of news sources, the weeks, months, even years, of painfully inching toward that impossible interview. The stories she filed barely hinted at the dangers, the discomforts, the grueling hours, the personal sacrifices.

This book, which should be read by anyone interested in foreign affairs, journalism, and the professional growth of a woman—as well as anyone who wants to read one hell of an exciting story—finally tells us what it was like.

Gee Gee is now a syndicated columnist based in Washington. But that doesn't mean she is a Washington columnist. Not if that means working the cocktail parties, the dinner parties, the press clubs, the carefully rehearsed official briefings.

That's not Gee Gee's style, thank goodness. Her style is still to grab a suitcase and catch the next plane.

BUYING THE NIGHT FLIGHT

So we still don't know where Gee Gee's byline might pop up next. El Salvador? Warsaw? Oman?

But we do know that wherever it originates, her name on the story means we're getting the best.

MIKE ROYKO
Chicago

I.

To Die in Guatemala

> "The guerrilla war in the mountains . . . is the only
> way to revolution."
> —FIDEL CASTRO

The hut they led us away to that moonless midnight was a long wooden shack that stood alone in the forest. It sat on the far corner of one of the aristocrat's big haciendas, and the sardonic joke of the whole thing was not lost on us—we were with the Guatemalan guerrillas and the _hacendados_ or landowners were precisely the people the guerrillas were sworn to destroy.

As we groped in the darkness, we found a hard dirt floor which was used mostly for storing machinery. It must be little used and the area sparsely populated, or else why would they bring us here? Miguel, our guide, led us with a very dim lantern into a small separate room at the end of the hut. In it stood two canvas cots with blankets, and not much else. There we were. Henry Gill, the fine photographer who worked closely and collegially with me on the _Chicago Daily News_, was already getting testy over this whole unwholesome situation. Our guide, the mysterious Miguel, a handsome, curly-haired young student obviously of excellent lineage, carrying an attaché case full of obscure books, was playing the revolutionary game to the hilt. He would do at least one thing we wouldn't do: he would eventually die for its curious satisfactions.

Miguel left us for a moment, then returned with two rough-hewn

1

pots which he delicately placed several feet apart in the other room. *"El servicio,"* he said with a comical gesture. One was for me, one was for Henry. It did not bother me in the slightest, but Henry was mortified. I was far more worried about other things, like getting out of this whole thing alive.

"You are to remain here for twenty-four hours," Miguel told us in a low whisper before he left. "We'll come for you tomorrow night. While you're here you must observe absolute silence. There will be workers on the hacienda passing right by the shack from the early-morning hours on. Some might come into the other room for tools. We'll bring you food when it's safe." Then he bade us sleep well and was gone into the opaque black night that was all we yet knew or felt of the Sierra de las Minas.

As he turned and twisted and tried to settle down on his canvas cot in the darkness, Henry kept muttering, "We must be out of our minds, we must be out of our minds." I couldn't, in truth, totally disagree with him.

For my part I curled up on my cot too, but only after taking a sleeping pill and accommodating myself psychologically to the new situation. In situations like this I reconnoiter the territory like an animal, sometimes only in my mind, and make my peace with it by absorbing it into myself and making it mine. I was doing that as I lay there, and soon I was perfectly and even peacefully part of this new place and time.

That left me free to acknowledge and experience several other waves of feelings. I felt a tremendous, euphoric excitement because I knew that we were on our way and that it was unlikely now that anything could turn us back. I also felt the journalist's special excitement of doing something that not only had not been done before but that would be of encompassing interest. Only two months before I had stood in the Plaza de la Revolución in Havana, listening to Fidel Castro rant before 300,000 persons, "The guerrilla war in the mountains . . . is the only way to revolution. The people of Latin America will see that we were right." Now Henry and I were part of that revolution, which had the added piquancy that it was also a revolution our own country was trying desperately to destroy.

The morning broke bright and hot through the shutters, and the long, tedious day came and went slowly, very slowly. We waited there like Trappists, each lost in his and her own thoughts and feelings about this strange adventure. I ate whenever they brought food and found it good: campesino black beans squeezed out of a plastic bag onto tortillas, fried meat, boiled eggs, plain white bread, and strong coffee. But Henry refused adamantly to eat and I observed (for only one of many times) how much more finicky men are than women in situations such as this. In the muted whispers in which we occasionally communicated, he argued that he might get sick if he ate. *I* argued cogently that he would be too weak to take the trip if he didn't eat.

"Try a boiled egg," I insisted at one point. "How can a boiled egg hurt you?" I sat there peeling them and eating them.

"All right, all right," he finally growled, as one might placate a nagging wife. He hit an egg on his knee to break it and the gooey fluid ran all down his pants leg. He had got the only uncooked egg in the batch and smelled very much like rotten eggs during the whole trip. I kept my advice to myself from then on.

By nightfall we had both grown edgy. This was as far into the details of the plan as we had been entrusted and, trust notwithstanding, one had to wonder what would come next. "Put-yourself-in-their-hands" seemed the only possible approach to guerrilla journalism; but it did not rule out moments of doubt and even terror.

At 11:00 P.M. we heard stirrings outside. Was it the *hacendados* or the military? My throat closed. But it was Miguel. "We're going," he whispered, still cheerful, and we started walking up a side road. Then suddenly the word went along the line of twenty-nine men in Spanish. "Everyone down." We lay for an hour in the cornfield, as a new moon inched up over the trees, while every soldier and police-man, rightist terrorist, and American official in Guatemala was searching for us. That was how it all began.

3

*   *   *

Actually, of course, the situation had begun a long time ago. One would have to say it began that day four hundred years ago when the Spanish conquistadores marched down from Mexico to take the rich Mayan outpost cities of Guatemala. But while the other Latin American countries, led by Mexico in its 1910 revolution, eventually changed the traditional oppressive triumvirate of dictator-church-landowner and moved well on the way to becoming prosperous modern societies, only Guatemala, along with El Salvador and Nicaragua (and Paraguay on the continent), remained in this squalid feudal isolation.

By the time we got there in 1966, while the rest of Latin America was on the move—changing, developing, spurred on by each country's own internal impulses and by the excitement of John F. Kennedy's "Alliance for Progress"—Guatemala was not only stagnating, it was actually moving resolutely backward. In 1950, to cite just one indicator, 70 percent of the people had lived on a subsistence level. By 1963, 73 percent lived at that level. You could not even argue "trickle down" here.

At the bottom of everything lay the huge Indian mass—65 percent of the population, stubborn, long-suffering, fatalistic, and jealously protective of old customs that had remained unchanged since the Spaniards came. It was this inert mass that allowed the military, sometimes cynically employing the fig leaf of a party and often without one, over and over again to overthrow democratic regimes without the danger of any public uprising. It was this mass—its ignorance, its disease, its isolation, and its utter passivity—that shamed the university students and intellectuals and sent them into the hills in the 1960s as guerrillas. It was this mass that brought us there.

But we were dealing with far more than just another guerrilla movement, or else it would certainly not have been worth the time, the expense, and the danger. We were seeing firsthand what could be *the* next post-Castro guerrilla movement of our era in Latin America, and the first one in Central America. Since Guatemala had

had for a brief moment in 1954 a Communist government, the FAR guerrilla movement was looked upon by most analysts and diplomats as the next "Castroite" movement to attempt to take power. And if that happened, it would mean that Castro was not a single, isolated factor at all, but a movement that could crumble the stability of the Western Hemisphere with the force of his charisma, the simplicity of his message of revolution, and, of course, his guns. This was what we were testing, and, though doubtless it was more dramatic "to die in Spain" during the Spanish civil war, in the sixties in Latin America "to die in Guatemala" was a respected business.

How does one make contact with an underground guerrilla movement in a country where every security force is searching for them —and more than eager to kill to find them? By looking around. I mean *really* looking around. One must psych out the society and judge where are the weak points, the soft spots, the places where one can probe and possibly make a breakthrough.

But when I went to Guatemala to make contact the first time, in March of 1966, after studying the situation carefully I really couldn't find any weak spots. So I asked an old Guatemalan friend, a person who was extremely well connected politically, "Look, is there any way at all to make contact with the FAR?"

"It's highly unlikely," José María told me frankly, as his mind roved over the possibilities, "but I can give you one idea. I know a lawyer who is a member of the Communist Party, and I will call him for you. You go to see him—make a social call and mention *nothing* about his party connection—and at the end simply mention the fact you would like to see the guerrillas."

That same afternoon I was climbing the stairs in a modern building set in the picturesque old streets of downtown Guatemala City, and soon I was chatting amiably with a well-spoken man in his forties. At the end of an innocuous conversation I said directly but softly, looking him in the eye with an innocent manner, "I am very eager to meet some of the young revolutionaries. . . ."

He offered not a single giveaway gesture. "But you know I have

5

nothing whatsoever to do with them," he said, a trifle too fast but at the same time looking me straight in the eye.

"Oh, I know, I know that," I interjected.

"But it has been a pleasure meeting you," he said. "Do come by if there is anything I can really do for you."

As it happened—and as these things virtually always happen—I didn't have to "come by" again at all. The next day he appeared, suddenly and without warning, to have coffee with me at the hotel. And, strange, the day after that he called me in the morning and said he had a student leader friend I might like to meet. I was, of course, delighted and grateful.

It is always the same with these clandestine affairs. You make the contact, you behave correctly, you let yourself be known, you are as honest as humanly possible if only because the slightest suggestion of guile will immediately destroy the project and put you in danger, and you persist without giving the impression that you are nervously or abnormally overeager. It is a fine—a very fine—balance, and you fail to strike it at the danger of extreme loss. You're not playing games; you're playing with temperaments tuned to calculated and sometimes spontaneous brutality, all revolutionary collegiality one moment and calculated savagery the next. You have to realize that you as a human being are nothing to them because the cause is everything; these are people who dehumanize themselves in order, in *their* thoughts, to humanize or order the world in their image.

At 3:00 P.M. the next day Humberto, the student leader, "dropped by" again. This time we sat for a few minutes in the big overstuffed sofas in the Pan American Hotel's inner lobby, and he mentioned nonchalantly, "I would like to take you somewhere." I nodded without speaking.

We began by walking casually around the blocks near the beautiful old central plaza, with its fountains and its flowers and its whispers of the cruel ballads of the old conquistadores. Once he said to me in a low voice, "You are lucky. You are going to see someone important." I nodded. I still assumed I was simply going to see some of the Communist students.

6

Then we got into a car with a driver and rode a few blocks.

Then we got out of the car and walked around the block precisely three times and waited under a tree.

Then we got into a station wagon and drove for two hours around the city, gradually easing our way to the outskirts. I had lost my sense of direction and bearings completely by now.

Then we drove down dirt roads and stopped several times. When no cars came, we drove on.

As this dramatic ballet continued, I became more and more fascinated. I didn't feel afraid, which in retrospect was quite foolish. Instead, I felt intensely alive, with nerves whizzing and singing and blood flowing. Indeed the process in itself became so interesting to me that I very nearly forgot the purpose and end of our odyssey.

Two and a half hours after Humberto had picked me up at the hotel, we walked into an unfinished, creaking modern house somewhere in the suburbs and sat down on a simple cot and some stools. Almost immediately two very young, very eager, and almost merry young men swept in, doors banging behind them, with all the casualness of a neighbor dropping in on a summer afternoon in Wisconsin. It was as if the wind had suddenly dropped some brightly colored leaves at my feet, instead of the dark wraiths of history they actually were.

There was the notorious Luis Turcios, a lithe, liquid figure wearing a stylish black sweater, black pants, and white shirt and tie. A handsome young man, he carried about him a distinct joie de vivre. With him was the slight, blond, intense Cesar Montes, who had the pitiless air of "the revolution" engraved on his every action, instilled in his cold eyes and in each taut answer.

Montes, indeed, struck me as so thoroughly different from Turcios that I had to wonder—and this question has recurred to me constantly in nearly two decades of interviewing "revolutionaries"— what they had in common besides revolution. Montes was only about five feet tall, with high cheekbones and moody, sulky eyes. He occasionally wore glasses and then he looked scholarly and deceptively young. But after a few hours with him I realized he had a certain forcefulness as a leader.

Turcios, on the other hand, was full of the very devil, in love with being a "revolutionary" and in love with life. His ideology was fuzzy, and he called himself a "Communist without a party." There was no such relativity about Montes or his ideas. He knew exactly where he was going. He was a member of the central committee of the Guatemalan Communist Party, even at his young age; and although his family background was shrouded in a mystery that he most definitely encouraged, it was believed that his parents were originally Mexican Communists.

He and Montes began by explaining their classical "three-stage" movement. "Now we are only entering the first stage," said Montes. "We are teaching the peasants and preparing for the moment when we can fight the army and take power. The second stage will be to transform the guerrilla war to a regular war, and the third stage is the general offensive when the whole people will rise in regular and irregular fashion."

Turcios, who, with so many other Third World revolutionaries, had studied as a Guatemalan soldier at Fort Benning (and insisted that the experience taught him a good deal), explained that they were already building *"focos"* or centers of resistance in the rough, barren Sierra de las Minas area east of Guatemala City. From there, the dream went, their "peasant army" would sweep down eventually upon Guatemala City just as Castro's army had ostensibly swept onto Havana in 1959.

In years to come I was to infiltrate and write about most of the major guerrilla movements in the world, but this one was to turn out to be archetypical and even prophetic. Their strategy was to become one of the major strategies of those fanaticized young men and women of all of the developing world—and, as it happened, I was the first outsider to see and study it in a Central America that would soon be in flames just because of young people like them.

We talked for two hours before Humberto, our driver, and I drove back to the hotel in silent satisfaction. Mine, indeed, was so great

8

that I could scarcely contain it. I had no idea why I had been chosen from the list of eight correspondents who had somehow gotten their names to "the movement," but never mind. I had the interview and I had it at the most difficult and dangerous time.

It would be nice to say that at times like this I thought only of conveying information to the world, but that, frankly, would not be true. That responsibility is certainly the dedication of my life; but I have to admit that first I felt only the most delighted sense of personal accomplishment. I sat in my simple little room at the Pan American, with its woven Guatemalan spreads and heavy furniture, and laughed aloud out of sheer joy. The laugh seemed to hang for a moment in the silence. Then I walked around and looked at myself in the mirror. I walked out on the balcony, and the whole bustling world down on those narrow streets seemed lovable and friendly, even though I had spent most of the day talking with people whose lives were devoted to killing. Such are the crazy little victories of journalists!

At moments like this the sacrifices one makes to be a foreign correspondent—husband, children, the house with the view of the lake, the comforts of normalcy, and the reassurances of conformity—seemed, quite simply, irrelevant. The joy is a matter both of personal transcendence and at the same time of a deep penetration of the world: of an odd sense of movement both ways.

I wrote the interview—or it wrote itself, really—in less than an hour. By then it was still only 8:00 P.M., and the plane to El Salvador, where I had to go in order to file safely, did not leave until 11:30 P.M. So I tucked the story away in my purse, dressed up, and went off to an elegant cocktail party at the American residence given by the American ambassador, John Gordon Mien. I took an almost catlike pleasure in chatting, drinking, and wondering together with my fellow correspondents about where Turcios could be, when all the while I had him quite literally tucked away in my pocketbook.

A short while later Ambassador Mien, a splendid man, was killed by Turcios's men. By then Turcios also had died, ostensibly in an auto accident. Guatemala in those days was an endless celebration of dying, and I was soon to be tentatively included in the program.

Since the Turcios interview was widely published and had worked so well, I expected no trouble at all when Henry Gill and I returned to Guatemala that next fall. But when I telephoned Humberto at home, he sounded a little put-off and strange. "I'm going to be at the hotel at noon," he said hurriedly and with a weak voice, "I'll meet you then."

It turned out that he was going to be at the hotel for the weekly *Rotarian luncheon*! Humberto, my guerrilla page, my first revolutionary, my leader into the clandestine labyrinths—in six miserable months he had been graduated from the university, had been reformed into a bourgeois, had gone into his father's business, and become a Rotarian! My tempestuous lady of the afternoon had become a Tupperware saleswoman!

The chargé at the embassy cordially warned me of the danger of "what we know you are trying to do."

The police chief of Guatemala City looked sideways at me and gazed at me for a long time at a public meeting.

Meanwhile I was having no luck at all in making new contacts. And I was getting nervous.

By the time two weeks had gone by, I was growing discouraged. We were too obvious, and I had not been able to make even one miserable contact.

It was seven on a bright Sunday morning when the woman manager of the hotel knocked on my door. In a low voice she said, "I thought you should know—some detectives are downstairs looking for you." It was precisely all we needed.

I telephoned Henry and we decided to walk boldly downstairs. It wasn't difficult to pick out the two detectives (let God be my witness) because they were standing *behind two potted palms*!

There was always this Keystone Cops/banana republic aspect of Guatemala, but I knew all too well how lethally "comic" it really was: how many hundreds of mutilated bodies of prominent and

10

not-so-prominent people appeared in alleys in the dark of the night, some killed by the Left, some by the Right, some through the intervening providence of some private passion that often did not answer to, but used, any ideology around.

The two skinny, illiterate kids behind the palm trees had obviously been given the job of following us everywhere. We'd be walking down a street and suddenly Henry would pivot around and snap their pictures, while they would break out into peals of laughter. They hid behind bushes for us, waved through the leaves, and flirted with me.

We would walk in one side of the cathedral with appropriate dignity, then dash out the side door and lose them.

It was all endlessly diverting, but it was a deadly, defeating diversion. I understood their tactics all too well: no one from the guerrillas would dare to contact us so long as the skinny ones were about. That was their final card in this strange game.

And it was precisely then, during that already irksome period, that the desk clerk one morning handed me a letter. I opened it and saw the outline of a hand drawn across it. It was a letter from the "White Hand," the infamous "Mano Blanca," the rightist killer organization directed clandestinely by the big landowners and by the military and in particular by Colonel Carlos Arana, later to become president of the country. The "Mano" killed and mutilated everybody it suspected even of sympathizing with democracy, much less with Marxism.

And the letter? Naturally it was filled with dirty sexual references —this is the way Latin men deal with women who get in their way or break from the macho's cosmic plan for them.

"We are speaking to you as we speak to the men of America; we are telling you the entire truth so that you believe what we say and not just to frighten you," the letter began. "Since you arrived in the country before the elections in March, the services of security, the A1, the G2, the army, the Interpol, and the private espionage of the MDL and the White Hand knew that you had arrived in the country to spy. . . ." (At this point I paused to notice that I was even a little pleased by the sheer weight and variety of the attention I was

11

receiving.) It went on, with frequent references to me as a *"puta"* or "whore," something that also rather pleased me since I had always resented my Illinois corn-fed looks. Then it went on to warn: "Now you are being watched, body and soul; wherever you go, there are eyes following you. Only a few days ago, four men were waiting for you to take you to a night interview, but you did not trust them, and it was a shame that you didn't go because we would have given you chase, you spy, and we hope you will go to a guerrilla camp because upon leaving the city for the mountains, you will never again return and your death will appear an accident during a gallant adventure." But I was considerably aggravated by the fact that they then accused me of also being the "mistress" of the former rightist dictator, one Colonel Peralta. It is one thing to have one's politics attacked, but Colonel Peralta, a little, gray-haired gnome of a man, was one of the least attractive men I had ever seen.

Now everyone in Guatemala City obviously knew where we were, who we were, and why we were. For the first time, I forced myself to contemplate the unthinkable—that we just might not be able to do it. Henry and I passed days sitting lethargically in the lobby, drinking beer and feeling "eyes" on all sides. Worst of all by far was the humiliating thought of returning to Chicago without the story.

But, as it happened, just then our luck broke. The guerrillas got word through one of the contacts I'd made and contacted me by phone (in Guatemala, at least then, phone-tapping was not a problem) and we spoke in German. Since our skinny detective guards went home for lunch and dinner every day, I made a date to meet the envoys—two very young, very polite students—in a coffeehouse during the lunch hour. This ruse somehow worked. I suggested we leave the country (to El Salvador), and leave very obviously and ostentatiously, as though we had given up. They gave us the name of a third-class hotel in which to stay upon our return and arranged to contact us there on the following Sunday morning. When we left, we kissed so many people good-bye, it was like a Mafia wedding. And we draped ourselves in such a sad air of failure that our hunters apparently were properly confused.

In El Salvador we rented a Volkswagen and, in a frenzy of activity, prepared immediately to start the eight-hour drive back to Guatemala. But when we went to the Guatemalan embassy, we had another moment of terror. It was Saturday and the consulate was closed; we couldn't get our Guatemalan tourist cards until Monday and our rendezvous with the guerrillas was on Sunday. If we missed this meeting, it would be virtually impossible to re-create it.

Henry looked at me. I looked at him. I almost cried, and then he got an inspiration.

"We'll go to Pan American and buy plane tickets to Guatemala and get our tourist cards from them," he said. And the next morning we were indeed in our third-class hotel in Guatemala City talking to Miguel, the German-speaking, upper-class guerrilla who would be our guide.

Now we could only wait—until that moment when they would come for us. The hotel, one of those back-street hostelries that seemed created deliberately for intrigue, was our prison. We did not dare go out for fear of being seen. The staircases creaked. The dining room was always deathly silent, and everyone entering was followed by suspicious looks that slid and slithered from eye to eye and from table to table. And then there was the bellboy.

It was perhaps not unnatural that my nerves were on edge. One night I heard a slight movement at my door—just enough of a rustling to terrify me. I looked out the keyhole and looked into two eyes. For a moment I thought I might faint. Then I swung open the door to find myself facing the little, pockmarked, phantomlike bellboy, who, I had noticed, had a certain feral look about him. We finally decided he was simply a twenty-three-year-old voyeur—exactly the next thing I needed.

By this time no one except one Guatemalan friend knew where we were. We were out of touch with the office and I left dated letters to be sent to my family, who had no idea what I was doing. If anything had happened to us, only my friend would have known or could even have guessed it.

Then one day they came for us. "This is the time," Miguel said

13

with a strange smile, half excited and half wistful. But there was still more waiting. In a small *bodega,* or bar, they left us for four hours that seemed an eternity. "This is some kind of ruse," Henry kept insisting, suspended between anger and frustration. And in many ways it was this last waiting that turned out to be the most frustrating: Could it be that even *now* it might not work?

But I also knew that we had gone too far now to turn back—and that gave me a strange new feeling of repose. A major rule of dealing with revolutionary movements is this: You put yourselves in their hands and you demonstrate every kind of trust. (This, of course, comes *after* you have made all your careful calculations.) For all intents and purposes you no longer have any will of your own. In our case our lives and wills were quite simply held in abeyance—held captive by these fanaticized, inexperienced, idealistic, often cruel, often immensely kind, sometimes crazy young men. Already two Americans, Ronald Hornberger and Robert Moran, were known to be dead; they were killed in trying to make contact with these very "boys." One was most probably an innocent scholar, the other probably a Vietnam veteran bent on revenge. We really never knew everything.

And sometimes it was simply better not to think too far ahead. I called the waiter and asked for another sandwich and beer. And after four hours they came for us.

Twenty-nine persons stood up, slim profiles thrown against the sky, with packs on their backs and machine guns thrown casually over their shoulders.

"The *compañera* is ready," one of the boys joked. "I'm calling her *compañera* already." *Compañera*—the Spanish term for female comrade. It seemed I was accepted.

The group fell into line. There was one group of armed guerrillas in the front, another behind, and our "unit" in the center. "Follow the person directly in front of you," they told us. "Make no sound. And show no lights."

It would have been a splendid idea to follow the person in front

14

of you if you could have seen the person in front of you. But it was midnight and the sliver of a moon was sliding rapidly behind the trees. Somewhat to our surprise—and soon to our horror—we found that the guerrillas used no paths or roads. Their idea of going up a mountain was simply going up a mountain. Up the rocks, over the bushes, through the thorns, down into the canyons!

As absurd as it sounds now, I had on only flat walking shoes. I wore brown pants and a light blouse with a patterned sweater over it. Most of the time I looked simply terrible, and every once in a while I had to creep away and vomit, while Henry, who was very proper about manners, would look at me with an expression that was a mixture of reproachfulness and "I-told-you-so" embarrassment. I was not embarrassed. I was just intent upon getting through the whole thing. But the final absurdity was my black purse. I have always carried a certain type of good, practical black purse with pockets in the sides where I can put my various notebooks and cards. Of course I carried this black purse to the mountains. It was a friendly, familiar thing in this strange new world.

For the next four hours we staggered, we fell into ditches, we dragged through creeks, we climbed huge rocks and generally suffered for what seemed an eternity. "We had thought of taking you farther into the *montaña*," Cesar said to me once, with a distinctly ironic twist on his lips, "but we decided the walk would be too hard for you." It struck me that I'd never heard a wiser decision. At 4:00 A.M., just as I was wondering whether I could go any farther, Cesar declared, "All right, we'll stop and sleep here." He motioned toward a grassy place on the side of the mountain; it seemed to bother him not a whit that it was sloped at a forty-five-degree angle.

He curled up in a checkered blanket with his machine gun in his arms and promptly fell asleep next to Henry. Henry complained later that Cesar's machine gun dug into his ribs all night. I complained that every time I tried to relax on the slope, I began sliding down —and that directly beneath me was a sixty-foot drop into a canyon with a waterfall. When morning came two hours later, all around my feet were gullies where I had dug into the mountain to keep myself from sliding off of it.

The next three days that we spent with the FAR were among the strangest of my life. I felt totally suspended in time—I no longer was sure what or where I was. We spent our days sitting around in the sunlight chattering endlessly in Spanish. Henry took pictures of guerrillas jumping, guerrillas talking, guerrillas posed for battle. All around us were the three thousand troops the army had sent out— we could hear their shooting all day long. It was we whom they were seeking. The days had a certain rhythm and timing. Three times a day the old peasant man would come. He would deliver the sacks of tortillas and the plastic bags filled with bean paste. Then he would sit back on a rock for a full hour gazing fondly at the young rebels.

"Tell me," I asked him finally, "why do you help the guerrillas?"

This time he climbed down from the rock with apparent eagerness and walked over to me. "For humanitarian love," he said. He looked me straight in the eye as he added, "They are the first ones who ever cared about us."

Cesar, so slim, so sure, so cool, then motioned to another, younger peasant who had come up with the older man. "Tell her everything," he said emotionlessly.

"Do you have any land?" I asked the younger man, as he scrambled dutifully down to face me.

"We pay twenty-five dollars a year to the landlord for the land . . ." he began. (That was a lot, given their meager incomes.)

Montes cut in. "The landlord they never see," he added scornfully. "They have just enough land to live on a subsistence level."

"We're not allowed to live in our village anymore," the peasant began again.

"For helping us—they were forced to move here," Montes inserted. "The police burned their houses, and burned down their chapel—they are Evangelicals."

The peasant nodded. "And they destroyed our honeybees. I was four months a prisoner."

"Did they torture you?" the guerrilla commander asked.

16

"No," he said, shaking his head. "But my brother—they put that thing over his head and hit him."

"That thing" was a bag they wrapped over a prisoner's head until he couldn't breathe. Meanwhile they were beating him until he was almost dead, or frightened nearly to death from fear of asphyxiation.

"My boy, he was eighteen, died of malnutrition while I was in jail. One of my relatives had to pay one hundred fifty dollars to get free. I only had to pay eighty dollars."

Cesar and his men kept prodding the peasants: "Remember this . . . Remember Justo de la Cruz, whom they killed and he didn't even know us . . . Think of all the injustices. . . ."

It was an effective teaching method, I could see that. Besides, they were organizing the village into political cells, even though the final word came from the directorate general in the capital.

Most of the guerrillas had been to Cuba for some training, but when I asked Cesar about money from Cuba, he drew himself up proudly and said, "Haven't you read about our bank robberies and our kidnappings? We're entirely self-supporting."

"Say," Montes went on, "did you know the robbery of the Bank of the Occident was by the FAR? The papers say forty thousand dollars, but we haven't finished counting the money yet." He paused devilishly. "The bank was right in front of the police station," he added, grinning.

Another time Montes pressed me for what I thought of Fidel Castro. I demurred. I never did believe in expressing my own beliefs while on assignment. Finally he demanded, "Don't you think he's a big egocentric?"

"Well, frankly, I do," I relented.

"I do, too," Montes said with a big smile. "But we won't be like that."

I looked long and hard at him. I didn't say anything more. In years to come I would hear that phrase—"We won't be like that, we will be different"—so many, many sad times.

Little by little I drew them out on their *acciónes*, trying to find out what they really did—and how they justified it.

17

There had been an "action" at Jocotales, for instance, a small working-class district of Guatemala City where the guerrillas' "city resistance unit" had attacked that November, killing three of the policemen in ten minutes of steady machine-gunning of the miserably poor adobe section. One of the men killed was a young sergeant, Rigoberto Parazzoli, and he was buried in a military funeral that punctuated the suffering and the senselessness of so much of all that was going on. His body was carried to the cemetery on the shoulders of a police guard while his widow sobbed and tiny barefoot boys sold water in tin cans for the flowers—five centavos a can.

He was carried past the tombs of all the assassinated political leaders of the last two decades, for here the cemetery is the *Who's Who* of Guatemalan politics . . . Colonel F. Javier Arana, hero of the Right in the 1940s (assassins never apprehended). . . . Mario Mendez Montenegro, hero of the democratic Left until he died mysteriously in 1965 (case never solved). . . . The list was endless, the tombs are solid rock, the assassins were in the palace.

After the funeral, where the sergeant was praised as a man who "defended Guatemala from political restlessness," Henry and I drove out to the police station, seeking out every bit of information and insight. A simple, honest-looking man, Lieutenant Antonio Anselmo Pineda, who was chief of the station, got up from an old wooden table and pointed out the holes in the ceilings and the small caves in the dirt floor where the grenades had exploded.

"What do you feel about the guerrillas?" I asked him frankly. "Do you feel any hatred for them for doing this?"

"Hatred?" he repeated, and he blinked his eyes. "No," he said slowly, in words that came to be haunting to me. "We don't know them. They don't know us. We wouldn't have attacked them, but they were attacking us. I don't know why they did it. I don't know what their motives were." He thought for a moment, and raised his eyes questioningly up to me. "Perhaps they know."

This touched me deeply. So few people could really understand the depths of this tragedy that had grown only more and more desperate over the last twenty years.

18

When I asked one of the more sensitive of the guerrillas about the sheer strategic sense of killing poor, ordinary policemen whom, after all, one might expect they were waging the revolution *for*, he responded by saying thoughtfully, "It is really very complex. If you kill a military officer, usually the people will agree with you. But if you kill a regular policeman, the people resent it. Very often the police are poor people themselves, who work on their days off painting houses and doing odd jobs, so they are well known. Too, we have to keep clarifying things. After we attacked the electric plant, the opposition phoned the firemen and threatened that we would attack them for putting out the fire at the electric plant. This was very clever because the people liked the firemen. We had to put out a statement saying it was not so."

The third day the shooting intensified. It was all around us, it was constant, and it was coming closer and closer. A barely perceptible nervous hum seemed to ride through our campsite like a phantom stallion. When I heard Cesar, Miguel, and the others speaking in Spanish about continuing to walk all night deeper into the mountains, I felt distinctly faint.

I was so exhausted from lack of sleep that I knew neither Henry nor I could do it, so I went over and sat down next to Cesar on the ground. "We've got to get out," I said. He looked at me—a long, harsh look—and shook his head.

"It will be very hard right now," he said thoughtfully, his eyes narrowed. "But do you really think you must?" I argued forcefully. After talking with some of the others, he returned to tell me, "We'll send two scouts back to see if we can get your car for two o'clock tomorrow morning. That means—*if we can do it*—that you'll have to start out about eight. We'll have to get you to the car so our men can get back here before dawn. It means . . ." He paused, and gave me another one of those looks. "It means going through the army lines twice."

Suddenly I awoke from the torpor and from the relative safety of those three strange days. Suddenly everything was again deadly serious. I realized that part of me feared going back, that in only those few days the side of that hill had come to be home, a protection, roots. Leaving was a new uprooting, a ripping up of a strange new security. There were no farewells; we shook hands with a hushed gravity. We all knew we would never see one another again, and I knew that for all the days of talk and interviewing I would also never really know who or what these young men really were or would be or do.

The walk out was even more grueling than the walk in. Once we had to pass within sixty feet of the outskirts of a village, Gallo, where we knew army troops were entrenched. As our little group of twelve passed by, a mangy horde of dogs in the village set up a resonant cacophony of baying. "Down," someone whispered, and the word traveled like a stone thrown through the column. For five or six minutes we all lay on our stomachs in the mud and waited. Although I had lost faith in any protective God some years before, I whispered a fervent prayer. We are all basically so weak.

No one came, and we crept by, phantoms in the charged night.

An hour later, after we had been pulling ourselves up the steep, often nearly vertical mountainsides by grabbing the dried, bristling stalks of the corn, the boy leading us admitted, *"Miren, compañeros . . .* look, comrades, I must be honest . . . we've lost our way."

He didn't need to say it. We had literally been going around in circles in the mountain; we were all exhausted, and the time for getting us out and getting them back was rapidly running out. At one point Henry was so worn out he sat down and said, "I'm staying here until morning."

I told him, "If you do that, the guerrillas will kill you. And if they don't, I will."

Gasping for breath and feeling our legs would not hold us, for four more hours we wandered on the stark, fall-away sides of that damnable mountain. More times than I care to recall, I asked myself, "Can I make it?" Could I even take another step? By the end when we finally got back in that opaque blackness to the "path" (whatever in God's name that was), one of the bigger guerrillas was literally

20

pulling me up and over the rocks and another was pulling Henry, who, however, doggedly refused to let them carry his beloved cameras!

My heart was pumping so hard that my breath came in spasms. Time after time I thought I could not take another breath. Occasionally we would stop and our guide would make a strange birdcall in the endless darkness of this hostile universe we had entered, to be sure we were not lost also from the rest of the group. Luckily, they always answered in the same call. Occasionally we would overhear someone in the darkness giving the code words: *"Guerra del Pueblo* —People's War."

Some ancient Mayan god must have led us, not much before 2:00 A.M., back to the same little road and to our little Salvadorean Volkswagen. I nearly cried for joy when I saw the squat, practical little car standing there, waiting, with that Germanic deliberation. Two well-dressed students were waiting there, and they drove us back to Guatemala City. It was over. The next day we drove out to El Salvador.

What came out of it all? Was it really all worth it?

Professionally the whole series was an incomparable success. It was printed all over the world, even in the Rumanian paper *Scinteia*, and I felt enormously gratified by the journalistic recognition. It also laid the basis for doing many other such things.

But I understood clearly the limit of our work. Ethically I was disturbed by the sheer impossibility of reporting the entire situation; I simply had to accept the fact that there was very little I could do about this. Of course I had found out a good deal about the Guatemalan government and military forces beforehand, but there was no further way, once I had been to the mountains, to report directly on activities of that side. I was a marked woman so far as they were concerned, and I still remain so.

The episode also taught me that you never really *can* outgrow your image. Roy Fisher, the *Daily News* editor and a man I admired immensely, wrote in his column at the time, "Hollywood couldn't

21

imagine a foreign correspondent like Georgie Anne Geyer, our man in Havana. She would be better cast as a pretty school teacher than as a cool, nerveless foreign correspondent who thrives on hazardous assignments." *Editor & Publisher* did an article on "Gee Gee Finds a Revolution," and repeated the schoolteacher part; they cast me as "your child's seventh grade teacher."

All my life I had tried to outlive my image as wholesome, blond, smiling girl next door. What more could I do than I now had done? I guess it all just goes to show that one is eternally stuck with oneself.

I did not return to Guatemala for several years. When I did, I contacted no one in the government and was very, very careful. Then I went back on vacation with my mother and some friends. By then I thought I had been forgotten and I gained what in retrospect was a foolish confidence. So I went back a third time, in 1972. That was the mistake.

One evening I was returning to the Camino Real Hotel after dining with one of my closest and dearest friends, the former Bolivian diplomat, Julio Sanjines. Julio is a unique spirit. He is a tall man of fine features and matching manners and intelligence whose aristocratic Spanish-Bolivian family had large land holdings in Bolivia before the revolution there in 1952. "We thought that by giving them the land right off, we could save the machinery," Julio used to joke. "But they took the machinery, too."

Julio and I had and have a special friendship that has prevailed across the years. We have always helped each other whenever one of us was in trouble. Each called the other and something just always happened to make things right again. It is an enormously precious thing.

This night, after a lovely dinner, he bade me farewell at the door and I crossed the elegant lobby, headed toward the elevator. At that moment a very tall, strung-out, dark man with the gaunt cheeks and sunken eyes of an El Greco character was headed toward the bar. Seeing him, I remembered clearly that he had been watching me that afternoon in the lobby. Now when he saw me, he made a swift, 180-degree turn and walked rapidly after me to the elevator. To my relief—the breath suddenly caught in my throat—the doors closed, seconds before he would have entered. On my floor, I ran from the elevator and opened my door as quickly as possible. As I rushed into the room, I heard the click of the elevator, signaling its opening, and the sound of his footsteps *running* down the hall toward me. Inside, I swiftly closed the door and somehow thought to secure the special bolt lock. Within seconds I heard him outside and saw the lock turning and turning—he had a key to the room! I stood there, utterly frozen, hearing the turning as though it were something deep in the furthest corridors of my mind. Only because I had secured the special lock was he unable to get in.

Then suddenly I could move again. I ran to the phone and told the desk to send some men up immediately, because someone was trying to break in. Within minutes they had sent a bellman. The El Greco man had evaporated. I also called Julio and he did something with the government—he never told me what, precisely—and came immediately to the hotel.

The man, ironically, was now in the bar. We dragged him out and confronted him at the desk. "But I am just a German businessman," he said, looking at me from behind those sunken cold eyes. "I got off on the wrong floor by mistake. My room is just above yours and I thought it was mine."

Julio took care of things. But that night, I half lay, half sat up against the wall of the room, trembling with fright. I knew that the Mano Blanca had tried finally to fulfill the portent of the old letter. But it was thwarted—Julio and a special lock had saved my life.

The bigger story of Guatemala and young guerrillas and American involvement will certainly not end in our lifetime—all of Central America was in flames by 1981 and eighty thousand by then had died in Guatemala alone—but the Guatemalan story continued for me in the summer of 1974, when I spent a fruitful week at the U.S. Army War College as a civilian guest at its annual defense seminar.

At one of the cocktail parties, on a glorious spring day on the perfectly manicured lawns, I noticed one of the young colonels studying me rather carefully. Finally he came over and asked, "Aren't you Georgie Anne Geyer?" When I nodded, puzzled, he laughed and said, "Well, I know you, but you don't know me."

The colonel turned out to be the officer who in 1966 had been the Special Forces adviser to the Guatemalan military at the brigade at Zacapa, the town nearest to where we were. This brigade was the one that eventually sent out every sort of military and civilian killer it could find to wipe out the guerrillas. The only trouble was that they were rather indiscriminate about the whole business: they managed to wipe out not only a few hundred guerrillas, but even by conservative embassy estimates at least ten thousand peasants just like the ones we had met.

It turned out that the American military officers on the scene, whom we identified in the stories by numbers if not by name, knew we were with the guerrillas. In fact, I learned that night, they were after us.

It was one of the stranger experiences of my life, but not untypical of our times, to sit there in a neat, pleasant, orderly American house on the army base at Carlisle Barracks, Pennsylvania, calmly discussing with this decent and thoughtful chap how he was encouraging and advising part of an army that was out to kill me. Not only was I being stalked by the Guatemalan military, I was being stalked by my own. And it was all too typical of the manner in which all too many Americans of my generation were to become so often angrily divided and alienated from our government.

At the end of the evening, after several drinks and a warming dinner and excellent conversation, he leaned forward and said, "You know, I was never sure that you weren't the one who was on the right side."

II.

Starting on the South Side

"Women have a much better time than men in this
world; there are far more things forbidden them."
—OSCAR WILDE

Like so many things, it all started with a small obsession.
When I was only seven or eight, I used to lie in my comfortable old
German bed at night, in every respect a most loved and blessed
child, and think about it. What, I would wonder for reasons I have
never totally understood, if only one person had the truth and that
person was a woman? She would not voice it because the women I
knew did not speak out; and so the world would be denied this
crucial truth.

Years later a famous Chicago architect told me that when he was
about the same age, he was tuning in to the same waves when he
also wondered, "If I knew the truth, would I tell it to a woman?"
Even to his mother? The male answer: "No."

The life I started with was circumscribed to create the perfect
young wife and mother. The expectations were clear, and until I was
well into adulthood, I never knew anyone who questioned them. In
the forties and fifties, there was no women's movement, and the old
feminist movement of the twenties had left little residue for our type
of world. Too, World War II had left the United States with men
who craved the hearth and women who craved their men.

25

My future seemed engraved in stone. I would be the first generation of our family to receive a college education. I might work for
no more than two or three years (but only as an "experience" in life,
certainly not to support myself or for the joy of some desired work),
and then I would marry some stable, nonabrasive, amiable, boy-next-
door "good provider" with whom I would settle down (nearby) and
raise no more than two children. They, in turn, would then proceed
to replace *my* life just as I had replaced my parents' lives.

When I was a young teen-ager—interested in all sorts of young
men—my aunts and cousins would assure me, with that intense
certainty of women throughout history, that this brief time would
pass and I, too, would be accepted as a wife in the world of men.
"You will be married before you are eighteen," they repeated solemnly. It was a promise and at the same time a benediction; it was
one's entire and only reason for living.

I remember with absolute clarity how I would look them straight
in the eye and say, quietly and respectfully but slowly and stubbornly, *"I will not!"*

But then I had always been extremely willful and often blindly
determined. When I was a baby, I in effect named myself. They
would say to me, "Georgie . . ." and I would say back, "Gee Gee,"
and that was the name that always stayed with me.

Perhaps it all never would have happened if the women around
me—women I loved very deeply—when asked their opinions on
something, even something domestic, wouldn't have always said
with such resigned submission, "I only think what Joe thinks." Or
Jim, or Bob, or Louie, or whichever "good provider" they had opted
for. I remember lying awake at night, not brooding but repeating to
myself with a deep obstinacy, "They won't get me." It was T. S.
Eliot's "Music heard so deeply that it's not heard at all."

Despite the fact that I was born in 1935 in the midst of the
Depression and that my parents did not have the fifty dollars to pay
the doctor, I was always what one would now call, like some bogus
FBI poster, a "wanted child." My adored brother, Glen, was ten
years old at the time, so I came as rather a surprise into a difficult

26

world. The country was collapsing into bits, and our family was not spared. Relatives moved in with parents or with the one person in the family who had work. We were lucky because my father had his own business and helped everyone else in quite extraordinarily generous ways. Across the ocean, darkness was settling over Europe and my brother would soon almost be killed in the near-sunset of Western civilization, but our immediate world remained solid. There was always about our family, and inside us, like a hard rock of certainty, a strong sense of good and evil, of white and black, of sureness about the world and the generosity that comes from that. Moreover, in concert with this was the absolute assurance that the United States was not just "a" country—the United States of America was the lodestone, the central planet from which the rest of the world spun off.

Our house, too, was the center of everything, and this does certain very special things for a child. It was just a little house, a simple dark brick bungalow no different physically from the endless streets of bungalows and big comforting trees on the Far South Side, but it was very different inside. Everyone came to us. We did virtually all of the entertaining, and in the summer everyone came to our Wisconsin summer home. It seemed quite natural, and it also gave me a strong, secure sense of "being" very early on. Because of an odd mixture of personalities in the family—a mixture that could have been as disastrous as it was creative—we were the first ones to try everything. Much, much later, when we were both adults and he had children of his own, my first boyfriend, Richard Siegle, said to me, "Your family did everything first. You water-skied first. You were the first to slice open the hot dogs before you barbecued them." Big, important things like that!

When my mother died in 1979, handing me the one unsustainable blow in life that I never quite believed would or could come, the minister praised her so correctly as a "woman who created neighborhoods" wherever she went. This was so true; it was a gift of God that was hers. But we were also infinitely blessed in our neighbors, who became—and still are—our real extended family. There were the

27

Siegle family next door, the Lengeriches across the alley (we had real alleys in those days too) and the Beukes and Bialleses next door. Our homes were extensions of each other. These wonderful people are still my rock and my solace.

But if ours was first of all a happy, prosperous family life, on the other hand hard work in the Germanic sense was expected of everybody, and everybody, moreover, was expected to *enjoy* it.

My father had a dairy business at 7749 South Carpenter Street that thrived precisely off the sheer amount of blood and sweat he and my grandmother, "Oma," poured into it. He would get up at three in the morning and run two of the most important routes, then come home for a big lunch that was really a European-style dinner, sleep, and go back to the dairy to work. Oma, who had come over from the German section of Poland near present-day Poznan in steerage when she was sixteen, heaved the milk pails around with the best of the men. But when she dressed up in her fine lace and beaded clothes, in her elegant big house with the Czechoslovakian china and the German crystal, she was the envy of any grand lady.

In contrast to the hardworking but fun-loving nature of the house, my religious life hovered like a slightly threatening angel. I was sent to a Baptist Sunday school with a straitlaced, terribly decent and highly puritanical family down the block. Not only did I believe in God, heaven, and angels, but I took totally to heart the Baptist maxim that one must also "convert" and "bear witness to" one's loved ones. Whenever my mother's father and mother came out from the North Side, I became anxious and puzzled. My grandfather, Carl Gervens, a lovely, gentle, scholarly man from the Rhineland, was a German socialist and skeptic. He was not about to be "saved." I simply did not know what to do.

But this early experience with religious absolutism is not something I really regret. It helped me to gain a strong moral sense—and a sense that life was meant to be a dedication, not simply a pastime. When, during my university years, I gradually lost an organized faith, it was a great and disturbing loss for me; I have wondered since whether work, when central and crucial to us, does not become an internal search or a substitute for the lost or wayward outer God we now seek inside us.

My propensity for otherworldliness fed by constant reading, I divided the world into two spheres, both of which were deep and sometimes terrifyingly real to me. One was the world here and now, the hearty bourgeois world around our breakfast table. The other world was the "heaven" of our Sunday school . . . the languorous clouds in the sky . . . the world beyond worlds beyond the horizon. I remember how excited I became one day when both worlds collided with a great *Götterdämmerung* crash in my mind. I was poring over the atlas, one of my favorite pastimes, and I discovered that Bethlehem, which had always been a metaphysical concept for me, really existed. On a map! I was overcome with a throbbing excitement for days.

Juxtaposed to my literary dreaminess was a very, very real world. There was Chicago with its political corruption, its racial hatred, and its Mafia operations and a citizenry that accepted all of this as natural. It was this tribal morality that fed the growing flames of my hatred for injustice and my desire both to protect myself from this parasitical world and to fight it and to try to change it.

Perhaps most important, hovering always just over the horizon, both terribly appealing and terribly threatening, was the black community. It hung there like a cloud on the horizon—but I had always loved the rain and the wind, and so I was fascinated by it. Most of the people in our neighborhood feared or hated blacks; to me they represented my first fascination with another culture. It was forbidden—and thus needed desperately to be known. I probed it, but carefully; occasionally I would venture a little way into it and sit on the stoops (we had stoops in those days and in those neighborhoods) and talk to the old "Negro" men and try to learn about them.

Much later, when I worked on the *Chicago Daily News,* I tried to repay the black community just a little for all it had suffered at our hands: I initiated and got printed the first series on the black community that any Chicago paper ever printed. We had thirty-eight parts to it—in fact, once we did it, we overdid it!

But in many ways life was also so snug and cozy that to this day my closest and most loyal friends are those from the "old neighborhood." We had "old countries" and "old neighborhoods" and "new neighborhoods" then, you see, and those who "made it" might move away but were never really hated for it—envied a little, maybe—because they always came back and never forgot their friends in the "old" neighborhood. Indeed, one success was everyone's in this basically tribal milieu.

In this environment my big, stubborn, honest father stood out like a beacon of honesty, if not always of understanding. Both an admirable man and a difficult man, he was a typical "mountain man" of southern Germany. He had hands like great hams, and he stood well over six feet tall and weighed sometimes more than 250 pounds. He terrified my boyfriends. He was absolutely incorruptible, with that dire, unforgiving honesty of self-made men whose honesty is both a heartfelt thing and a dare against the world they have bested.

In the midst of the Depression, before I was born, the dairy business on the South Side of Chicago was fraught with corrupt building inspectors looking for payoffs, with Mafia "enforcers," and with big dairies driving out small dairies like ours with bribes of five thousand or ten thousand dollars—substantial amounts of money at that time. If you were not Irish or one of the "machine" ethnic groups, you weren't in—especially Germans, with their individualistic tendencies toward their own businesses. My father had the dubious "honor," when he was a boy at Twenty-first and Lowe, of having to avoid the Reagan's Colts, an Irish gang that included such boys as Richard J. Daley and his cronies. This left him with a deep hatred for "the machine" and its bullies. He overcame by being so big he simply threw Mafia bullies and others out physically.

I inherited this white, burning hatred. I was capable of being moved to tears when I was only seven or eight by the pictures in the paper of mobsters bombing union leaders' homes. I was never one of those suburban relativists, bred in suburbia where liberalism was easy; life for me was real because there was always a very real bully on every block.

30

In the early days of the Depression, before I was born, the White Castle route, a large and money-making route of hamburger stands all over the city, opened up for bids. They were little white-brick "castles" and the hamburgers were flat, good, and cheap—five cents in those days.

A story that became one of the little myths by which we lived was born when my father, Robert, went to Mr. Lewis, then president of the White Castle chain, and told him flatly, "I'm not going to offer you one cent in bribes. I couldn't, and I wouldn't if I could. But I'll give you the best milk and the best service you'll find anywhere."

Mr. Lewis, another rare, honest man, accepted the offer on the spot. The Geyer's Dairy chocolate milk was so rich that the White Castles just whipped it up and there you had creamy milk shakes. Thanks to all of those little white "castles," we became moderately well-to-do.

But my father worked so hard—and he had been forced to do so since he had to quit school at thirteen when my grandfather abandoned the family—that he had little time or few emotional resources for bouncing a blond little girl on his knee. Robert Geyer was an endlessly good man, but he was often, like many self-made men, remote, given to fitful rages, to lengthy soliloquies, or to endless silences.

I loved my father, and I never blamed him for anything, for how can you honestly blame someone for not giving you something he didn't have to give? I reacted with his same stubbornness and determination, by turning to work and accomplishment in order to "earn" love. I dealt with everything by going my own way; by doing, doing, doing. Later in my life it took me a long, painful time to figure out why my accomplishments didn't bring me love from other men, either, but instead only competitive resentment and rage of a new sort.

I guess I realize most poignantly what I missed when I was sixteen, already graduated from high school with highest honors, and we were out in Palm Springs visiting relatives. On a particularly pleasant starry night, after visiting relatives whom my father especially liked, we were walking across the moon-baked desert and my now more relaxed father put his arms around Mother and me. It was a singular, transcendent experience, just having my father put his arm around me. Although no one ever knew it, tears filled my eyes. It was the first time I could ever remember his touching me.

That a man as rough in manner and as remote in emotions as my father should have married my mother, a beautiful and refined young "lady" from the North Side, was still another curiosity. She was just as refined as he was rough; she was just as needing and giving of love and emotional expression as he was incapable of giving it. He was a "good provider," she always stressed, and he was certainly a good man; but he was a damned hard man to live with.

When I was born, for instance (and the birth took some forty-eight hours), my father used the time to put in the cement driveway beside the house, never once calling the hospital. He wasn't being intentionally cruel at all; he just thought that was a good time to put in the cement driveway.

It was my mother, Georgie Hazel, named after her grandfather, who taught me to read and write when I was four, sitting at a little table out in the sunlight at our lake house; it was my mother from whom I got affection and, generally, approval for my work. We traveled together. She laid the foundation for the curiosity that drove me to Siberia, up the Tapajoz, and down to Abu Dhabi (perhaps I *did* overreact a bit). And while the Geyers gave me their stubbornness and determination, I think it was her far more cultured family of Rhineland Germans who gave me whatever sensitivities I had.

But it was my mother, too, I think, who quite unknowingly instilled in me a deep dissatisfaction with the "woman's role." She always insisted she wanted nothing except a family; yet she always complained bitterly about "all the work" at home. I realized much, much later that this tall, graceful, lovely woman was complaining not about "all the work" but about the fact that she was not rewarded by my father with the outward shows of affection that she, a tender and affectionate woman who would have bloomed under the lifelong

32

gaze of a man capable of tenderness, so needed. In turn she became somewhat possessive of her children, wanting us always by her side and wanting, I am certain, me to replace her in her position, as unhappy as she had often been with it. My choosing a profession, I am sure, struck her as a betrayal until late in life, when she came to understand and even prize it.

The third great influence on my life was my brother, Glen. Ten years older than me, tall, handsome, charming, and far too generous, Glen was in many ways a young, surrogate father to me. When I was just a baby, he took me under the long wing of his long arms and unwittingly prepared me for a world that would be a stage.

Glen, later to become a leading dress designer, had a genuine artistic sense that I never even approached; everything he touched turned to beauty. For me he created a marvelous fantasy world. He turned everything into a kind of theater for me, and so I learned early how to move in the kind of world of half-reality and half-fantasy that I eventually created for myself. I could have done little that I have done without him, his constant support, and his love.

But no amount of scrutiny of my childhood can explain why I wound up in Guatemala stumbling through the mountains . . . or in Cairo talking with Anwar Sadat . : . or in the rice paddies of South Vietnam . . . or listening during a vicious sandstorm in Khartoum while American diplomats were gunned to death by Palestinian terrorists. . . . But as far back as I can remember, I wanted to know —I *had* to know—everything in the world. At ten I wrote a 110-page book (with myself as the heroine, naturally). In high school, in the absence of any guidance, I read right through the library. Even as a child I was terribly concerned about truth—truth, that is, in the sense of "what is" in the world. I was also concerned about those "couriers" who carried truth. I looked outward for truth, not inward, and broadcast it with the ardor of the missionary I once wanted to be. Eventually I chose journalism because—in opposition, for instance, to philosophy, where truth was theoretical—our truths were concrete and approachable, if only because they were small, relative truths.

33

*   *   *

On a sunny fall weekend in 1952 my parents delivered me, an expectant package of sixteen, to Northwestern University, in Evanston, Illinois. Very soon I felt I had arrived in paradise. This was the era of campus fun, of university joy, and of sorority parties—but of great intellectual inquiry, too. All of the doubts of high school fell away. Suddenly it was not the cheerleaders of high school who were the popular symbol; it was the serious though socially-minded coeds. The conformity of high school also suddenly disappeared. We were free to dream, to be socially angry and intellectually productive; those of us in the prestigious Medill School of Journalism took these possibilities particularly seriously.

We of Medill were a close-knit, elitist group, no doubt about it, despite the dour ugliness of the old dark-brick building that stood on the lakefront. Indeed, on graduation, my closest friend, Mary "Miki" McDermott, whose father, Frank, had been the Irish boss of the South Side, decided to do something unthinkable in those times—we gave a party in an off-campus apartment from 2:00 P.M. to 3:00 A.M. and invited all of our professors! They all came in a state of surprised and pleased shock; that was an era in which professors and students stayed a formal distance from one another.

We were suddenly free to dream, and Miki and I saw ourselves as adventurers. We were going to live: fully. And love: fully. It was Anaïs Nin's "I will not be just a tourist in the world of images." Or, said in a heavy Bogartesque whisper, "He travels fastest who travels alone."

Despite the unfair image of the fifties generation as socially unconscious imbeciles, we had our very real causes. I did a paper on Paul Robeson and the prejudice against him and broke down sobbing as I wrote it. When the Supreme Court decision on integration came, we applauded wildly in classes and walked around the campus singing. And I made wonderful friendships, friendships that have lasted until this day: Lucy Woods Wiesner, Lynne Reich Basta, Carol Krametbauer Petersen, Phyllis Oakley. . . . People most definitely were not interchangeable in those days, nor did we have

34

discontinuing selves. We were loyal and loving, and relationships lasted.

I also had my own feminism, and I researched it and wrote about it and talked about it in an era in which it was not even suggested as an historical subject. Everybody thought me quite dotty but I really didn't care much; I have never been much of a philosopher, but it just seemed frankly wrong to me that women should be considered inferior or that they should be expected to do only one thing in life. It was wrong, it was inhuman; and I wouldn't put up with it. It was only much later that I found out how hard the world made it not to put up with it.

Much, much later, actually in 1982, I expressed to a young woman student at Rollins College in Florida what my real idea of feminism was, really from the very beginning.

Lizz Jacobson, a thoughtful young woman, asked me: "There are two types of women that can be very successful in this 'man's world': the woman who becomes like a man, and the woman who retains her femininity. What do you think about this?"

I answered: "I think a lot of women, and I don't want to be critical of them—the ones who sort of become male by taking on male qualities in any profession in order to get to the top—are denying their female qualities just as much as men have denied the value of female qualities. Even from the beginning I didn't want to change things so that women would become like men; I wanted to change things so that what was female would be respected by both men and women. I think the women who in effect have become men in their working habits and in only prizing work in the professional work-place have done exactly what men have done throughout the centuries, which is to degrade whatever women do."

There was only one thing I really wanted to be: I wanted to be free intellectually. I wanted to be able to investigate and see and know the world and everything in it. But every one of my experiences with men—and with the idea of marriage—showed me with desperate clarity that I could never have that freedom tied to a man. It was a terrible choice to have to make—and I never quite gave up

35

my anger at a world which would tell a human being, of either sex, that you could not have love and "knowing" too. And so I made the only choice that, in my heart and soul, I could make. I made my way by myself.

I hated the journalism nuts-and-bolts courses: reporting, copyreading, in particular typesetting. What I loved was the humanities, and I drowned myself in history, in political science, and in literature. But even this education, which most people would think of as pretty good, left a great deal to be desired. I am still suffering from the fact that I never had a single course in philosophy, physics, anthropology, sociology. . . . If anything allowed me to know cultures in a special way later on—and if anything helped me to form the judgment necessary for making quick and right judgments on events, it was this much-maligned "liberal arts" education. There is no shortcut, and why, with all the joys of learning history with all its passions, should there be? You've simply got to know everything if you are to be a good journalist, and in particular you have got to know how this race of man made its way to those of us today who are suffering over the same dramas and joys and tragedies that men and women have always known.

Our third year Miki and I decided to do something daring; we would go to Mexico for the winter quarter to a hedonistic school in the mountains outside Mexico City called Mexico City College. Medill allowed us to transfer credits but not grades, so we had the best of all possible worlds.

If Northwestern had been paradise, Mexico was the next higher level of paradise. Almost all of the students at the college—and three quarters of them were men, most of them GIs on the GI Bill from the Korean War—lived in upper-class homes with Mexican families. This was nice and very proper, but it also meant that you had to keep very strict hours and take part in family life. At first Miki and the two other girls who came with us were horrified when we saw where *we* had been put. It was a big, gray, penitentiary-style building on the Avenida Melchor Ocampo, and the apartment could at best be called lower-class functional. Our "housemother" was a handsome, fortyish divorcée who had a big "friend" who came every afternoon at four o'clock to "visit." Clearly, if the college knew about the "unhealthy" aspects of our housing, it would have changed us to one of those dull rich houses, but I soon instinctively made one of those mutually convenient trade-offs. We would not tell on *her* if she did not enforce hours. We became the four most popular girls at Mexico City College, if only because at any party we could outlast all the others.

When it came time to leave after three months, I died deaths. Life had finally been precisely as I had dreamed it: adventure in a strange culture, joy, mystery, intensity of act and emotion. Miki and I soberly agreed we would never again in life be so happy.

In the fall of 1956 I went to Vienna on a Fulbright scholarship. Vienna was then still a haunted city, her body whole but her soul ravaged by all-too-recent holocausts. It had only been the year before that the four-power occupation government—one of the most unusual arrangements of all times—had ended. Now, with the Russians blessedly and miraculously gone, there was an arrested sigh of relief, but it remained arrested. They were so close, and Vienna was such a desirable, somber jewel. Yet it was also a world that was once again pulling itself together. The assurances that all of us felt in our world, in our Western world, remained unbroken.

Then one morning that October I woke up in Vienna to the German-language radio broadcasting the last cries from Radio Hungary: the Hungarian revolution had begun.

With other students from the university I traveled in a bus to the border. It was already wintry cold in the rolling hills that flowed between Austria and Hungary, and the sky was gray and forbidding. The people fleeing across those snowy hills had the empty, searching faces of refugees everywhere (I was to see many too many more of them in my life) and their dark, dreary clothes expressed their suffering. The Austrians behaved like heroes in those first months, when every school and hotel and municipal building in the charming old villages of the border provinces were opened to the waves and waves of refugees. They slept on floors, on makeshift beds, on the ground. They stood in silent lines waiting for the food we students were dishing out in the cold old Hapsburg courtyards. I was filled with the excitement of it all—but for the first time I was to realize that "living intensely" also meant suffering and observing suffering and absorbing suffering. I was heartbroken. Heroism had failed. Goodness had lost. What was the matter with the world?

Naturally I had to fall in love with a Hungarian, and naturally I chose a handsome, blond, charming one. We worked together on the border, we suffered together over the Hungarian tragedy, we stayed up listening to Radio Hungary. On New Year's Eve—a bitter cold, white afternoon and evening in which the whole world was lost in the undifferentiated whiteness, the kind of day when it seems that there will never be another—we drove out to the border and watched a refugee "show" that moved us to tears. In the crowd of hundreds in this hall one after the other would get up, dance, sing folk ballads from his village or recite poems, while tears flowed freely down every face.

But there was something else that year in Vienna that left me with a new kind of joy: I learned, rather quickly, actually, to speak good German. I am always so saddened for people who, seeking the fickle outer joys which never seem to make them happy, do not or cannot understand these inner joys. Learning a language—and then finally experiencing this magnificent world it opens you to—is like having a creature growing inside you. Suddenly you have something new inside you; suddenly you can recognize an entirely new world. The day I finally could speak German was a day of sheer joy for me; after that, I studied languages whenever I could. It was almost an addiction.

When I left Europe in the fall of 1957, as heartbroken and emotional as I had been when I left Mexico City after my magic time there, our relationship gradually died out. But I also came home with a dire case of hepatitis. It was serious indeed, because I was in bed with it for a full year, and I was in a coma for two full months. But it, too, taught me very special things: It taught the girl who thought she could will anything and everything that she could not; it taught her the patience that people must have who cannot raise their hands higher than one inch more each month; it taught me respect for patience. And I thought a lot.

The *Chicago Daily News* that I joined in the winter of 1960 was still considered one of the great papers of the nation. What's more, it was the "reporter's newspaper." Ben Hecht, Carl Sandburg, John Gunther, Ernest Hemingway—all of them and many more had passed through its generous and creative doors.

Ben Hecht's description of this unique and scurrilous and wondrous band in the twenties held up still when I arrived forty years later. "We were a newspaper tribe of assorted drunkards, poets, burglars, philosophers, and boastful ragamuffins. We were supermen with soiled collars and holes in our pants; stone broke and sneering at our betters in limousines and unmortgaged houses; cynical of all things on earth, including the tyrannical journal that underpaid and overworked us, and for which, after a round of cursing, we were ready to die." It was a heady and wonderful atmosphere in which to start work. My dear friend David Lazar many years later perhaps expressed to me best why we were all so enthralled with newspaper work. "I used to stay up until two A.M. on the old *Sun-Times* when the first bulletins came in," he said. "It was so damned exciting, because I knew that I was the first one in all of Chicago to know those things." That was it—that was the addiction, the bait, the hooker: "knowing" things before anyone else did.

The *Daily News* was a feisty paper, a little raw like Chicago itself, but one that revered and spawned and showcased good writing. It was, in its way, quite literary. But it was not, in those days, for women. Despite my minimal experience (only four months on the *Southtown Economist*, a neighborhood paper), the city editor wanted to put me on the city desk, but the staid old managing editor, Everett Norlander, flatly told me, "We've had two women on the city desk and we'll always have two women." Within a year I became the third, thus breaking a real quota and the first taboo to irritate me.

But the *Daily News* was also a paper quite unlike papers today; it was a journalism quite unlike journalism today. We quite simply "reported" what was going on. We did not write columns or our own personal interpretations on the news pages. We reported fires and murders and investigations and the statements of institutions. It was a much straighter and much more honest job then, and it was also a hell of a lot of fun.

We loved one another on the paper—and for a very special reason. We competed brutally with the other papers (there were four then!) but we didn't compete among ourselves. We were out to get the world but nobody was going to divide and/or conquer *us*. It was another bit of the Chicago tribal morality perhaps, but it was grand. So when one reporter got a prize, everybody celebrated because everybody shared in it; it reflected well on everyone. It was very, very different from journalism today, when *The Washington Post's* "creative tension," in which everybody is pitted against everyone else and everybody ends up hating everybody else, has become more the dreary norm.

In those days we also called ourselves simply "reporters." No, not even "journalists" and certainly not "media" or "media celebrities," good God! Nobody came into journalism in those days for power or to be celebrities; they came in because they wanted to write, or walk the streets, or booze around and raise hell with the world. But those reporters knew the city; they lived in it, not the suburbs, like the editors today, and they loved the city. It was our clay and we were its.

The *Daily News* reporters were almost caricatures of themselves: Ed Rooney and Bill Mooney, the tough-talking reporter's reporters; my longtime boyfriend, Harry Swegle, and Bill Newman, who wrote so well and so sensitively about the city; the brilliant Lois Wille, who helped so much in easing me on as the "third woman"; the rowdy, wonderful Howard Ziff, with his big black beard; Ed Gilbreth, who knew Chicago politics backward and forward. . . . I wish I could mention them all, for in truth I loved them all. And I sat in the most extraordinary seat in the city room, as fate would have it. In front of me sat Mike Royko, then simply a rewrite man but later to become "the" satiric genius of our generation and a fellow columnist. On my right hand sat Jay McMullen, the crack and wry City Hall reporter later to become the celebrated husband of Mayor Jane Byrne. And on my left was the wonderful Bill Newman, with his elegance of expression and his subtle charm. What a triumvirate!

Then one Thursday our wonderful city editor, Ritz Fisher, called me up to his desk and said, "Gee Gee, we've got a good one." One of the reporters who covered the Mafia had arranged for a "waitress" by the name of "Irene Hill" to cover a big Mafia wedding that Saturday. I was Irene Hill.

I spent hours in our morgue studying the mug shots of the leading Mafia figures, and I dutifully bought my waitress uniform in the cheapest place I could find. What perhaps was most strange was how very easy it was. Late that Saturday afternoon, dressed in my "costume," I simply went out to the Tam o'Shanter Country Club. On the road outside, as usual, FBI men, reporters, and others waited to catch glimpses of the hoods rushing in, in their big black limousines. I walked by and in, in my uniform.

To my chagrin, however, I was initially placed in an upstairs room where I would not be able to see the participants at all. So as soon as I could, I slipped out and began serving drinks on the patio where everyone was arriving. I quickly spotted Tony Accardo; his right-hand man, Jackie Cerron; Murray "The Camel" Humphreys. I made sure to serve *them* drinks, noting down every little comment and gesture in my mind.

Then once again I was relegated to Siberia. After serving *my* designated table in a corner of the enormous room filled with some two thousand, I realized that since cocktails I hadn't seen any of the "biggies." So I began to wander around with my champagne and finally, to my delight, found the entire bunch, all men and about thirty of them, seated together in a dark side room. I had started pouring the champagne when, to my horror, a swarthy gnome of a man jumped up and pointed his finger precisely at me.

"Don't give us none o' dat," he virtually shrieked.

I froze in place, then fled back to the kitchen.

"You're pretty dumb," said the bartender. "That's the eleven-dollar-a-bottle champagne. That room gets the twenty-five-dollar-a-bottle stuff."

At 2:00 A.M., weary but happy, I walked out to the road where the FBI and the other reporters still were waiting. A guard motioned us over. "Now, girls," he said, "be sure not to talk to those reporters." I assured him I would certainly do no such thing.

The next Monday my front-page story appeared, with a picture of me primly attired in my waitress uniform. It began, "The mob went to a party and I went along for the ride."

But those stories were unusual. More and more, pursuing my early passions, I covered race relations. In those days a white woman could still drive around most black sections of Chicago, even to night meetings; I only had one threatening scene—and that taught me a great deal.

In the middle of a bright and sunny weekday I had driven out to West Madison Street to attend a Planned Parenthood meeting in a very poor and particularly dilapidated black section of the city. The once-proud old buildings now had only their fronts to recommend them; once inside, you found that the hallways stank and you picked your way with revulsion over the filth, feces, and refuse. As I walked to the building from across the street after parking my little Volkswagen convertible, I noticed four nice-looking young black men standing on the corner and I greeted them cheerfully, with a big "hello." They responded in kind.

But up on the third floor, where the meeting was supposed to be, I found only two very drunk, very disreputable black women, their eyes glassy with drugs. I left quickly only to find, as I approached the front door, two strange and very threatening black men entering. There was no question of the threat—a look passed between them and on to me. And they stopped just inside the front door. I took a deep breath and rushed through them, pushing their arms aside. To my continuing terror, outside they continued to follow me. But the four men I had greeted were still at the corner. Incredibly, they formed a line facing the two threatening men and stopped them from following me across the street. In my memory until this day is etched the scene of that strange and fortunate standoff.

The experience also represented something else to me. Reporters working in a different neighborhood—or another culture—must always establish themselves in the turf. The Press must always act as though they belong and also establish friends and collaborators, who become protectors. This is the law of the street. That first time I didn't do it calculatedly. I liked the four young men, but I was also from the South Side of Chicago, so it all came quite naturally.

Around this time I also met a man who was to influence me deeply, Saul Alinsky. Saul, a big husky man from a Jewish family from way, way behind the tracks, was to become the organizational genius—and conscience—for many in his and my Chicago generation.

He founded and ran the Industrial Areas Foundation, which trained organizers and organized neighborhoods or groups that were powerless, in order to gain power. Saul's methods were highly confrontational, always putting the big powers like corporations and city governments and universities on the spot, and he was not above doing a lot of awful things to empower the "people" he believed in. If you were a friend, Saul could be wonderful company, full of wit and irony and gentler than the most dedicated big puppy. If you were an "enemy," his wit became scathing; his instinct was to kill. In short, people either loved him excessively or hated him excessively. I loved him, but not without an understanding of why he was hated.

What his critics never understood was that Saul was quintessentially, almost embarrassingly, American. He would never, for instance, go overseas—he would never go outside the borders of "my country." He loved it with the mystic, stubborn, unquestioning patriotism of the immigrant, even though he was second generation.

What many—City Hall, the Democratic machine, big companies, others in power—hated him for was his "revolutionary" or "radical" philosophy of organizing. In *Reveille for Radicals*, for instance, called a "manual for . . . revolution," he wrote, "This is the story of People's Organizations, ever-growing in number and irrevocably committed to the rallying cry of democracy: 'We the people will work out our own destiny.' They are on the march toward a common goal—full democracy for the common man."

It all sounded very radical, but in practice what Saul did was very conservative: to organize the down-and-out quarters of American society *into* the American system. Thus he might strengthen and in his mind even save it. But it was the way he did it that made him a lot of enemies. He organized *against* the biggies, whether the University of Chicago or City Hall or Eastman Kodak. What they couldn't see was that in many ways he was saving them and their way of life!

After I interviewed him for a long series I wrote on The Woodlawn Organization, the first successful black neighborhood organization in Chicago, Saul and I became close friends. There was never anything overtly romantic about our relationship, but there was a special kind of "romance" about it, even though he was some thirty years older than me.

He would tell me the most outrageous stories, and I adored them and him. Once, when TWO was challenging the Daley machine, he told me of being called into Mayor Daley's office. The two men were much alike in character, but with such different callings in life. The mayor wanted Saul to call off a particular TWO offensive (Saul was always thinking of things like having members take over all the toilets in the Loop and just stay in them for several hours!), and Saul, for all his sophisticated knowledge of politics and personality, was stunned by the idea that Daley even thought he would do it.

As Saul, angry and miffed, got up to leave, Daley called him back. Then the mayor pounded his fist on the desk. "All right, Alinsky," Saul quoted him to me, "tell me what your price is. I'll pay it."

Saul laughed as though he would burst when he told me that. Saul didn't have a price, just as my father did not, and it said something about Mayor Daley that he thought even Saul did. But then the Chicago machine thought everybody had a price.

People didn't understand Saul. They called him a "radical," not realizing that he was basically the most fervent possible American and the most conservative anti-Communist. They never understood he wanted to enfranchise the "outs" in order to save the "ins." Nor did he take any guff from anybody, whether liberal, black, or whomever. When black students at one university announced to him arrogantly that they wanted their own black student union, he said, "Cut out the crap. You don't really want that. Now, say it." And they did. They were playing some of the games of their time, and Saul knew it, if "liberals" didn't. He didn't want this country to break up. And he didn't play fashionable games.

What he gave me was something very special. I disagreed with a lot of his thinking and even tactics. He could be extremely cruel, although usually only to people he thought could take it. (Often they couldn't.) But Saul was a great balance to my excessive romanticism and to my extreme idealism. *He taught me tactics.* Just in watching him all those precious years that I knew him, I absorbed what is practical politics, what is strategy, and how one moves tactically in the world. I learned not only how much better it is to win than to lose but *how* to win and how to win in one's own way.

Father John J. Egan, known as "Jack," another fantastic, bigger-than-life man and priest, worked closely with Saul in those days—indeed, this Jewish iconoclast and this Catholic believer were like the oddest pair of loving brothers. They got the Archdiocese of Chicago to support a good deal of controversial community organization, among other "impossible" things. In later years, Jack Egan told me this story about Saul:

"One day we were walking down Michigan Avenue, and I was a little worried about some of the things we were doing and how people would criticize me. Saul stopped in his tracks. 'Why does everybody have to like you?' he demanded. 'Jack, you do what you have to do. Some people don't like little bald men, some people don't like priests, some people don't like short people or Irishmen. For God's sake, be true to yourself and do what you have to do and everything else will fall in line.'"

Midwestern "radical" impulses—and they are not that in any other sense of the word anywhere else—were everywhere around me. Hull House held another deep and very special attraction for me at that time. Jane Addams, Jessie Binford, Edith Hamilton—they offered another, kinder but no less tough radicalism and love, "social feminism." And they were women: strong-minded, determined, idealistic, tough, politically sagacious women. We had one such woman in my own family, a great-aunt, Alma Foerster, who had been a Red Cross nurse working in Archangel, Russia, during World War II. She was a true heroine, but she was never mentioned to me.

In the early sixties I repaid Hull House in small manner by saving its buildings. Although I am not at all an organizer myself and hate the very idea of "mobilizing" people, preferring to sit in corners and on the edges watching others, or else singing at a piano bar, I became so angry when the city was going to raze Hull House, along with the entire Near South Side neighborhood, that I organized a "Save Hull House" committee that utterly tormented City Hall. And we won: we saved Hull House. It was during that experience that I had the enormous pleasure of knowing Jessie Binford, a little sparrow of a woman who became, with her myriad social causes, the "conscience of Chicago." She told me of her first meeting with Chicago, straight out of the Iowa cornfields, and of her first meeting with Jane Addams: "I arrived in Chicago on an awfully hot July day. Every other place was a saloon, the streets were dirty. The air was heavy. I had left the beautiful Iowa countryside and I wondered if I hadn't made a mistake. And no one paid much attention to me. The next morning, I said to Miss Addams, 'I want you to tell me what I am to do.' And then she said what seemed to be the most wonderful introduction for a young person, 'I wouldn't do anything if I were you for a while. Just look around and get acquainted and perhaps you'll think of something to do that none of the rest of us have ever thought of before.' I don't know, it gave me a kind of freedom. Of not having to conform to an organization right away."

It was exactly the way we reporters in Chicago started—by just "looking around."

46

III.

From the Streets of Chicago to the Whorehouses of Peru

"When you see a country in chaos where 200,000 people are trying to get out and 12 people are trying to get in, those 12 are foreign correspondents."
—A foreign correspondent

At the *Chicago Daily News,* in the early sixties, we would sit in the city room overlooking the muddy, churning Chicago River and watch the foreign correspondent "greats" as they came home, sometimes battered by the fray, having waged their battle against ignorance and evil and having at least so far survived. From Istanbul and Seoul and out there east of Suez, they came. The gallant, cultured Paul Ghali, an Egyptian Copt who smuggled the famous diaries of Count Ciano out of Italy during World War II. Bluff, literary George Weller, who was always swimming the Bosporus or virtually any other waterway that had the misfortune of crossing his path. And lean, mean Keyes Beech, with his bedroom eyes and his taut thinking. They were all tough, but Keyes was especially tough —he had covered every war and had been in a large number of battles since World War II.

Watching them stride across the city room as I imagined they strode across the world, I would groan inside with yearning. But there seemed, in those first years, not the faintest indication that I could or would ever be a foreign correspondent. I was twenty-seven. And I was clearly a woman. All the correspondents were men in their fifties and sixties.

But in 1964 I "escaped" the Chicago city desk through a ruse—
I applied successfully for a small grant, the Seymour Berkson Foreign
Assignment Grant, which allowed me to work in Latin America for
six months. The paper would perhaps never have sent me, and so
it was the grant that broke the professional logjam. Larry Fanning,
our editor, said simply, "Fine, you can just continue to work for us
down there." They fully expected I would then come home, and
there seemed no need to burden them with the fact that I knew
clearly I never would.

Why did I without question choose to go to Latin America, thus
unwittingly putting in motion for the years of the '70s an impulse
which would bring an entire group of women correspondents to the
South? Was it because there were so few correspondents there?
Because it was so relatively uncovered? Not at all. I went to Latin
America because I loved it; because in my blood and soul I had some
deep subterranean affinity for it. Perhaps it was the old, old pull of
the South to the Byronesque men and women of the North. I only
know I followed my love—and that is the only thing without question I would tell young people for them to be happy: Follow your
love. There is no other happiness.

So it was that I traveled south—south across the Caribbean, down
the Andes and the gray sea coastline to Peru. I found myself a little
third-floor apartment in an elegant colonial building at 440 Avenida
Arequipa, right in the middle of Lima, and I began to learn how to
be a foreign correspondent.

While tutoring two hours a day in Spanish, I was trying to make
elementary contacts and interviews, and one of my first subjects—
and lessons as a correspondent—was Víctor Raúl Haya de la Torre,
the great old man of the Aprista Party. In the thirties, when reform
and democracy were basically still unknown in Latin America, it was
the brilliant Haya who sparked the call for democratic revolution on
the entire continent. I had long admired him. I *had* to meet him.

Although I was now an experienced reporter at home, I did not
know—and there was nobody to tell me—how to work in a foreign
country. So instead of psyching it out and adapting to my new

culture, I tried to work as I always had. And it was a mistake. With Haya, for instance, I felt very clever indeed when I got his private phone number from a friend at the American embassy and began systematically phoning him there, day after day and week after week and sometimes hour after hour. Every time I called, a male servant's voice would tell me politely, *"Víctor Raúl no esta."* Víctor Raúl is not at home.

I knew very well he was in the country. I knew very well he had to be home sometime. After five weeks of compulsive calling I found myself breaking into tears of frustration. It was not only Víctor Raúl —I had been in Peru for a full month and had not had one single major interview.

Then, by chance, I was introduced to two Peruvian journalists. We were drinking pisco sours in the wood-paneled corner bar of the lovely old Hotel Bolívar when I poured out my tale of frustration.

"But it is so easy," one said, shaking his head in wonder and confusion at the innocent *gringuita.* "We will take you to the Aprista Party newspaper. It is through the editor of the party newspaper that you arrange interviews with Víctor Raúl."

The other seemed properly embarrassed when he mumbled, "In Latin America, we never call a man at home. It is . . . not quite polite. He would never answer professional calls at home." I was appropriately chagrined.

That very afternoon we went to the Aprista newspaper and were ushered immediately into the editor's office. He was a charming young man, and within half an hour he picked up the telephone to arrange the interview. The next day I met Haya.

I learned more than one thing that day. Besides the American embassies, one of the best sources in any foreign country is the local journalists. They *know* their country. What's more, they often have information that they cannot use in their countries, particularly when they are under dictatorships or in countries with censorship. They are glad to get certain information out, which then often comes back to them in a way that they can use. Of course, this is an exchange, both of information and of help and protection.

As I worked, I became aggravated by such accepted journalistic "truths" as James Reston's "Americans will do everything for Latin America except read about it." I became as defensive about Latin America as a mother cat about her favorite kitten, and later when a Chicago woman told me at a party, "You were always angry about your little countries . . . because other people didn't love them as much as you did," I had to admit she was right. In this I was different from many of the sixties and seventies generation of journalists—I didn't want to "be" something, I wanted to "do" something very particular, in line with my beliefs and my temperament—I wanted to interpret Latin America because I loved it so. Too, my countries were "people" to me; I loved them, I hated them, but I always interacted with them.

In trying to figure out *why* Americans did not care all that much about reading about Latin America, I realized that in part we correspondents were acronyming Americans to death in the area. Every story was about the PRD defeating the MNL, which had just merged with the GDU and the splinter HYU for the first time in history. Many of the stories were simply unreadable. At the same time, the really great movements of history were hardly being observed or interpreted—like the Indian land rebellions in the mountains; or the descendants of the Incas sweeping down from the Andes and becoming citified *cholos;* like the new priest-guerrillas; or spectacular movements to develop the interior.

I thus determined to cover trends, to try to pull together the great social movements and to explain them in their entirety and cross-nationally. Whether covering the new populist military or the Cuban-Russian split over guerrilla warfare in the sixties, I tried to go across national lines and trace the changes in all the countries. By writing in terms of real people, in terms of history, and in terms of tales and legends and adventures, I began to be published widely— people *would* read about Latin America!

And there were tales and legends—and even present-day legendary kingdoms—everywhere in Latin America. One year, for instance, while visiting Colombia, I went out to see the military about going to Marquetalia. Marquetalia was one of five "Communist republics" that the Moscow-line Communist Party in Colombia had established during the terrible years of "La Violencia" in the fifties and sixties, when 200,000 persons were killed. That awful and pathological violence was the exact predecessor to the Central American violence of the '80s. Marquetalia could survive, in a kind of peasant agrarian socialism, because it was so very, very isolated in the great black mountains of southern Colombia. It was "autonomous" and it was ruled by the infamous Tiro Fijo ("Sure Shot"). A brutal bandit boss, with a flat face and slit eyes, Tiro Fijo ruled Marquetalia, the hidden republic of three thousand persons, with a mailed fist that was only very secondarily "Communist."

By the time I went to Marquetalia in 1966, the army had pretty much taken over all the republics. We flew in a helicopter over the massive, barren mountains, which then gave way to lower, greener ones that flowed into precipitous valleys, which in turn seemed themselves always to fall off at some point into still lower, hidden valleys.

The copter whirred down on the even ground amidst a number of small wooden houses that later, much later, reminded me of another doomed colony: Jonestown in Guyana. We got out. We were going to stay the night there with the small contingent of Colombian soldiers. Already the Marquetalians, whatever was left of them, had fled into the mountains. Soon darkness came. We sat around on the floor of Tiro Fijo's simple wooden house and talked for some reason in whispers.

"The farmers raised oranges, avocados, papaya, sugar, coffee, bananas a . . . oh, yes, yucca," the colonel explained. "There were some cows. There were also thirty to forty tax collectors who collected six pesos a month and a share of the harvest from surrounding farmers on pain of death for failure to pay."

The "ideal" society ended up as such societies always end: with force and intimidation.

A male nurse whom I also spoke to, Pedro Antonio Ardino, had lived there. He related to me how, after he had been there for a while, "suddenly the mood changed and they thought I was a spy. One night they came after me and shot eighteen or twenty times. I ran away into the forest and finally made my way out."

By 1964 the Marquetalians had grown in pugnacity and were even shooting down planes—and that was too much for the Colombians. Three battalions were deployed and Colombian soldiers spent two months struggling up the nearly impassable canyons, cutting new paths painfully as they went. The "agrarian Communists" were finished in those final campaigns.

That night was one of the stranger ones I spent, a harbinger of things to come. As the guest in the hut I was given the "bed" of Tiro Fijo to sleep in. It consisted of four boards jammed together and a piece of leather tied across it. It was freezing cold and even the rough army blanket didn't keep me warm. I didn't sleep, but at least I didn't dream.

My little trip to Marquetalia showed me the very beginnings of guerrilla warfare, albeit in an odd form, and the wellsprings of Marxism ideology and banditry in Latin America which I was later to see a lot of and understand much better.

"This violence is the outcome of a frustrated revolution," Fals Borda, Colombia's greatest sociologist, told me afterward, in Bogotá. "You can't compare it to anything else. It's a new type of violence. It became respectable to use violence. But this went out of bounds. It became something new, amorphous, much more dangerous." These were prophetic words. I was to think of them later, in Santo Domingo, in Cyprus, in Beirut, in Teheran, in El Salvador. I didn't know it then, but I was to live and work through most of the post–World War II new cycles of violence of the twentieth century and often in the most disturbing and incredible firsthand manner— and my own revolution, the revolution within me as a woman, was to parallel that in strange ways. But everything was not ideological.

While living in Peru, I decided at one point to go up the coast to Chimbote, a wild and woolly frontier-style town where the poor *cholos* or mixed-bloods were making fortunes in the anchovy trade that rode in with the cooling Humboldt Current. Actually I was going up there only to "look around" (that old simple secret of journalism, looking around) when the Associated Press chief in Lima asked me to do a piece for him on the less-than-thrilling subject of the "sister city program" between Pensacola, Florida, and Chimbote.

Chimbote was sand and millionaires in shabby little huts and brawling bars and raucous women and mysterious ships sailing illegally to sea and . . . a half-finished stadium which "the children of Pensacola are building for the children of Chimbote." I started out doing a freshness-and-light story on this sisterly exchange, thinking it would take a couple of hours.

I paid a visit to the American bishop in charge of the committee. Tall and austere, the bishop assured me the program was "just fine." I paid a visit to the more voluble American-educated mayor. He assured me that the Chimbotans just *loved* the Pensacolans. I paid visits to local journalists. They hemmed and hawed and hesitated and indicated that there were strange things going on—but none of them knew exactly what they were.

Was something wrong with this project? I talked with Ralph Guzman, the Peace Corps chief; yes, he agreed, something was wrong. Perhaps it had to do with the fact that the local man who had given the land for the stadium was the vice king not only of Chimbote but of the entire coast. Moreover, his biggest whorehouse, "Acapulco," was right across the road from the stadium.

Three, four, five days went by. I was due back in Lima—what the hell was I doing still in Chimbote? Chicago wanted to know. Finally, with a Peruvian journalist who was helping me, I decided to go directly to the man himself. The journalist kindly arranged it and we found ourselves at one o'clock one desperately hot afternoon drinking a bottle of red wine in the vice king's house.

"García" was one of those typical short, squat *cholo* types: half Indian, half Spanish, and filled with the special guile of each side. He was tough and cunning and I soon saw that he was also notably vain.

"I am giving this land to the children of Chimbote," he was

53

telling us, with a sticky benevolence. "These poor children without a place to go, in this city of sin, in this . . ." He looked at us, sipped another glass of wine, and went on.

This went on for two hours and still we had learned nothing. Impatience led me to try another totally instinctive approach. First I found myself smiling and saying, "You say that you are getting nothing from the stadium." He smiled and nodded.

"But I can see that you are an intelligent man."

He smiled self-effacingly and nodded again.

"In fact," I went on, "you are extremely smart." He looked appropriately humble. "I just cannot imagine," I went on, critical now, "that a man as smart as you would give up something without getting something for himself. After all you *are* smart. . . ."

He had had just enough wine. His eyes blazed and his nostrils flared. He would show this *gringuita* that he was not dumb. "Wait." He jumped up and rushed into the other room. Within moments he was back. Breathlessly, for the red wine had taken its toll in the heat, he unrolled a very large roll of paper that held the entire design for the stadium on it. "There, you see whether I am smart or not!" he proclaimed.

We went over it, studying it. First we saw nothing unusual. There was indeed the regular part of the stadium—a large, round circle. But then I saw that carefully drawn in all around it were little, tiny, individual squares. Rooms. I looked at my journalist friend and he at me. García, meanwhile, was standing upright, all five feet four inches of him. How could we think for one moment that he was dumb. Never, never, never!

"The rooms," he said, pointing to the rooms lining the outer wall of the stadium. "Those are mine. And I also get the concessions for all sales inside the stadium. *Muy vivo, no púes?*"

I congratulated him. He was, I told him, indeed the man I had thought he was.

The journalist and I wandered back in a kind of comic daze. García had given the land so he could locate his girls right *in* the stadium. What's more, he had signed a contract with the city council. Knowing this, it was easy to get the contract from the mayor, even to make him bring it over to me at the hotel.

The bishop of Chimbote waxed ashen when he got the full story —then he was enraged.

Pensacola, once knowing "the truth," withdrew the project. No more Girl Scouts went door to door to collect for the boys (and girls, we now knew) of Chimbote.

Alistair Cooke once described best the special work and opportunities of the foreign correspondent. "It is the stimulating duty of a foreign correspondent to cover everything," he wrote. "Whereas a domestic reporter, even at his best, graduates from general reporting and hops up the ladder to success towards a single specialty, a foreign correspondent is required to act on the preposterous but exhilarating assumption that he takes all knowledge for his province." Cooke also answers well the nagging—and utterly incorrect —claim that no one can ever really know another society in a short span of time, as an outsider. "The best stuff ever written on the Constitution was by Bryce, a Scotsman," he pointed out, "and the best thing on Peru is by a Bostonian. But, of course, you start from scratch. You don't take things for granted. You don't think you know. That's an important thing. The resident of a country thinks he knows. The foreign correspondent has to go back to the origins of things every day. You can't write about a violation of interstate commerce without explaining to the British where the whole concept started. So you teach yourself."

Although some newspaper editors maintain that regular street reporters are the same as—and can be exchangeable for—foreign correspondents, they are really two very different types of people. To be a foreign correspondent means being of a particular, somewhat manic temperament, always seeking to conceptualize and bring things down to their roots. To be a foreign correspondent is to love the entire process, in fact, to love the life.

The life. When I would go home, in between, exhausted and needing nurturing for a bit, people would always ask me the very same questions: Don't you get lonely? How do you pack? Isn't it hard being in different countries all the time, and alone? Don't you get tired of hotels?

It is just the opposite. I *love* hotels. I love the days. I love the mornings, the breakfasts alone. I love unraveling the mysteries around me. Once unraveled, I hold them for a moment, then pass them on, for if we correspondents are anything, we are couriers between cultures, carrying messages from people to people.

In later years I discussed my love for hotels with my friend, the great Egyptian writer, Ihsan Abdel Kuddous. Ihsan had a lovely wife, Lula, who liked to visit her grandchildren in California for weeks and weeks. "When my wife and I go to visit our son," he told me, "for three days I am very happy with the grandchildren. Then I need to move to a hotel—I need to—where I can watch people." I understood so well. For people like us hotels are a microcosm of life. Life there is distilled; it is all there at our fingertips.

But being a correspondent is also very intricate work. You are called upon every moment and every day to exercise not only your romantic and adventurous propensities but also persistence and judgment. You have to judge constantly—facts and people and why people are telling you things—and you'd better be right. You certainly always need a healthy skepticism—I have never found someone who believed in the perfectibility of mankind or of human systems to be a good journalist—and you absolutely need a tough-minded reading of history, of political science, of anthropology, and of literature.

Intuition and training mingle in this work. You have to learn or sense what another person's "thing" is, what his or her interests are, how honest a man he is, why she is telling you things at all. You put things together, month after month and year after year, by going back and back and back to people and seeing how they change—and then often judging the information by subtleties such as how that person has or has not changed. The whole process becomes narcotic, a little like a tournament in Riga for a chess maniac.

But actually there are basic journalistic questions that can be applied to and used in any society: "What is the nature of this regime? What is the present stand of the opposition? What is their policy toward national culture? Which are the groups that are trying to carry the country back to the past? How does the present military institution feel about the present as compared with the past? Who holds the real power? What is the position of women compared with the past? Who is the official leak?" I could go on and on.

One strange and compelling aspect of a correspondent's life is the way everything in life becomes speeded up. Because you are covering, day after day after day, things that other people might see only once in a lifetime or never, you live in a distinctly different "time." Sometimes I have felt as though I had lived five years in five weeks; by the time I was thirty-five, I felt as though I were 150. In a sense it is what the Old Testament scholars sometimes call "biblical time," the time that counts because it is so meaningful and so intense.

In this life friendships and working relationships—and loves— become speeded up, too. Friends and lovers tend to be people in the same floating-crap-game circle—other correspondents, diplomats, men and women in international finance, missionaries, priests and ministers, and just seeking people who are curious about things. These people whom I like and love and count on were best described by E. M. Forster, when he wrote, "I believe in aristocracy, not an aristocracy of power, based upon rank and influence, but an aristocracy of the sensitive, the considerate, and the plucky. Its members are to be found in all nations and classes, and all through the ages, and there is a secret understanding between them when they meet. They represent the true human tradition, the one permanent victory of our queer race over cruelty and chaos."

This kind of life can of course also come to be too much. For some correspondents the price became too high. They retired back to Montana or Oklahoma or Michigan. Others became alcoholics, too many of them. But then some of those became antialcoholics. And for all of us there are times when we have just seen too much—too many riots, too many bloodied heads, too much ugliness—and couldn't absorb any more. These were times when the only thing

57

that saved us was the black humor that correspondents so often indulge in.

In these early years I soon confronted the disadvantages, and advantages, of being the only woman most of the time, in this odd and wonderful profession. Male colleagues, much as I loved them, could be counted on eventually to say, "You have all the advantages." This, of course, began only when I began to be successful. (Apparently before that I did not have all the advantages.) What they supposedly meant was that because I was young and blond and female, I could get things from men. Frankly, I never quite understood the principle at work here. I just couldn't picture waking up at three in the morning with some stranger lying next to me and saying, "Eh, Che, *mi amor*, tell me where your missiles are?" Men apparently think this is the way it's done.

Once in Bolivia, when I had been having a good time—and an awful lot of lunches and dinners—with a bevy of dark-haired, attractive men, my friend David Richardson, of *U.S. News & World Report*, quipped, "Gee Gee, you should write your first book and call it 'I Always Buy My Own Breakfast.' Then you could call your second book 'Well, Almost Always.'" We seemed to do nothing but laugh in those halcyon days.

In real life the "advantages" and disadvantages, indeed, turned out to be quite different from what I originally thought. When men had lots of time and were relaxed, no question about it, they would rather be with a woman correspondent. People in "out" positions also preferred women, at least American women. I am convinced that I had success in reaching guerrillas because they, being anti-American and generally pro-Marxist, hated American *men*. It was American men who were the representatives of the *métropole*, not American women. Indeed, not only were we just women, but we were the women of the conquerors (how delectable!). What's more, if you were straight and honest, they would be extremely honorable about you to prove themselves as honorable men in contrast to the capitalist libertines. All of this most definitely came into play in Guatemala.

When men in power were in crucial or dangerous times—which was precisely when you needed to see them—then it was something else again. Then they wanted to be with important correspondents, and then it was men. It was a syndrome it took me some time to understand and to work around.

But these were minor things. Most important were the joys of the profession. Our odd little group of wanderers and seekers-after-little-truths was quite simply the most splendid set of princely misfits I have ever known. We had the equality of the hobo and the grace of the aristocrat. It was a splendid way of life—and a deep commitment.

IV.

Santo Domingo: "You Didn't Have to Be Here"

"No man knows whether he is a coward until he
has been in a civil war."
—ANTOINE DE SAINT-EXUPÉRY

My first chance to "be there" as a correspondent almost
never happened.

In 1965 I was back in the *Daily News* offices, fresh from my first
gypsy year in Latin America and speaking perfect Spanish. I didn't
have much to do except plot how to get back there as soon as
possible. Then one day the news flashed over our machines: The
Dominican Republic, long the personal plantation of the heinous
Trujillo family supported by so many of the corrupt political and, in
particular, senatorial groups in the U.S., had erupted in a democratic
revolution.

I found myself literally trembling with excitement: for the poor,
long-suffering mulatto Dominicans, for the future of the Caribbean,
for us. Of course I would go. Of course they would send me. Of
course they would choose me. Like the good girl I had been raised
to be, I waited. "Any minute," I kept thinking to myself that first
day, as I sat in my chair and waited, "any minute, they will walk right
out of their editors' offices and down the aisle and point their Uncle
Sam fingers at me and say, 'Gee Gee, get packed for Santo Domingo.
We want you!'"

By the second day the waiting was becoming intolerable. I got the

clips out on the Dominican Republic and sat there reading them
avidly. Then late that day I got the news: the office had sent to the
"D.R." Jim McCartney, a splendid journalist with our Washington
bureau but one who had never been in Latin America and did not
speak Spanish.

At that point I did what all little girls, then at least, were taught
to do. I sulked, brooded, spent hours and days going over every unfair
and unjust thing that had happened to me at the hands of men—
but I didn't *say* anything. Not a cross word passed my lips. I kept
this up for a week, then finally on Saturday I walked into the office
of our editor, Larry Fanning, and exploded in wrath, "Give me a
leave of absence. I'm going to Santo Domingo." Then I added, "No,
I'm going anyway."

"Gee Gee," Larry responded, his voice showing clearly his astonishment, "Gee Gee, what is wrong with you?"

This was all clearly quite crazy, but in fairness to me, if we early
half-"liberated" women were more than a bit mad, what would you
call the men? For at this point Larry tried seriously to explain to me
why he had not sent me immediately to this revolution in my South.
"Santo Domingo is too dangerous," he told me soberly. "It is a street
war, and you might get shot." Then he brightened and said, "Look,
what I'll do is this: I'll send you to Vietnam."

Vietnam? I stared at him in disbelief. This was 1965, and the war
was at its height. "There," he went on, with total sobriety and
deliberateness, "you don't have to be out on the street. You can stay
in Saigon."

Aghast at this incredible offer, I refused to abandon Latin America, and the resolution of our little conflict was for me to be sent
down the next week, as the second string, when Jim left.

Then, as I started to plan for the trip, a sense of panic struck and
another "little obsession" took over. I became convinced that the
moment I stepped off the plane, I would be shot. There would be
no grace period. It would happen right away. And then we would
have no correspondent at all. I walked around in a trance. I was
terrified. I thought about leaving letters behind to my loved ones,

for the end was clearly in sight. On the plane from San Juan to Santo Domingo, I spoke to none of the correspondents, thinking only of the moment when the plane door would open and I would step out. Saint-Exupéry wrote that no man knows whether he is a coward until he's been in a civil war—and now I would never even get to find out what women felt.

When the door opened and I stepped out into the sunshine, what I saw were dozens of marines, some of them lounging shirtless in the assuring tropical heat. In that languid scene I lost forever that kind of inordinate, unspecified, undifferentiated fear. There were times when I was afraid later, but never like that.

Santo Domingo, in retrospect, was a revolution made to order for a young and idealistic correspondent. Totally unlike the wars of today, it was a nice clean revolution against a perfectly awful tyrant, with the U.S. government on the tyrant's side, and we young reporters on the side of goodness and light.

The island itself was luxuriantly lovely. It was the island of Hispaniola, the first land in the New World discovered by Columbus on his epic voyage, and it was—and is—green and mountainous and surrounded by magically emerald seas. But its human history had contained only misery and tragedy. The dictator, Rafael Leonidas Trujillo, had ruled his fief throughout most of the twentieth century with a brutality and totality rare even for the Caribbean. A gnome of a little man, he bought off U.S. senators and politicians while oppressing his countrymen with brutish secret police whose trademark was the yellow Volkswagen. When one pulled up before your door, you knew your hour had come. Often Trujillo did the torturing and killing himself; he was an innovative sort.

Trujillo's Dominican Republic illustrated the quintessential mixture of independence from and dependence upon the United States that typified most of the Third World, and especially these countries of the Caribbean, and that I, as a woman, particularly understood. In the last century the Dominican Republic had voted twice to join the United States, for instance, only to be turned down twice. All of the intricate psychological traumas of poor peoples who both love and hate rich and far more blessed neighbors were present here in intensified fashion.

Trujillo's attitude toward women was in the purest Latin tradition. He adored his little, gnarled, peasant mother. He visited her every night after "work." He built a phallic statue in her honor on the precise spot where he was born. All other women were to be used.

Trujillo had, finally, been killed by a courageous cabal of Dominicans in 1961. His squalid and ruthless reign had been followed, with John F. Kennedy's blessing, by a true democracy. Juan Bosch, a genuine "democrat" (and a fine writer), had returned from three decades of exile in Cuba to be the island's first elected president. But then in 1963 the old Trujilloite military, who were still very much around, overthrew Bosch's fragile regime. By the time we got there in 1965, what we saw was another heroic attempt by the Dominican democratic forces to regain power from the Trujilloites. But with a difference—President Lyndon Johnson had by then abandoned the Kennedy dream. Convinced that the democrats were "Communists," he had sent thirty thousand American marines to put down this highly desirable, moral, and workable revolution.

The situation was a journalist's dream. Into the big, then-elegant Hotel Embajador poured the foreign correspondents, the diplomats, the generals, the Haitian leaders in exile, the Norman Thomases on endless fact-finding trips, and every kind of curious hanger-on. After the 7:00 P.M. curfew every night we argued, drank, brawled, and fought the Battle of Santo Domingo. Everyone became deeply and emotionally involved. Indeed, the arguments were so bitter between the "democrats," who supported the Boschist *"constitutionalista"* rebellion, and the conservatives, who supported the Trujilloites (as much in the name of power as of anticommunism), that we divided up on two sides of the bar every night. Once, at the oceanside Vesuvio Restaurant, feelings ran so high that we had to separate two tables to keep the diners from strangling one another. In the U.S. contingent people like Dan Kurzman, Jack Skelly, Bob Boyd, Dick Reston, Ward Just, Jim Pringle, John King of the State Department,

Les Whitten, and I shared a tremulous sense of mission. We had the irreplacable unity and comradeship of firemen, rushing every day to the same fire.

Every morning, filled with excitement for the coming day, we would set off in cabs (our "democrat group" usually packed in together, naturally) through the marines ensconced around the hotel, through the war-wracked streets, and down to the "Old City," which the rebels held as their ground. There at the checkpoint only the journalists could go across. We were the only people to "be there." In the to-become-famous Coppelia Building, we usually found Luis Caamaño, the colonel who had suddenly been swept to power in the coup. Caamaño, a laconic, mustachioed, square man, would regale us with the news of the day.

What seemed wonderful to me, and still does, is the fact that we —and only we—could go to all sides. Only we could know everything. Only we could put *all* the pieces of the complicated puzzle together. They were relative truths, these truths that we dealt with. They were not "the truth" that philosophers or theologians deal with, but they were perhaps even more important because they were things that you could come with certainty to "know."

Despite my editor's worries I encountered only one problem as a woman, and it was a problem apparently impossible to resolve. Even in the rebel zone, with fighting going on all about us, the Dominicans, with their Latino spirit, would bring out chairs for me. Folding chairs. Hard-back chairs. Whatever was available. Larry Fanning wanted to send me to Saigon where I couldn't get hurt. And here the Latino revolutionaries insisted upon my sitting down during battle!

One day I was covering the official, highly formal signing over of the National Palace, a center of the fighting, from the Dominicans to the Brazilian or "neutral" troops. Four Latin generals, all resplendent in medals, gold braid, and red epaulets, sat on four folding chairs under an almond tree. We—thirty male correspondents and I—were pushing in closer to overhear the military chatter when suddenly one of the generals, seeing me standing, which was intolerable, got up with a little flourish and brought over his folding chair. *"Señorita, por favor,"* he said.

Gritting my teeth, I sat down on the chair for a few moments and then, as soon as I courteously could, got up and pushed in closer.

This little drama was repeated four times. After half an hour I looked about and the entire Yalta-esque little scene had changed. I was standing, the four Latin generals were standing, and four of my unregal male colleagues were lounging on the vacated folding chairs.

First revolutions are like first loves: one works through the webs of one's personality in both. I was determined to do things my way, and that meant working as a woman and staying very much a woman. To have become a clone of the male journalists would have been not only to deny my own female identity, but to lose values that should be incorporated into this and every craft. This also had to mean never asking for any quarter; I did my job, I never asked for favors, and I tried to help other correspondents whenever I could. The result was a group of magnificent friendships, filled with affection and with humor and with irreplaceable memories, lasting to this day. The firemen (and one firewoman) at the fire!

I had very distinct ideas about the woman's new role—and about what our values should be and about how we should behave. Early, for instance, I made two hard and fast rules for myself. First, I would never use my sex in any way and, second, I would not allow anything outside myself to change me in any way that I would not change myself. I saw quite clearly that women really had a double moral-ethical indemnity, for we were or should be ethical persons in our work at the same time that we were also constantly called upon to be moral women in our personal lives. I didn't mind this—what I minded in life was not that it asked too much of it but that it asked so little.

Inside myself I was also beginning to discover what I wanted from this life. The little girl who had burst out in pique at Larry Fanning instead of expressing from the beginning what she wanted (which would have meant acknowledging that she had a right to express her wishes) was just beginning to give way to an adult woman. I was learning what the fashionable young people of the sixties never seemed to grasp: that you learn "who you are" not by pondering over it but by first learning "what you are" by "what you can do."

In a sense I suppose I was an interim woman journalist—a creature between the harder, tougher, and basically antifeminine generation of a few women journalists just before me, and the more fully liberated and very female reporters of today.

The old approach can be seen clearly in the legendary Dickey Chapelle. I met Dickey once in the lobby of the Embajador. Small, slim to the point of pinchedness, and very intense, Dickey had covered every war she could get her hands on. Now she was dressed completely in marine gear, from the boots (heavy boots in the tropics?) to the water can (in a city with wonderfully scrofulous bars on every corner?), to the *entire uniform.* She was a brave woman and very nice as a person, but I couldn't figure out who it was beneath all that gear. She was later, tragically, killed in Vietnam—standing up in the middle of combat. That was not my style. I was not only a woman wearing sundresses and sandals every day in Santo Domingo, I was also a life-lover.

We all felt the killing and in truth we all suffered over the war. One day I remember was the day we were called down to the house of one of the *"constitutionalistas"* to find that his guard had been murdered in an attempt on him. The children were running up and down the street with the dead man's brains on a stick, while we stood there staring at the pools of blood. Then there were the other days, the light days, like the days of the "Scotch war," when both sides deliberated over the fate of a warehouse of Scotch whiskey which found itself dangerously poised in a twilight zone between the two sides; what resulted was a lot of carrying of bottles back and forth, backed up by heavy strategic thinking. There was the Polish correspondent from *Trybuna Ludu* who (to his astonishment) was carted around by the American army just like any other accredited correspondent, and who was ecstatic that he had finally found a "real people's revolution."

It was in Santo Domingo, too, that I began to see my job not only as reporting the day-to-day news but also interpreting the deeper sense of what was going on—not only political analysis but also psychological interpretation.

Indeed, in the troubled and fanatical young men (the best in the country) who were fighting the revolution in the rebel zone of the Old City (against the American troops), I found the first signs of a kind of pathology that was to spread through an increasingly troubled world. When we would go down to the Old City, for instance, the young rebels, driven to despair of a special kind, would say, "Kill us," and, "That's all you can do to us," or they would threaten to "burn the city." Jaime Benítez, then the brilliant head of the University of Puerto Rico, who had done the prime negotiating between the groups, told me then in words uncannily prescient, "What you have here is the problem of desperation. They get a suicidal feeling that is aroused by conflict with a great power. You have a small person, who's proud, and he feels that he has nothing to lose but his life, so, 'Go ahead and kill me.' This is what the rebels maintain as their final card. Or, they might kill themselves—or burn the city. That is in the tradition of the Spanish civil war, for instance. *We see this in all weak peoples.* We saw it in the South with the Negroes and in Vietnam. They are willing to take the act of self-immolation. This is a new factor in the sociology of conflict. The United States discovered, to its amazement, that some of our people are willing to be killed. It did not take this into consideration when it got into this kind of conflict."

This was long before Jonestown and Beirut and Iran—but it anticipated brilliantly and frighteningly the new pathologies of politics that were arising in the world.

Those of our "democrats group" were doing some deep and often angry psychological soul-searching, for it was all too clear to us that it was decades of American policy—plus the present policy—that had brought these decent and idealistic and courageous young men to this intense appointment with history. Washington had shamelessly supported Trujillo until the end when the CIA wisely helped the Dominican patriots who assassinated him. But now, again, we were behind the old Trujilloite killers, and for many of us this was simply more than we could bear.

One of the most disturbing things that had happened—and that unquestionably contributed to the later stages of the revolution—came in the behavior of the American ambassador, W. Tapley Bennett, Jr., a tall, cordial man of the American South. At the crucial moment of the revolution, the leaders—four of them—came to Bennett in the big, white American embassy building to ask him to intervene and stop the carnage. These were not any ragtag revolutionaries; they were leading people of the country, including the respected leader of the Senate.

Ambassador Bennett told me the story, as he told it to other correspondents, apparently not even aware of what he had done. He told me he received them in his office only after they had agreed to leave their guns outside. He told me that they disgusted him because they were physically so "dirty," although the Trujilloites he was backing were morally the filthiest people in the world.

Their message to him was a crucial one: They were appalled at the killing; they remained convinced that they would win, but they were ready to accept a truce; they wanted him to negotiate for them with the Trujilloites. In effect the revolution could be ended honorably for everyone.

Even today, as I write this, I can feel the rage rising in me. Here an American envoy had an incredible opportunity, in a little country friendly to us which had suffered for scores of years from our policies, to do something good and decent and workable. And what he did was to turn them away! He told them he would do nothing for them. He seemed quite ready to give the country back to the old killers.

The Dominicans left his office in the darkest despair. They felt, they told me later, that the only thing left was to go back to the bridge over the river, where they had been fighting, and die there, if necessary, fighting to assuage the shame he had felled on them. That is what they did; and, in one of those drama-filled and paradoxical moments of history, now they began winning. Bennett's errant dismissal fueled their historic rage at the United States and gave them the fanatic, libidinous energy to win. By noon the next day they were clearly winning. It was then that Bennett, from under his desk while bullets ricocheted through the embassy building, telephoned Lyndon Johnson asking him to send the marines. In short, none of the ensuing months of agony and the hundreds of deaths would have needed to happen.

It was stories like this that the press, and the press alone, could tell to the world. At least we of the press there were able to show what had really happened—because we were "there." We were not only a corrective on the American side, we also served the function of relieving the trauma on the rebel side. We were a defusing element, for, as Americans and as the press, we gave the "good guys" hope. Journalists were becoming a power in their own right, but we were not thinking about that at all. Santo Domingo preceded Vietnam in this development; this beautiful and tormented tropical city was actually the first place where the new powers of the press were worked out.

Despite the seriousness of the situation, there were many opportunities for light stories. One morning early on, our "democratic group" was taxiing down the road to the Old City when I noticed the zoo. "The zoo," I murmured, "the zoo . . . my God, is anybody feeding the animals?"

Our entire car burst into hilarious laughter. "Here we are in a revolution," Dick Reston (James's son) said, between hearty guffaws, "and you're thinking about the animals."

Indeed I was. But I didn't *say* another word. The next day I just strolled by myself to the zoo, and what should I find but the marines in there feeding the animals C rations and other appropriate foods! What's more, I soon discovered that Mrs. Barton Connett, wife of the American chargé, had thought about the animals and had found them alone and forgotten, the ape dragging his empty paws out between the bars. It was she who had organized the feed-in.

It made a great story, and the next week I got the most wonderful revenge. Dick Reston, then with the *Los Angeles Times,* received a copy of his paper. My zoo story had the top of the front page— his political story, serious and important beyond question, was on the bottom of page six.

Juan Bosch, the white-haired, moody, writer-politician who had been ushered in with such Kennedyesque hope in 1961, the very symbol of the democratic revolution in Latin America, now was the leader of this revolution to return the country to constitutionalism —and of the PRD or Dominican Revolutionary Party. But he was not here. He was somewhere, hiding out it was said, in Puerto Rico. One Thursday, without any clues but filled with hope, I boarded a plane for Puerto Rico, with the return trip for Sunday. I had no idea whatsoever about how to find him. As it happened, on the short flight I began talking with a husky, bright German correspondent who thought he had Bosch's phone number. I could come along. When we called, we found that not only was the number right, but that Bosch would see us. That night.

There he was, hiding out in a small suburban house outside of San Juan, and we were the first journalists to see him. It was hardly a dramatic redoubt, but then at heart he was always a consummately bourgeois man. The house was busy even in its supposed secrecy. A number of dark-haired men were always hanging around (in Latin political circles, people polish and perfect the fine art of hanging around), and Bosch was charm and cordiality itself.

Somewhere in the conversation this man with the craggy face and the grizzled white hair argued passionately that his side of the story was not being adequately told—he was particularly incensed about a *Life* magazine article by former ambassador John Bartlow Martin.

"Dr. Bosch," I said suddenly, "why don't you write your side of the story and I'll get it published in our wire service?"

His eyes lit up. "Of course," he said. "Of course, I'll do it."

He had it for me the next day. Still trembling with a sense of the drama and the luck of it all, I rushed back to my hotel, where I meticulously translated his elegant Spanish into English. Then I took it to Western Union . . . to be transmitted by telegraph to my office. When I returned to Santo Domingo the next day, I had seldom felt so happy. At that moment—when the "scoop" came to be known by the other correspondents—I no longer felt like a kid: I was accepted along with the older "pros."

The revolution went on. Day passed into day and week into week as we Americans interfered in this strange island melodrama on this bitterly hot and bitterly divided island. The American administration tried to impose leader after leader, one worse than the other. The rebels held their desperate lines in the Old City, until, in contravention of everything we were supposed to be doing there, the American marines let the Dominican military through their supposedly "neutral" lines to attack the rebels. Those of us in the press corps and embassy who believed in a different United States were sick at heart—and bitterly angry at our country.

About this time, in May, the tension, the shootings, the long hours, the bodies, suddenly got to me. I had been in Haiti for a few days, where I saw the *Tonton Macoutes* batting schoolchildren outside the palace with baseball bats. The night I returned from Haiti to Santo Domingo I suddenly developed a strong and terrifying wrenching of muscles on the right side of my face. Soon it was out of control. Then the wrenching began in my back. It was not painful, but it was the most terrifying physical ailment I have ever had, because of the total sense of helplessness.

Then the very army we were all criticizing for being there came through. They evacuated me by helicopter to the army hospital, and the doctor gave me strong tranquilizers. In the morning I was fine, but it made me aware, and wary, of the tensions we were all constantly under.

Every day brought some new, almost always fascinating and quite often repulsing, development. One day, by chance, Jim Pringle, then of Reuter's, and I happened to hear at the same time from an American priest of mass executions out at a bridge called Villa Mella. Now, I knew what Villa Mella was: it was the sickest banner of the sick age of Trujillo. It was the area outside of Santo Domingo where the former dictator had had his palatial "summer home." Here he and his sons would personally execute their enemies in the most appalling ways. Then they would drop the bodies over the Villa Mella bridge and they would float out to sea. History apparently was repeating itself.

Jim and I decided to go out to Villa Mella, but we needed a good taxi driver, and this is where the real heroes of these pieces come in. At this period, as opposed to later, American correspondents still had a lot of protection, much of it a psychological extension of the realities of American power. Americans still ran the world, particularly this part of it. No one would "dare" touch us—or they would face the consequences. But for a Dominican cabdriver—that was another thing. He had to stay on his tormented little island long after we grandly swept off, and he had no protection at all.

Yet we found another of these very brave simple men to take us out to Villa Mella, and the three of us drove through the pastel-colored shacks of this strange island in silence. By some strange piece of luck that day there were no soldiers at the bridge. We stopped and climbed down below it. I don't know why I was not even more sickened than I was. Perhaps it was because of the danger. But there were bones burning, open graves, bodies in the river. We looked quickly. There was no need to hang about—and we drove back to Santo Domingo as quickly as possible, now in a new kind of silence.

The same night Jim and I filed our stories, and the next day we had the pleasure of going out—again—to Villa Mella, this time with a United Nations investigating force. At least there were no more killings at Villa Mella. Our stories had been effective.

Much later, the spring of 1971, I got off at the Santo Domingo airport and climbed into a taxi driven by a little brown-skinned man. Driving into the city along that sparkling azure sea, I sat thinking back to those bittersweet days of the revolution there and all they had meant to me.

Suddenly the little driver turned around and looked at me in a beseeching manner. "Aren't you," he asked, "the *señorita-periodista* (the "Miss-Journalist") who went out to Villa Mella during the revolution?"

I looked at him, astonished and fascinated. No, I did not know the man—how could he know that? "Yes," I finally answered, "but how in the world could you remember that?"

"Oh, señorita," he said, "we will never forget a thing like that— you stopped the killing."

Whenever things get bad and whenever I question why I chose to live such a crazy life, I think of that little man and what he did for me and it all seems quite wonderfully worthwhile.

Yes, in many ways it was surely in Santo Domingo that I first learned, the hard way and the only way, why we had to "be there." Actually, it is what it is all about, because nothing out there is ever what you thought it was or would be before you got there! It is always, always different from what you had supposed. You have to be there because if decent people are not, the brutes of the world certainly will be. You have to be there because you want to be: because it's the most exhilarating and satisfying and doggedly difficult profession in the world. And finally you have to be there because if you are any kind of responsible human being at all, it is your moral down payment. It is your part of the risk of living.

I saw Juan Bosch several times after our initial clandestine meeting in Puerto Rico, and each visit gave another glimpse into the character of this very complex, brooding man who was shaping history.

In Puerto Rico, in hiding in 1965, Bosch was very much the leader: sure of himself, angry with history and in a rage over the United States, ready to go back and lead his people back to democracy. Then during the winter and spring before the elections in the spring of 1966, another Juan Bosch emerged. Many called this Bosch the "coward." He sat inside—and I mean far, far inside—a big, old white house on the main boulevard with his guards and party members constantly in attendance. He held PRD party meetings there and gave out orders from there. It took me a while before I was willing to admit that this man with so many fine leadership qualities, this man with the face as craggy as those on Mount Rushmore, this man who still electrified the poor Dominicans with his words every day on the radio, was indeed "afraid." The generals, who despised him, were clear enough about it: "If he takes thirty steps outside his house, we'll kill him," one told us clearly. I never understood the "thirty steps." Why not ten? Why not five? There are clearly imponderables when dealing with minds of this size.

But the fact was that Bosch never, never once went out of that house the whole time of the election campaign. Many of us were convinced that it was this isolation that cost him the election. And he lost to the little old Trujilloite, Joaquín Balaguer, who, not being very discriminating, had written of Trujillo: "Trujillo is God and God is Trujillo." The young men who had fought in the revolution for Juan Bosch were devastated. One said to me just afterward, standing in the Old City where we had all seen so much, in words approaching Greek tragedy, "Our wine is bitter. Did our comrades die for the return of this man?" This, for us, was the hardest blow.

Years passed. The next time I saw Juan Bosch was in 1970, when I returned for the next elections. Part of what I wrote then captures, I think, the mood then of this kind of man scorned:

> The bitterness and trouble etched in the craggy face of Juan Bosch are like canyons in an ancient wilderness. If he were not so much a man, he would be the essence of the woman scorned.
>
> He is back in his native land after three weary years in exile, so angry at the United States that he seems all by himself to be a chorus of Greek furies.
>
> He lives in his sister's home near the blue sea that edges this tropical city, and he seldom goes out.
>
> Each day, this troubled-looking man with the clipped haircut cries out to his countrymen. His early afternoon radio broadcasts, with their homey parables about Dominicans, love, politics, and life, reach into every corner of this convulsive green island, enlivening a torpid existence with questions that only God could answer.

Yes, Bosch—the mystical, temperamental, tough core of so much of the torment of this island, is a different man today than he was five years ago. Though he is only 61 and looking fit and splendid, he is painfully aware of his age. . . . He is the democrat betrayed, so betrayed he now has turned his Cartesian mind to the delineation of a "solution" for his country that he obscurely calls "dictatorship with popular support."

Much of the fascination with Bosch is that he is a man who weaves perfectly constructed, slim and shiny theories about his Dominican country (a most random and undisciplined world) with the natural, even thoughtless, avidity with which a worm spins silk.

So it was no surprise to me, having known him for six years, to find that the furies within him had erected another perfect construction to explain his disillusionment with the United States and with democracy, both of which he had perhaps loved too much.

"Every day here people have less and less interest in representative democracy," he began. I thought back to the time when he was Mr. Democracy in the Caribbean. "Even in the United States it doesn't work. Luckily, the American intervention opened the eyes of our people," he went on, rocking gently in a rocker on the open porch of the attractive modern house. "If not, we might have gone years without realizing that representative democracy would never work for us."

I was only being facetious when I asked, "Dr. Bosch, are you suggesting we did you a favor?"

"Yes," he answered, "this is the way history works."

But that, still, was not the final denouement, not the final scene. That, for me, occurred in 1976, when I again found myself in the Dominican Republic, drawn as by some strange magnet to this mulatto kingdom of suffering.

I finally found Dr. Bosch in a nice but simple apartment up from the sea. He was totally out of politics, and he had drawn about him, like a protective cloak, an ingrown far-leftist group. He had his own ideological salon. As soon as I saw him—as soon as he welcomed me in his usual gallant way—I could see the change in the man. Before, his face had always seemed on the brink of suffering. He always looked as though about to break. Now he looked comfortable and happy, but most of all at peace. We chatted for a few minutes, while he rocked back and forth in his rocker, and finally I said, "Dr. Bosch, I have never seen you looking so good."

He responded eagerly. "It is true, Georgie Anne, it is true. I have never been so happy." He then went on, with a gentle enthusiasm I had never witnessed before in him, and talked about his "group," which I knew gathered at his feet with the spirit of the young Greeks around Socrates. He loved the exchange, and the teaching, he loved the living and working only with ideas.

When I left, I felt a certain peace too, for I always liked the man. Perhaps this was always the place for a Juan Bosch; he was meant to be a professor, a thinker; being a leader had often, I know, driven him to the edge of madness. He had finally come home.

But that was not the end of Bosch; the end, for me, was sordid and tragic, considering what he had earlier represented as "Mr. Democracy in the Caribbean." Drawn ever back to this island where I had known so much happiness and so much sorrow, I returned in 1982 for the elections. Now Bosch was running as an all-out Marxist for the presidency. His young followers, wearing red berets and running in march time, were a new kind of social fascist. But Bosch, running on his bitterness against a country which he now felt had never appreciated his genius and not on ideology, lost badly. Times had changed.

My close friends who had sculpted the revolution and the democracy and who time and time again came close to giving their lives to it and for it now were in power. Despite everything, they stubbornly remained total democrats. There was the great young black leader, José Francisco Peña Gomez, leader of the PRD party and now mayor of Santo Domingo, and Sacha Volman, the wonderfully crazy and dedicated and deeply democratic Rumanian. A legend in the Caribbean, Sacha had been behind or adviser to almost every democratic movement in the years he spent there. He was and is a political genius, not to speak of being the most delightful of companions. Sometimes, thank God, the good win.

For those of us in the press Santo Domingo was the harbinger of all that was to come. It was where we learned not to trust our government. It was where we learned firsthand the palpability of evil in banal people. It was where soldiers first told us, with common amazement, what they tell journalists in all wars: "What the hell are you doing here? You didn't have to be here." And it was, even more than Vietnam, for those of us who were there, the place where the press began the steady process of becoming not only the describers of events, but the interpreters and arbiters of "truth." Once it started there, this process was to appear everywhere, and it was my generation of journalists which had the special curse or blessing of having to live through and work through this too.

V.

New Cuba, Old Cuba

"You have all the advantages, being a woman."
—Practically every male correspondent
I have ever known

I stood on the pier in Puerto Rico, watching the ship moving away in the night. The lights of the ship first skimmed the water like tiny stars; then they glimmered on the horizon; then they dimmed, and dimmed, and dimmed. And I stood there . . . and stood there . . . and stood there, before I finally turned in despair. Suicide seemed not at all an unreasonable response.

A week and a half before, I had finished the Dominican elections of April 1966 and felt I needed to "get away" for a few days (if a foreign correspondent can properly use that expression). So I went over to San Juan for the weekend. Al Burt, then of *The Miami Herald,* and I had breakfast and he told me jovially, "I suppose you know that José Llanusa is here with the Cuban contingent for the Caribbean games." Llanusa, then the Cuban minister of education, was very close to Castro and, Burt pointed out, was offering certain journalists a rare chance to get into Cuba at a rare moment.

My weekend of peace and my dreams of beaches dissolved. No correspondents had been allowed in for more than a year and Fidel himself had not been seen for upward of four or five months. The rumors were gaining in crescendo like a crowd forming around a sudden accident. "Fidel is dead" . . . "Fidel has been replaced" . . . "Fidel is in prison" . . . "Fidel is out" . . .

I took a cab out to the Olympic Village. My best estimate was that my chances were no more than one in one hundred, but I couldn't *not* take the chance. At the gate the engaging little Puerto Rican told me that Llanusa was out. I waited. I waited and waited. In fact I waited all day. I had lunch with the Puerto Rican guards and was just beginning to get tired of it all, wondering why I hadn't stayed on the beach, when Llanusa returned.

A rangy, dark-haired man who looked as though he belonged in Montana rather than in Cuba, Llanusa stood, his hands on his hips and his sport shirt casually open halfway down his chest, facing me on the little patio of his "Olympic" villa.

"You want to go to Cuba?" he asked. I nodded firmly. "All right, come back with us on the boat." It was all accomplished in less than five minutes. Again, "hanging around" had paid rich dividends.

But the Cubans were not returning for at least ten days—the duration of the games. I became impatient. Since I had not been home for a long time and since my father had been very ill, I decided to use this time to return to Chicago for a week. They *promised*, the Cubans did, that they would not leave under *any* circumstances before the end of the games. Besides, I had a Puerto Rican friend in the Olympic Village administration, and we arranged for me to call him every night to be sure that there was no mix-up. I left for Chicago.

Everything went fine for six nights. Then, on a Friday night, I was at a party at our editor's, Roy Fisher's, and I put through my usual call. There were still four full days left until the scheduled departure.

"Something changed," my Puerto Rican friend now told me worriedly. "The Cubans got very angry at the games rules today and they're pulling out tomorrow." Tomorrow!

I boarded the first flight to San Juan on Saturday. It was three hours late. Every minute that passed was a deadly reminder to me of my mistake in not staying in San Juan. When we finally arrived at 6:00 P.M. instead of 3:00 P.M. I raced to the dock. I could still see the ship on the horizon. Going to Cuba. Going to Cuba without me.

"They waited about forty minutes for you," the dockmaster told me matter-of-factly, as though I had missed an Amtrak to Philadelphia. "Then I guess they had to go." I said I guessed they did. I went down to the hotel, contemplated suicide, and instead went to the bar.

The next few days were filled with a particular brand of torture. Every day I had to read about the ship. About how Fidel had taken the unprecedented action of meeting it there and riding with the athletes back to Havana on the train. I pictured myself . . . arriving in Cuba . . . sitting with Fidel on the train as he talked with the athletes. . . . My mind and conscience were equally unforgiving.

But if making mistakes is part of the game, so is recouping. I tried to pull myself together and decide what to do next. Talking with the office, I decided it was worth it to make another last-ditch, desperate try. So I flew to Mexico City through Miami and prepared for a long siege of trying to telephone Llanusa in Havana and see if he would give me a visa to come through Mexico, where there was an embassy. I now expected the odds to be about a thousand to one.

The first morning I put through a call. To my astonishment it went through right away and I also got Llanusa on the phone right away. "Of course," he said, to my astonishment. "If you go right away to the embassy, perhaps you can get the one P.M. plane." I was on the 1:00 P.M. plane; I had dinner with Llanusa that night in Havana.

The next night Llanusa's wife leaned across the table at the Tropicana. "We have to go," she said suddenly. *"Bueno, muy bien,"* I said agreeably. "No, you don't understand," she went on, "you're going to see Fidel."

Our car sped back to the Havana Libre, the former Hilton, and there, in front of the hotel, was Fidel Castro, leader of the revolution, hero to young revolutionaries throughout the world, premier of

Marxist Cuba, pacing back and forth. Two jeeploads of men, their machine guns poking out like sticks out of a green garden, waited by the curbside.

My first impression of Fidel Castro remains with me. And still, frankly, bewilders me. There before me was what everyone sees from the pictures—the big barrel-chested man with the neat khaki uniform, the heavy overhanging forehead, the little and tight eyes, the strange irregular jaw. But what surprised me then, and all the times I saw him, was the strange mixture of almost abnormal sweetness, like a favorite uncle's overly affectionate attitude toward his young kin, and a piercing and quite frightening coldness and ruthlessness —bordering on a total lack of feeling for others—behind the eyes.

It was also strange to me that I felt virtually no normal sexual attraction for him at all. I say this with hesitation, because it is so easily misunderstood. I never looked at leaders or anybody else I interviewed as sexual quarry, and never ever confused professional and personal relationships. (Men are equal—they shouldn't be sex objects, either.) Yet usually there was some very normal degree of sexual interest.

Castro, who was after all a big, earthy man, left me with no feeling at all. I even felt a certain effeminacy in him, something I would not have trusted had not other women who met him backed up this view. I am not in the slightest suggesting homosexuality. Castro had had lots of women. Rather I think I was seeing for the first time a man for whom women and sex were simply instrumental and unimportant, for whom power—in the name of "the revolution," with which he totally equated himself—was everything.

The rest of his entourage immediately fell asleep. I found myself, thirty-one years old with two years of experience in Latin America, face to face with one of the most charismatic and sought-after leaders in the world. My notebooks were in the hotel, but I could take no chance on losing this apparition. So I began to work out a certain method I later perfected. I learned to focus—virtually to set my mind on—certain important phrases as he uttered them. I had the conscious feeling of a hand coming out of my mind and grasping them and freezing them for a moment. I found that with this method I could keep quotes perfectly for at least three days.

And Castro was indeed a marvelous interview. You never had to ask him a question—he began, and seven hours later, or eight, he stopped.

But there was one curious pause. At 1:30 A.M. Fidel paused for breath. He looked at Llanusa, who was asleep. "José . . ." He jostled him to awaken him. "Let's get some ice cream."

Llanusa looked groggily at his watch. "It's too late," he said.

Right across the street from the hotel there was an enormous, super-modern ice cream parlor. Since it took in a full city block, was the only modern building about, and was tied to the earth by none other than flying buttresses, I sensed it represented more than a taste for ice cream.

Fidel looked at me and said with deadly seriousness, "We now have twenty-eight flavors."

I was astonished, confused. What was I supposed to say—"Do you have chocolate ripple?"

Then he said, again with total seriousness, "That's more than Howard Johnson's has."

Now I was absolutely nonplussed. Howard Johnson's? Was I in Communist Cuba or was I Alice in Wonderland?

Then he answered the riddle—and gave me some good insight into the Fidelian mind. "Before the revolution," he said, now with just a touch of humor in his eyes, "the Cuban people loved Howard Johnson's ice cream. This is our way of showing we can do everything better than the Americans."

But the little charade didn't even end there. I described the little incident for a light touch in my first interview with Fidel. The paper called Howard Johnson's in Chicago and they replied, "Sorry, Fidel, but now we have thirty-two." When I told Castro this, the next time I saw him in the mountains, he laughed heartily and said, "That just shows we have to work harder."

The stories I filed to Chicago, by wire then, went from there all over the world: "*Castro* IS ALIVE," the banner headlines read. The Cuban exiles attacked me for saying that Castro took two showers a day. The pro-Castro people attacked me because I didn't eulogize him enough. That's the way it goes.

Despite all this, Cuba in so many ways turned out to be a peculiar kind of torment. It was my first serious bout with the total ideological personality. In Cuba, for the first time, I was troubled by the kinds of conflicts that were to become the leitmotiv of my generation of journalists. My conscience tormented me with the challenge of portraying things truthfully and correctly, many of them things I could in no conceivable way really and wholly *know.* I was always on the outside touching parts and portions. This was my first confrontation with Marxist communism and its absolute demands for suzerainty over not only one's body but one's soul. A year later I would go to Russia—and in subsequent years to many other Marxist lands, but this was my first and most painful confrontation.

I have to admit, even now, that at first I was attracted by the clear absoluteness of it, and I resented and rebelled against and hated myself for this attraction. The entire philosophy seemed so simple, so whole, so cogent. One truth, one revolution, one way for man. As a lone American on that island for two months the bombardment of ideology staggered me, crept every moment into my consciousness.

How, I kept asking myself, had this whole Western, Christian people—this whole nation—suddenly switched, like a light going off, to communism? How had such a rapid political and mental transformation been made? As in Santo Domingo, the very tropicality of the place was a dissembling factor; *tropicales* are not supposed to turn out to be impassioned ideologues. It was as if something darkly magical had taken place. Everywhere I went, I asked, "How did you come to communism?" And almost always the answer was, interestingly, the same.

At Veradero Beach, Alfredo González, the bartender at the restaurant that had been the old Irénée Du Pont mansion (family pictures were still displayed on the end tables) told me when I asked

83

him how he had become a Communist, "After the revolution, they kept making these laws, and they were good for the people, and then one day they said they were Communist."

In the Third World countries that had gone to communism in the postcolonial period this change was never out of choice. It was because the people were following an all-powerful leader who had already been won to Marxism, which offered him eternal dictatorship. They were following the all-knowing traditional Latin American *macho líder máximo.*

Then there was the continuous game of watching Fidel, trying to understand this prototype of the man who becomes "one" with the people: the leader, the caudillo, and, ultimately, the dictator. Dr. Claudio Palacios Mesa, a Cuban psychiatrist, described the relationship between Fidel and the people in "la Plaza" in these words: "It was a kind of dialogue between him and the people. Oh, the people didn't speak, but from time to time they would applaud. They would find he was saying exactly the things they were feeling."

I watched Fidel's New Class firsthand. I stayed at the Communist Party guesthouses (all very cute and swish) all over the island. I dined with Fidel at his beach house with Llanusa, and he talked endlessly about the types of yogurt he was producing. I stood for hours with him on the beach while he talked to the crowds that gathered—often speaking elliptically about sharks, which I knew of course represented the U.S. I watched him take little scraps of paper from people's hands with their requests written on them. This practice had begun centuries before in Spain when people brought notes to the bishops. It was, even now, continued with the dictators all through Central America. I went to the old racetrack and watched the gaunt, jaded faces of the "Old Cuba" watching the horses.

One day we all went down to a collective farm at Banao, where I observed how Fidel worked. Everybody was "waiting for Fidel"; this was why the country was working so poorly and why the Russians stepped in in 1970 with their intergovernmental economic commission, which meant in effect that the Soviets took over the total planning of Che's destroyed ideological economy.

The peasants, even officials, stood in a line until Fidel came. He emerged from his jeep, embraced many of them, then spent several hours walking up and down each line of beans, strawberries, corn. He would stand there, that special look of studied, theatrical puzzlement on his face—a look I got to know well.

"Why not move that over two inches?" he would say, speaking of an errant line of beans. *"Sí, Fidel,"* they murmured, as in chorus. *"Brillante,"* another would whisper. It didn't take a degree in economics to see what was plaguing the Cuban economy; it was the old Caudilloismo and the dependency of the people.

Everywhere I saw a blend of the old, traditional Latin characteristics and the modern, universal ones. At the beach one day, for instance, we stood for four hours while Fidel spoke to a group of Cubans, who stared at him as transfixed as their mothers would have stared at the Virgin Mary. They they began to offer him their problems. Each problem—a roof fallen down because of the rains, an overcharge of rent, a child not cared for correctly in a hospital, was written down on a scrap of paper by Fidel and placed in his upper right-hand pocket. He then took these back and gave them to his lover and assistant, Celia Sanchez, who personally took care of them.

Then we had the lunch in Banao. To my surprise Fidel very deliberately sat me down directly across from him at a long table. Approximately thirty of his inner circle were with us. It soon became clear that I was being used—as a foil.

"Now, you are a decent person," Fidel would say, and I would wonder what was coming next. "Every decent person has to support the revolution."

"Not journalists," I said. "Even if we personally support much of it, we have to keep a distance. Nothing is so perfect or so pure in the world that it does not need outer criticism, that it does not require some people who stand apart . . . and outside."

85

He focused on me in a strange manner. "Nobody can stand apart," he cried. And he began the ideological lecture, using me as a foil. "Everybody must take part. You cannot serve the imperialists if you are a decent person, you cannot. . . ."

I could see this was going to go on for hours. And though my Spanish was good, I was certainly at a disadvantage. So, in the heat, and exhausted after several hours, I unconsciously hit upon a successful stratagem. One of Castro's own speaking tactics, when he was addressing the crowds in the Plaza de la Revolución, was to say, "and what do the Yanqui imperialists say now? They say Cuba is going to fall into the sea. And what do *I* say, I say '*Mentira, mentira.*'" [You lie.]

And so, subconsciously, I found myself mimicking Fidel. When he said something particularly outrageous, I found myself shaking my right arm in the air—at him—and yelling, "*Mentira, mentira.*"

To my relief and amazement it completely broke the tension. His aides roared with laughter, and even he laughed. The spell was broken and the pressure was off me.

But when I got to my hotel room that night, I realized what a toll something like this takes. Never in my life had I ever been left so deeply, totally, emotionally exhausted and drained. I quite literally staggered into my room. I didn't even go down for dinner. Arguing with the Fidel Castros of the world is not invigorating.

But I did not think I had lost.

There was always the nagging question of "truth"—the basic question, of course. Do you "truthfully" report a society like Cuba's by reporting what they tell you, when you know they are lying? Do you report what you suspect? What dissidents tell you? In this, my initial experience, all I could try to do was to put together my observations and insights and judgments from all sources and try to arrive at a relative truth that would please no one. It didn't matter; journalists (as most people have already guessed) were not put in the world to please other people.

I did work out ways of doing things. I could, for instance, work on two levels: the stated and the effective. Even if I disagreed fervently with someone, say a dictator of some sort, if he were indeed doing a lot of good for his people, I could judge and say that with utter dispassion and fairness. Equally, as much as I loved my own country, I could always judge where it was being just and effective in its policies and where it was not. This, it seems to me, is as close as one can get to a mini-philosophy of journalistic fairness.

What was infinitely more complex was how to report this new ideological mind. How do we report mind control? Coercion, physical or psychological? The manipulators of souls? These were the new questions for the new era into which I just happened to be born, and they were utterly bedeviling. In 1966 Jonestown and Cambodia and Iran were still to come—but I glimpsed their beginnings that hot, long, troubling summer.

In 1966 Fidel Castro had only barely revealed himself. He was considered *the* revolutionary hero of his time, particularly in Latin America but also among many quarters in the States. I felt nervously uncomfortable with this definition of Fidel, even more so after I was in Cuba. When one looked into *his* psyche, there were certain things that stood out:

His rough and gross father, a Gallegan from Spain, sired Fidel and other siblings by his servant, a woman whom he married only after their birth. Fidel always hated him. Castro was typical of the charismatic personality described by writer Gene Vier: "No single person represented an absolute value. They were always seeking the universal, which implied a detachment from the particular, a detachment that pervades Castro's friendships—no particular person has an absolute value for him." We know now that he always hated—abhorred—the U.S. and set himself up as a Communist in order to fight it. We know now that from his earliest days in the mountains fighting Batista, he planned to make the U.S. his enemy and foil, just as he tried to make me, on an infinitesimal level, his foil that day in Banao. In my heart I knew after that summer that Castro would never have made peace with the United States, no matter what we did—he needed us, psychologically, and he needed us as the enemy against which all of his energies could rage, and thus become real.

But I learned more that summer than just how to peer into Fidel Castro's psyche.

The third day I was in Havana I had run into Chile's Salvador Allende in the lobby of the Havana Libre. I blinked. There was Senator Allende, not then the martyred first elected Marxist president in the world and certainly not anything near the martyr he was to become to so many people. He was still a charming, dapper, egocentric bourgeois. I had known him when he ran for the Chilean presidency in 1964. Only now he had been totally forgotten, by Chile it seemed, by the world, and certainly by his old "friend" Fidel Castro. Indeed, he was, in Fidel's eyes, disgraced. He had not only lost (Fidel never considered him a real revolutionary until much, much later, if then) but he had lost to Fidel's archenemy, the ethereal Eduardo Frei, and to Christian Democracy, which Fidel quite rightly considered his rival in revolution in the world.

So it was that he spent most of his time sitting in the hotel lobby, forgotten and forsaken. I immediately went up to him. "Senator Allende, do you remember me?" I asked.

It seemed he did remember me, perhaps because I seemed to be about the only person in Havana who wanted to talk to him. My guides looked at him sidewise with barely disguised looks of disgust. "He is always hanging around, waiting for Fidel to come and see him," one high party member told me, "and Fidel can't stand him." It all became rather pathetic, and I somehow felt sorry for the fallen Marxist, in his funny little hats. Every time I saw him, he would say something like, "I am sure Fidel will come for me today, I am sure of it."

Later, after Allende was elected the first Marxist president of Chile, it was all quite another thing. Then Castro would fawn on him. Then Allende couldn't get rid of him. Castro imposed upon long, thin, cultured Chile an incredible nonstop thirty-day tour which left the cultured, non-*tropicale* Chileans gasping. But that was later. History, like love, cannot be predicted. It cannot be rushed —and it certainly cannot always be trusted.

Soon Allende was calling me in the afternoon to go swimming in the pool. He would bring me books of Chilean poetry, which I gladly read. He was a good companion, proper with me and somewhat subdued. He certainly wasn't lonely. What the Cubans *had* supplied him with was a gorgeous girl with dark, languid eyes who seemed to be with him everywhere. Later, when I interviewed him in his stylish townhouse in Santiago three months before he became president, I saw placed prominently among the pictures on his fireplace one of him with his arm around Señorita Dark Eyes. The real Mrs. Allende didn't mind, despite her worldwide mourning after his death. They hadn't lived together for years.

The one thing that always stood out about Allende was his incorrigibly gossipy nature. He was always cornering me somewhere and saying of someone or other, "Is he sleeping with her?" Or, "But I see them together all the time, don't you think . . . ?" Then he came to ask of me, with a playful smile, "Is *he* the one in your life?" If I were with Mario, a Mexican editor whom I found out later to be on Fidel's intelligence payroll, it was, "It must be he." I'd shake my head. He was much like a meddlesome old lady. One day later in the summer he was out at Veradero Beach having lunch with his dark-eyed beauty and I was having lunch with a handsome young Cuban foreign officer nicknamed Paco. This time Allende's eyes met mine at a special time across the restaurant—serious, not jocular. He said nothing. The next day he said with an unusual solemnness, "Now I know."

This time I turned my eyes away and did not answer.

Allende had invited me to go with him to the Twenty-sixth of July celebration, the anniversary of Fidel's attack on the Moncada barracks. It was a big, fancy reception in the palace, and I was delighted to go. We were chatting with Mario when an impressive-looking, square-shouldered man in his late thirties joined us and was introduced as Manolo Piñero. It should have meant something to me, but in fact it did not. He had a very, very solid gray suit on, which contracted memorably with a most astonishing head of red hair and a great, bushy red beard. I soon forgot him. After all, I had Allende and Fidel to talk to, but I did remember much later that his very green eyes had fastened upon me with an odd intensity.

I forgot him only until 2:00 A.M. that morning, when the phone in my hotel room rang. "This is Manolo Piñero," the voice said. "I'm coming up to have a drink with you."

"You are not coming anywhere," I said with angry firmness. "I'll call the police." This turned out, in the light of things, to be rather funny.

"I'm sorry," he said. "I thought you might remember me. I met you at the palace with Salvador. I just got off work and I wanted to see you again."

The green eyes clicked into place. "I'll come downstairs," I said. When I saw Piñero in his real self—when I saw him in his khaki military uniform—everything fell into place. We sat all night in the stillness and emptiness of the Havana Libre lobby and talked. Talked about his years teaching literature in New York at Columbia, of his marrying an American girl who was a ballerina, of the years in the mountains with Fidel. Manolo Piñero, I now remembered, was the head of intelligence in Marxist Cuba—and the third most powerful man in the regime. It was Piñero who directed all the Cuban training of guerrilla movements in Latin America, who influenced the American New Left of the sixties, and who later godfathered the entire Cuban adventure in Africa and in Central America.

We sat up until breakfast in their dull coffee-less cafeteria and about 10:00 A.M. I went up and went back to sleep. My first thought was that Piñero's interest in me was political, but what political advantage could he possibly be seeking in a young journalist with no powerful connections? No, in the weeks that followed, it became all too clear that it was a personal "thing," made up most probably of extreme macho power play, but quite real and unquestionably intense.

To be perfectly frank about it, I found Piñero, or "Barba Roja"

90

(Red Beard) as he was widely called, attractive. Those strange green eyes stared out like inviting lights in the midst of all that ominous red hair. He had a razor-sharp mind and a nice wit. But he was the *head of intelligence for Cuba.* There was no way in the world that I was going to enter into any kind of a close friendship and certainly not an affair with the head of intelligence of Cuba! Besides, if I am to be honest about it, I knew it would bring me only a lot of trouble —and no information.

So it was that I politely "declined" any further involvement with Piñero, although I told him I was happy to have him as a "friend." How naive—in retrospect. I even outlined the rules to him (I was being "fair"). We could have lunch or go swimming in the afternoon but no more 2:00 A.M. meetings. He looked at me quizzically—I'm sure he thought me quite mad. But we never went swimming . . . and he never, never gave up. And I was already caught in one of those classical conundrums that women of my interim generation were constantly faced with and that would eventually poison all my Cuban relationships.

The day after our innocent 2:00 A.M. tryst in the lobby, the plot continued. This was the day Fidel spoke in the Plaza de la Revolución. For hours, and hours, and hours. People walked in and out in the celebrity stands where I sat and stood. They drank beer and talked among themselves while Fidel went on and on and on. I spoke for a while with Vito, a delightful CBS cameraman who was the only other American journalist around, and with him was the Cuban named Paco. Paco, who headed the press section at the Foreign Ministry, was six feet two, with curly brown hair, an ethereally beautiful smile, and stunning blue eyes. He kept staring at me, and I admit to flirting a bit, caught up as I was in the carnival spirit of the day.

That same night about ten o'clock I was back in my room writing my article when Vito phoned to invite me for a drink. To my surprise, when I knocked on his door, Paco opened it. While Vito kept a diplomatically low profile, Paco and I made an acquaintance quickly.

91

In spite of my caution, during the remaining five weeks I was there, Piñero managed to call me at two or three every morning, gradually building up in me a crescendoing fear.

With Paco the situation was different. I was keeping that in hand until one day, while we were walking down the street by the Associated Press office, he told me, "I've changed your assignment officer." I stared at him. "I've changed him to me."

I looked down and away. I knew it was wrong, and I also knew it was inevitable. "It's not a good idea, Paco," I said. "I don't think we should do it." What it meant was that he, and not the puritanical Communist guide I had had on my travels around the island, would travel with me. Alone. "No," I said finally, "no."

"It's done," he said, shrugging and pulling rank. "There's nothing more to do."

I stopped right there in the street and lectured him. I was absurdly like that in those days. "I suppose there's nothing I can do about it," I finally agreed. "But there is not going to be anything between us. Nothing. And if you try to make something between us . . ."

My upbringing regarding sex and sensuality had been very strict, and I moved through this very sophisticated world, at least in those early years, being extremely careful of involvements. I am sure that most of the men thought me quite crazy—I do, today, myself. Yet, at the same time, since I am a very passionate woman in personal feelings as well as political feelings, I think it protected me.

Eventually, however, my 1940s midwestern inhibitions gave way. We were both single, we were in love, we were harming no one. I had been honest with Piñero, and certainly nobody had told me that being in love was either mandated by or forbidden by the Cuban revolution.

Then one day I walked into my hotel room, having just arrived back from Veradero Beach and Paco, and the phone rang. It was Piñero's deep voice saying, "I understand you are going to marry a Cuban." My stomach tightened until I could barely breathe. Why was I so afraid? What was I doing wrong?

"Why don't you take me to lunch?" I suggested, for that was, among my "rules," allowed. He did—to a gorgeous restaurant on the sea, one of those reserved only for that "New Class" of Marxist Cubans of which Piñero was a charter member. The restaurant was nearly empty those days, for we arrived in the wake of the purge of the party's high livers. Piñero's green eyes fixed impassively on me. I was trying to find out how much he knew, but it was fruitless with someone like him.

"We had a talk about you," he said at once.

I looked quizzically at him. "Who?"

"Everybody said you were just like all the rest of the Yanqui imperialists—except two of us."

"Two?"

"Yes." His eyes narrowed. "Fidel and I."

In all of this, in spite of being a now-experienced journalist, I was still naiveté incarnate, still the girl next door from the South Side of Chicago. I was convinced Piñero did not know of my romance with Paco—in fact, I thought no one knew—whereas, in truth, everybody did.

Even here I held to my own ethical-moral female standard, always so much more complex than those of men. I suspected—strongly— that Paco was a thoroughly lukewarm Marxist, if one at all. But I never—never—asked him anything personal about communism. I didn't think it fair and I didn't want to know anything that could compromise him.

The night before I left, however, as we sat in one of the "New Class" bars, Paco for the first time poured out his heart to me. "I can't bear this anymore," he said, saying much too much. "I don't belong in this, I don't believe in it. And I love you and I can't get out and I'll never be able to leave." For the first time I learned that he had indeed been working *under* Piñero, although he was ostensibly in the Foreign Ministry. This didn't worry me in terms of intelligence, but it certainly worried me in terms of personal relationships because, it also turned out, he and Piñero were old enemies. All of Piñero's strange glances at me, growing more and more intense over the weeks, suddenly began to make more sense—to take on a dangerous new life of their own in which I was only the instrument for vengeance.

I left the next day, with the haunting image of Paco leaning against the airport building, his eyes seeming to stare inside himself. Allende, our paths again strangely linked, was sitting in the seat ahead of me on the plane. Then, ten minutes out of the airport, I was staring at the wing when before my eyes, one of the engines went out. At that exact moment the plane swerved totally and we made it back to Havana.

I immediately called Paco, who rushed back to the airport. By that time I was sitting with Allende and two others, having lunch. Paco came to the table, his face flushed, and said he would wait for me in the bar. And then Allende—a little man with a little man's envies —revealed so much. As Paco walked away, Allende muttered to me in Spanish, *"Ningun hombre merece tener hombros como estos.*—No man deserves to have shoulders like that."

Four days and another plane failure later, I finally did get out of Cuba, sitting all the way to Mexico city talking to Josephine Baker, who had her wonderful pack of mixed-race children with her. I did not know then that I would be forever banned from Cuba, irrespective of the fairness or unfairness of my stories.

The next morning after getting out of Cuba, I received word from Chicago: my father had died, suddenly and quickly, of a heart attack at our summer home in Wisconsin. It seemed that the world could not collapse enough around me. So he was gone. How does one go on living? It was desolation itself. In 1979, when my mother, who had been the true rock in my life—the point of strength from which I was able to go out to revolve around the earth—when she died I truly thought the world was ending. It became clear to me then how she had made everything possible, had given me the strength and the confidence to face down the world. For the first couple of years I came very close to falling apart. Then I began to rebuild the structures of support and sympathy; but life was never again the same.

The next year I applied for a Cuban visa again. No answer. My phone calls were not answered. I begged people for explanations. There were no complaints about my work—and no explanations. I foolishly kept assuring myself, as women do in these situations, that I had done everything honestly and straightly. I had—that didn't really have anything to do with it.

Finally, through a friend, I took out one of the top men in the Cuban mission in New York for lunch. I plied the chap with wine, but despite this all my pleas for answers were sidetracked. Finally at 5:00 P.M. after three bottles of wine between us, I was just about to give up, if only to go to sleep, when he narrowed his slightly bloodshot eyes at me and said, "You want to know why you can't go back to Cuba?" I nodded. "Did you ever offend Comandante Piñero?" he asked pointedly.

I had—and I never went back. Thirteen years later they still refused my visa requests. Manolo was still chief of intelligence, directing the thousands of Cuban troops in Africa and, by the eighties, Central America.

VI.

Chile: Reform and Despair

> "If we always look outside for our blame, that is in itself a form of dependence, too. We must look for our own blame to find our own personality."
> —EDUARDO FREI, President of Chile, 1964

Salvador Allende always reminded me a bit of a penguin. He was short and square and waddled slightly when he walked. He wore funny little hats that his vanity told him made him attractive to women, and his popping eyes sparkled with bemusement when he laughed. His "socialism" always seemed to me to be extraordinarily well buried under solid bourgeois egotism and the stolid bourgeois comfort in which he lived.

Frankly I never took him seriously until that fateful day in 1973 when he committed suicide in La Moneda, the battleship-gray presidential palace in sober Santiago, as the tanks and planes of his own country closed in on him and his disastrous Marxist experiment. Allende had a distinction: He was the first elected Marxist president in the world, and his regime should have or could have ushered in a new age of Marxist legitimacy. That was certainly what we were all watching for. Instead Allende's "experiment," in addition to killing the greatest democratic hope in the developing world, illustrated only the unrelentingly destructive and totalitarian nature of even this New World Marxism. This, I was to learn in my voyages through the revolutions of the world, was the way all attempts at the perfect society eventually end, destroying the possible good.

He shot himself with the machine gun given him by Fidel Castro, who had never liked him. And then even the effect of that dramatic act was mitigated a few days later when the military, which then ruthlessly took over, exhibited all the bizarre sex aids they found in the two grotesquely ostentatious mansions where Allende had lived with his mistress and his Cuban mercenary guards.

But why did he never appear this way to the world? Why should this man have become "the" symbol to the worldwide liberal democrats and free-floating radicals who took him as their clarion victim of American imperialism?

I had first met Allende the day of the fateful elections of 1964, which were to decide whether Chile would go Marxist or reformist Christian Democrat. Henry Raymond of *The New York Times* and I sat in Allende's office in the Senate interviewing him. In later years, when this world had changed so greatly and crumbled so tragically, I was to look back in my notes, which I always keep, to be sure what Allende had really said that day.

"Would a one-party state be good for Chile?" I asked him.

And he answered, thoughtfully but surely, "No . . . no, not right away. It will take a while."

I saw him last, personally, several months before he became "the world's first elected Marxist president," in his attractive townhouse in Santiago. He had been ill, but he looked all right and was utterly convinced that he was going to win. Since the entire fight about Allende and his Marxists revolved around the question of whether they would in the end still observe democratic forms, again I posed what I considered to be "the" ideological question.

"If you are elected, will there be elections again?" I asked him.

He paused. "You must understand," he said, carefully but revealingly, "that by the next elections, everything will have changed."

In that same interview, as a comfortable fire crackled in the fireplace of his study, Allende told me many things. "The whole thing is distinct from '64," he said. "The last time, the Right voted for Frei. Today it is different. We have different groups with us. Large groups of priests have clearly delineated a Christian-Marxist point of view. A large group feels that if you respect our belief, there is no problem. In '64, all the church was for the Christian Democrats."

Then he went on to say, "We are going to win within the electoral system, but we'll build new institutions, make a new constitution. We are not going to live under the capitalist system." He smiled. "If we nationalize all this . . . mess of American companies, if we control imports and exports and carry through a real agrarian reform, what other things can you do?"

In his speeches he had said that this is "not an electoral fight but the definitive battle," that there would be a "change of regime and of system." That was exactly what he meant; he was always an honest and forthright man.

But Salvador Allende, one of those fashionable Third World travelers in modish socialism who brought their peoples such unending and unfashionable misery, did not win the Chilean presidency that day in 1964. That day, Eduardo Frei, a tall, thin, dark man with a Catholic spiritual intensity that he applied to a love for democracy, was elected president. The country exploded in a massive outburst of relief and of obsessive joy. The importance of Chile was clear: In the age when everyone was seeking forms of development, Chile would show that rational democratic choosing and planning would win over Marxist totalitarian methods. Chile, a country with a long and revered constitutional heritage, was somehow chosen by history to show the way to a changing world—we were convinced of it.

Personally I was jubilant over the Frei victory, although I was meticulous in writing fairly and comprehensively about Allende. It would be difficult—impossible—to forget the night of Frei's election. With my colleagues I roamed about the city that night, and it was as if a whole people had gone mad with joy. The relief—to be delivered from Marxism—erupted in the streets. Open cars spewing confetti . . . floats with young people throwing streamers, music, impromptu speeches . . . the haunting music that land had so long composed to its special beauty. . . . It was heady stuff. We didn't know then that it would all die with the same terrible intensity.

The next day Eduardo Frei gave a press conference for the Chilean press and for the hordes of foreign press. Never before or since have I witnessed the jaded, arrogant, egocentric, wonderful foreign correspondent corps spontaneously stand up and applaud a new president of anything! We were supposed to be tough and mean and immovable. That day our human side was clear.

At that press conference, and for the next five years, we heard words we would not hear again in the Third World. Asked about the American "domination" that the Allende Socialists and his coalition Communists always railed at, Frei said simply, "We ought to have a word in the world because we have our own personality. We ought to be independent not only economically but spiritually. If we always look outside for our blame, that is in itself a form of dependence. We must look for our own blame to find our own personality."

Here, in Chile in 1964, were displayed very simply *the* two options for Latin America: reform by totalitarian Left or rational reform by the democratic, Christian Left. And in the next happy years of Eduardo Frei's term I covered Chile regularly and came to know it intimately. I stayed always at the elegant, continental old Hotel Crillon, with its perfect satin bedspreads and its old windows that looked out on the gray Eastern Europe–style streets of Santiago. I made contacts on all sides, and then the Marxists were all too delighted to meet with American journalists. It was a refined conversation with them, and then they agreed on the rules of the game: then.

The one I knew best was Augusto Olivares, then a newpaperman. A big, hearty man with laughing eyes and an enormous handlebar mustache, Olivares looked much like a Hungarian character actor whom no one could forget. We would go to lunch in one of the simple Chilean restaurants, with their reckless bottles of Chilean wine and excellent food, and talk and talk and talk until lunch blended into dinner and we had dissected the world and it was time for bed. One night at his beautiful home in the lush, British-style suburbs, I helped carve the magnificent fish he and his wife had brought. Later we sang and sang to the guitar of a friend of his.

Those were lovely days, days too good, days that always and everywhere should warn you that the winter is coming. Augusto became President Allende's top adviser. He never spoke to any of us "democrats" after that. He shot himself that last day at the palace, immediately after Allende.

But in those halcyon days of the sixties Chile gathered in everyone: ideologues of all shapes and shades, journalists, pilgrims to the new Jerusalem, to the Fourth Rome, viewers of the modern ideological mind. I covered it on a regular and deliberately unimpassioned basis. I went back regularly, drawn to a future that was indeed working. I sought out people on all sides, in particular the thinkers, because that was what it was all about.

Because Chile was indeed something new in Third World development. It was democratic but it was revolutionary. It was changing, but without destroying people in the process, and it was rationally redistributing wealth while building wealth. It was a combination of devout Roman Catholic reformism, of communitarian enterprise (capital and labor corepresentation in management), land reform, redistribution of income, and nationalization of mineral wealth. It was as totally and spontaneously an open society as I have ever seen, as Christian Democrats sat with Marxists of every stripe long into the night, discussing, arguing, dreaming, raging.

On the Catholic side one of the most fascinating characters was the brilliant, arrogant Jesuit Father Roger Vekemans. The Belgian-born son of a Marxist father, he had come from Europe and set up DESAL, which was the Christian Democrats' social arm aimed at promoting "intermediate organizations."

Vekemans was tall and imposing and so quick that his words and concepts had a kind of metallic brittleness. He strode about Santiago with his long cigarette holder and his bemused mien—a kind of Douglas MacArthur of the Church—and made a lot of enemies. But I greatly appreciated him.

"In classic Latin American society," he told me one day, explaining what the whole fight for the decent development of peoples was about, "you find the dichotomy between the state and the atomized

100

dust, and nothing in between; nothing in between the state and the individual. The individual takes no real part in decisions, for he is living only in a formal democracy. We want our people to live in an authentic democracy where all the decisions are participated in by them. A country like Chile is changing from a hierarchical society to an open society, from a closed society which prefers passive responses to an open society which demands active ones."

On behalf of the Christian Democrats and their ideology, he was out to establish the pressure groups that provide the give-and-take of any democracy. Self-help was a holy concept, in sharp contrast to the power-from-above ideas of the Marxists. "Nothing should be donated," Vekemans used to say to me, "no charity at all. In our thinking, charity is worse than communism."

But Vekemans and his social ideas were not the only ones developing in the now churning caldron of the once-static and oligarchical Roman Catholic Church in Latin America. There was the new "Theology of Liberation" in the Church—and I believe I was the first to write about it. Suddenly there were all these young priests talking about "liberation," not only in spiritual terms but in temporal terms. What this eventually came to mean, in a practice that came into its own in the eighties in central America, was the guerrilla-priest—priests who naively eschewed thinking about any differences between Marxism and Catholicism.

Of these priests unquestionably the most important then and certainly the one to become the most famous was the young Colombian, Father Camilo Torres. I interviewed him one Sunday at 7:00 A.M. just before he rushed to the airport. A medium-sized, well-built man, he had an ethereal smile and curly brown hair. "The perfect leader," I wrote at the time, "especially for Latin American women: handsome, sensuous and a priest."

Even then Camilo was rejecting the traditional idea that the Church should not involve itself in socioeconomic measures. As we sat in his little apartment in Bogotá that Sunday, he told me, "I consider the work of a priest is to take a person to God, to work toward the love of one's brother. I consider there are circumstances

101

that do not permit a man to offer himself to God. A priest must fight those circumstances, and for me they are political. . . . Decisions are now produced by the minorities and not the majorities. Because of this, the majority must produce pressure groups; it must take political power."

"Pressure groups": these were the same words that Vekemans used. But the intent of the two men and their view of the outcome were totally different. Camilo crossed over. He became a Marxist priest. He was defrocked. I wrote of him in my book *The New Latins:*

> He tried for a while to work with his mass movement idea. Then, impatient and driven by whatever devils or saints inhabited him (his friends insist there were quite enough of both), he joined the Marxist guerrillas. On February 15, 1966, the government announced that Father Camilo Torres had been killed in an encounter with Colombian troops.

I don't know consciously just why I pursued this type of Church-Marxist spirits-in-torment story so doggedly. But later—much later—this story was to erupt with fury: Jesuits in El Salvador smuggling arms to the Marxists; priests proclaiming the right to be "Christian Marxists"; my Maryknoll friend, Father Miguel D'Escoto, riding to power with the Sandinistas in Nicaragua and becoming their first foreign minister; the beautiful, rational Cardinal Oscar Romero being shot to death as he offered mass in the chapel in San Salvador. But, in 1964 and in 1966, these men and these extraordinary events were still shadows in the wings.

Perhaps I was watching these developments with such singular fascination—and perhaps I was feeling them so much more deeply than most of the men correspondents—because I, too, was deeply involved in these questions of independence and dependence. A woman's whole life, inner and outer, is if anything a complex of trying to learn how to deal with the inherent contradictions and demands of dependence versus independence.

As I observed these developing nations and peoples, I understood their complexes; I felt with them in their traumas; I comprehended their absurdities. The revolution within me and within women had many of the same components of the revolution that they were going through. This also gave me a kind of freedom and perhaps special empathy in reporting. For I treated these people with respect, yet I did not feel I had to pamper them because, in truth, I was one of them.

Other difficulties of being a woman in this profession took an amusing turn on one Chilean assignment. While traveling in the south of Chile with then-president Frei, I was working with (correspondents almost always just naturally teamed up) *Newsweek*'s Milan Kubic. I found him to be an exceptional journalist and a pleasant colleague. Our bevy of Latin and North American journallists had come down in a separate press plane, and the plane was not returning to Santiago for another day. That presented a problem, for none of us wanted or needed to stay another day in the remote southland.

During one of the rallies that took place near a large forest, while hundreds upon hundreds of people roved about us, while children ran and shrieked and while Frei himself was speaking over a loudspeaker, I stood for about twenty minutes talking with the minister of finance, a cultured gentleman named Santa María. He was a pleasant, gray-haired, elderly man, and we talked mostly about how they were trying to transform Chile through the economy. For some reason I mentioned to him my one problem: getting back to Santiago. To my surprise and then delight he responded at once.

"You can have my seat in the president's plane," he said pleasantly. "I am staying down here to visit with family. Just be at the bottom of the steps to the plane well before takeoff time—I will personally put you on."

I was delighted with my good luck, for getting about is one of the great problems of journalists. So there I was at the appointed time. Minister Santa María duly wished me well and put me onto a plane that was two thirds empty. I arrived quickly back in Santiago while the rest of the press corps waited it out in the South.

I did catch a glimpse of Milan, whom I had informed of this, standing well behind the stairs to the plane. It seemed to me, even at that distance, that he had a peculiar, petulant look about him.

I did not give this episode another thought until, as I continued to make my way around the world, I kept running into Milan's account of this little event.

First I heard about it in Vietnam, from astonished male colleagues. Then I heard about it in Latin America, again from the same sort of group. But it was the last time I heard about it that it really irked me. In the winter of 1969 I was driving from Beirut to Damascus for an interview with Yasser Arafat. When our car stopped at the always-troubled border, our group had a jovial reunion with a group of journalistic colleagues in the car just ahead of us, among them the *Los Angeles Times*'s Bill Touhy and Milan Kubic. It seemed to me that we had had a particularly jolly few minutes.

In Damascus and later in Beirut, however, the men in the first car asked me in various versions, "What is the matter with Kubic?" In effect, as soon as they had reboarded their car, Kubic went into a diatribe about me: that day in Chile I had taken "his" seat on Frei's plane; I had gotten it by "sleeping" with Santa María; that was the way that "blondes" operated in this field, in which women should be kept out, etc., etc. It was exactly the same story that he had been telling all over the world, and which had come back to me through close male friends in the profession.

At first I was angry. Then I grew more and more amused. Finally, one night in a madcap mood, I wrote Milan a tongue-in-cheek letter. I noted that, since this story had become so much a part of his life and was obviously so important to his well-being, I should and would help him spread it around. However, I felt it only fair that he include with it a "minority report": my side of the story. First I wanted to know: "Which seat was it that was really yours, since two thirds of the plane was empty?" I thanked him for the compliment—it was indeed hard and even tiring being a beautiful blonde and having to seduce every man, even for a plane seat, and even harder to seduce

Santa María while standing in the forest with hundreds of people around.

A month later I ran into Milan, whom I really liked and certainly admired, in the lobby of the Nile Hilton in Cairo. I walked right over and greeted him heartily. He took one look at me and quite literally fled out of the lobby.

But in one way he was right. It is very different being a woman in this business.

As I watched, Chile proceeded along its hazardous, hopeful path, as the Catholic Church and the Marxists fought it out over ideologies as different as olive oil and Perrier water, I was learning more and more about being a journalist. I was learning how to psych out a society, to find out where the weak points were, to discover who would talk, who had something to say, and where he or she hung out. Putting the intricate puzzle together: that was my great joy.

In everyday working terms I would come into the country and check into my favorite hotel and then spend perhaps most of the first day sitting on my bed and making call after call after call. From there I went on to interview after interview, and soon learned who were the interesting people. Usually these were not the leaders but the people just behind them. I kept notebooks (and have kept them still); they are the palpable representation of my innermost thoughts and, of course, of the work.

I also found ways of making myself "one" with a new place— rather like a puppy or a cat scratching into his bed. I would never, for instance, check into a hotel and go to sleep, no matter what the hour, without first walking all around the hotel and environs. In that way I made the place mine, I integrated it into myself; and I virtually never felt out of place or lonely. I was creating a reality out of pieces —and it, of course, was creating me.

And I learned how to pack. I always find it curious that people are so interested in how I pack, so . . . I take three light, washable dresses of different styles and for different needs; a heavy sweater with fur collar; a handsome raincoat; one long dress; a bathing suit;

105

a nightgown and light robe; and one kind of crazy thing so I don't get bored with myself. With this I can usually go from the Arctic to the tropics. My biggest problem is carrying along all the papers, files, and books I need.

If it is a solitary profession, it is also a kind of loving involvement with history. To insert yourself lovingly into another culture means a very special kind of love affair. The director Robert Bolt has said, "The comparison between a love affair and the making of a film is not so exaggerated as it sounds. There is the same day and night preoccupation, the same switchback of elation and gloom, the same absurd intensity. A film-maker gives to his film the sort of anxious attention which is only properly bestowed upon a woman." It is the same being a foreign correspondent. Sitting alone sometimes in a café, I would be overcome by the mystery, by the joy, by the sense of watching or of being watched. I got a sensuous thrill out of the travel, the excitement, the observing and exploring. I have always felt sorry for people who couldn't love other peoples and other countries; I *adored* each new place. And the mysteries became ever more mysterious.

One day at lunch in Rio, one of the United Press correspondents mentioned that Walter Rauff, the second-most-wanted Nazi, was living in Chile on the remote southern island of Tierra del Fuego. There had been an extradition fight over him, but the time period had run out, so he was able to remain in Chile. Yet while people knew where he was, no one had succeeded in interviewing him. Many had made the long trip down to the bottom of the world and had sought him out in the remote fishing village where he lived, but all had been coldly turned away. When I returned to my hotel that afternoon, I put a notation in my book under Chile (I have always kept a book listing countries and ideas and names and phone numbers of people there) and vowed the next time to try to see Herr Walter Rauff, mass murderer.

Several months later, when I again found myself in Chile, I flew down to Punta Arenas, the pleasant modern city on the wild and historic Straits of Magellan. The next day I arranged to fly across the Straits to the barren, isolated island. At the oil camp there the workers were nice—they even fed me lunch at the company dining room—but I was impatient to move on. Already it was early afternoon and I had another eighty miles to reach Porvenir, the remote fishing village where Rauff lived in utter seclusion. This last portion of the trip was taken in a jeep. Once in that barren cluster of houses that is Porvenir, I asked a policeman for the house. He climbed in the back of the truck. "We had a warning that somebody might attack him some time ago," he said, "and we try to watch his house."

Porvenir—the word means "future" in Spanish. It is a place where the cold gray waters from Antarctica slap at the black rocky beaches and the wind wails day after day. Black-necked swans fly overhead, white salt beds dapple the land, and the camellike guanacos race in packs of thousands across the unrelieved loneliness of Tierra del Fuego, the last place on earth.

When the door to the Pirata crabmeat factory opened to my insistent knock, there stood Rauff, a short man with chiseled Prussian features, now in his sixties and dressed in a neat brown tweed jacket with a tan neck scarf.

"Yes, come in," said Rauff. "It's nice to have company. But, no, I cannot give any interview. I am not news anymore, and I don't want any publicity."

I sat down and tried to convince him. I lapsed into German; I spoke Spanish with him. He was glad to have company, he said in both, but that was it. Even then I sensed that he was torn between wanting to talk and not wanting to talk. He was living a very simple, very quiet life there in Porvenir. The fishermen of the village could not understand how their kindly neighbor could be accused of killing 100,000 people.

He chatted informally as he moved about his cozy little room, with its shortwave radio and its Germanic touches, but of one thing he was certain—I had to leave. That very night. I knew of no realistic way to stay, so I said nothing.

It was 5:00 P.M. Rauff stood by his radio, trying to call the main

107

"airline" office in Punta Arenas. Then it was 5:05, and 5:10. He paced. "One thing I cannot stand," he said, "is when people are not punctual. I am always punctual."

Now it was time for the "evening plane," really a bush plane, back to Punta Arenas. But before going to the "airport" he took me for a ride in his truck with his big dog, Bobby, barking nervously in the back. We drove out the five miles to the Straits of Magellan, the historic passage that divides the island from the mainland, and this evening the Straits were wild, with stormy whitecaps.

Along the way Rauff showed me the fishermen's camps, wooden shacks huddled along the beaches. "And I, who loved big cities, have to live here," he murmured.

"Why do you stay now?" I asked.

"There are many people who would like to get me," he answered matter-of-factly. "Here—they see everyone who comes and goes."

Being with Walter Rauff was a strange experience. I knew he was wanted by West Germany as the second-most-wanted Nazi war criminal. Yet he could obviously be a charming and a cultured man. I felt safe with him because the evidence against him shows that he was what the Germans call a *Schreibtisch* murderer—a man who kills by signing papers at a "writing desk." He was as remote from his actions as the place he had now put himself.

How does a journalist relate or not relate to such a man? How should one? There are no rules; you make them up as you go along. My own feeling was to be outwardly nonjudgmental, in much the same way as good law officers try to be with criminals. Obviously, that would have been impossible were he still in power.

We were standing in the little shack, with its radio equipment, in the primitive airport. The man on the radio kept asking the distant bush plane, *"Cuando van a venir, chicos?"* And then I heard, in Spanish, the reply, *"No vamos a poder aterrizar esta noche a causa del tiempo, pero*—We won't be able to land this night because of the weather, but almost certainly we'll come tomorrow early."

I looked up and looked at Rauff. He looked stricken. I was staying.

108

Now it was 7:00 P.M. and he was sitting in his little living room drinking coffee, which he served with the impeccable neatness that attended every one of his efforts. The hot water for the powdered coffee was in a neat pitcher. His napkin was in a special holder. Everything was perfectly in order in the warm, wood-paneled living room with its simple furniture. Outside, the bay was darkening, and it was getting cold, very cold. "I like the house cold at night," Rauff was saying. "I have an automatic switch that turns the heat on at seven thirty in the morning when I get up."

Then, in a conversation that kept changing from moment to moment, I decided to wade in—I asked him of what he was actually accused. His face tightened.

"They say I killed ninety-six thousand Jews," he said unemotionally. "They know I never killed one man, and we never killed one Jew there." He paused. "That was a gentleman's war."

Again the conversation changed. "I usually make package soup in the evening," he went on, "but that is not good enough for a guest. So let us go downtown and have dinner at the hotel. I will show you the 'nightlife' of Porvenir."

Since it was still partially light, we drove out in his truck to "Useless Bay," a new moon of lonely sand. By now the sunset was exploding over the darkening water, and a luminous yellow light glowed behind the clouds. By the time we got to the Hotel Tierra del Fuego, a little low place in simple but comfortable style, it was after 10:00 P.M. A small band of men, all very Yugoslav-looking (not surprising, since they were Yugoslavs) were sitting in the bar, talking politics. We had a drink, a mixture of Chilean Pisco and vermouth, before retiring into the dining room, a little room warmed by a glowing stove.

And now Walter Rauff, the silent recluse of The End of the World, began to talk slowly, hesitantly, about his past. This has happened to me before. Something about a woman interviewer puts men at ease. They sit there and sooner or later everything pours out. Men forget that they are with a journalist and respond as they do to women who have always and throughout all time been the listeners and the comforters. At times I have felt guilty about this "advantage." But after clearly telling men that I am a journalist, I do not feel it is my duty to maintain eternal vigilance and keep warning them.

"There is no brief way to explain it all," he said as we drank a white Chilean wine. "Nobody can explain simply what happened in Germany. You have to understand what Germany went through in the twenties and thirties. It was a proud country, humiliated. No people can stand that. There were terrible things done, later on— I don't say there weren't terrible things. I'm not one who says he didn't know . . ." (He seemed, I thought here, almost strangely proud of not taking the "easy" way out on "knowing.") "I knew. But I was a soldier—right or wrong, my country. A soldier obeys. That's what he is."

I pressed him, because I still did not, then, know all the details of his case. "Of what exactly are you accused?"

"They say that I was in charge of technical things," he said, his voice sinking lower. "What did I know of technical things? I was the organizer. Organization—that was my strength."

Later I was to learn that he had started as a respectable career naval officer. He was already a commander when Hitler came to power and then joined the S.S. when Hitler began eliminating the Jews and other "undesirables." Rauff was in charge of the office that dispatched the trucks to the concentration camps; he personally approved of the "efficient" new method by which 100,000 people were gassed *in* the trucks en route. Organization: that was his talent.

Later, after he had fled to Chile, he was in jail briefly during an extradition trial that failed. "In the jail, I was so calm, so peaceful," he was saying, "as I have never been before. Once, one of the jailers came to me and asked, 'Now, tell us how it really was.' "

As the corpulent hotelkeeper's wife served us lamb from Tierra del Fuego, I asked him, "If you could go back, would you do the same thing over again?"

"Yes," he said slowly, "I would have to say I would do the same thing again. There was nothing else to do."

110

But now he was beginning to look drawn and depressed. Outside a ferocious cold had set in and we said good night.

When I met him for breakfast, he looked a different man. His face was agonized, his eyes bloodshot. "I didn't sleep," he explained. "I don't know why." He tried to smile. "Old things . . ."

He drove me to the little runway. "I know you will write something," he said, "but please don't say anything too bad about me."

And so I returned and left Walter Rauff alone at the end of the world. I still remember him, standing by the bleak gray shore, saying, "This is Porvenir, where there is no future."

The Chilean experiment in democratic change died. Eduardo Frei was unquestionably the most popular man ever to be president of Chile, but he could not succeed himself. And so, by a series of electoral quirks, Salvador Allende was elected president in 1970— the first Marxist ever to be elected president of any country in the history of the world.

Now the legendary free air of Chile hung with new fears. Now the two sides no longer sat and drank and laughed and loved together, for one side no longer respected the rules of the game. Whereas before I had always been on the friendliest of terms with Allende, now he refused to see most American journalists. The minute he became president, he was a different man; now he was in public the true Marxist he had always been inside himself. Worse, it was the same with Augusto Olivares.

I remember how my heart fell when over and over again I called Augusto's office at the national TV which he now headed. I was unwilling to believe what in my heart I knew—under their new regime we were now the enemies. The tolerant, loving, rational, arguing, decent old Chile was dead.

Yet the defenders and apologists for Allende and his regime will say smugly even today that Allende was only another democratic president; that he had no intention of changing the system; that he was unfairly overthrown by American involvement and imperialism. Why did some of us refuse to believe this?

111

For one thing there was the question of who was supporting and abetting a far leftist activist group called the MIR *(Movimiento Izquierda Revolucionario)*. This was a group of fanatic leftist guerrillas and activists in the South, particularly around the coal-mining city of Concepción, which was always a poor, leftist city. In sharp and total contradiction to everything that President Allende, dapper as always and now living in not one but two of the great mansions of the old rich in Santiago, was saying about obeying Chilean law, the MIR in the South was ruthlessly taking over small farms, terrorizing people, and driving out the small middle class and small farmer class that was the backbone of Chile. Apologists for Allende do not know or perhaps do not care that the big *fundos* were actually taken over by the government under Frei. Meanwhile Allende was angrily denying over and over in Santiago that he was a dangerous Marxist. He claimed to be simply a revolutionary reformer. Of the MIR, he said to all critics, "I can't control the MIR."

I decided to go to Concepción and look around; I had a feeling the answer to what Allende really was—and to what Allende really intended to do—might well be found there. An old friend, a professor in the university of leftist persuasion, gave me a letter to the leaders of the Socialist party in Concepción and soon I was knocking on the door of one of those scabrous, shabby old buildings in the southern city. I asked to see Rafael Merino, head of the party, and to my surprise they did not even look at my letter. Within minutes I was ushered into the presence of Merino and five other leading party members. I found myself sitting in a prim circle, almost like a ladies' sewing bee.

I decided to wade right in. "Are the Socialists leading the *tomas* [the land takeovers]?" I asked forthrightly. There was a moment of silence, then all broke into laughter. "It would appear that they are," said Merino, smiling broadly. A husky, well-spoken man who was a professor of philosophy at the University of Concepción, Merino explained that "the position of the Left and the Socialist Party is to push land expropriations even faster."

After that astonishing acknowledgment that they—Allende's own party—were indeed behind the provocations, I traveled all over the province. And it became even clearer that Allende's Socialists were indeed behind everything. I talked my way into the jail in Ñuble in the province harboring thirty-eight thousand farms and stretching from Santiago to the southern lake country, and there I talked to a young leader of the MIR. An engaging young man with a ready smile and intense eyes, "Ugarte" carried the Socialist line one step further. "We have to exterminate the *patrones*," he said, referring to the bosses of the big estates. "Soon the fight is not going to be only for land. Now we are preparing for war. Civil war. The type in Spain or Indonesia." Then he brought one fist down on a knee. "God, how I hate," he said, his voice nearly breaking. "It's a terrible hate, but I hate the *patrones*."

So it really was true. The Socialists were behind the MIR, behind the takeovers of the mini-estates. They were not only fighting for greater social justice within the system but for total revolution in which whole classes would be exterminated.

Already at this time the little farmers of the province had fled their farms and were staying in hotels, hiding out. Some would hesitantly meet me in a small park, looking over their shoulders at every word they said. When I drove out to the *tomas* or the little farms of ten and twelve acres that had been taken over in total contravention of all laws and Allende's statements, there were lines of hostile-looking men standing in front of the farms. They stared at me from behind hooded eyes, pointing always to the one man who talked for all: the Socialist organizer. This was a "spontaneous" revolution?

The sense of inner paralysis that so many Chileans felt in those days was perhaps expressed best by the youthful, open editor of the big Concepción newspaper, *El Sur,* Ivan Cienfuegos. "Why does no one act?" he said to me. "Because we're not accustomed to such things [the violence] here. We can't believe they're happening."

I came back to Santiago with, for the first time, a real understanding of what was going on. And I could see, too, everywhere I went in the South, from Chillán to Ñuble to Concepción itself, that the

113

army was waiting. . . . They were not going to interfere so long as Chile still hung on the brink of being a democracy.

But it was clear to me—it would have been clear to anyone—that the army and the forces of traditional democracy were not going to wait forever and let the Marxist forces establish a leftist dictatorship. As awful and as reprehensible as was the rightist dictatorship of Augusto Pinochet, which was to come, anyone who could not see that Allende's policies were leading directly to that certainly knew nothing of political dynamics.

Ironically, those who did know this were the Communist Party leaders. The Communist Party, which was the traditional Moscow-line party and far more sober than Allende's Castroite Socialist Party, wanted a long period of transition rule. They had a theory of history and they applied it, but they also saw that Chile, with its impressive history of democratic traditions, would not bear the kind of shock it was getting from Allende's MIR tactics.

In the winter of 1972, for instance, I stopped by the gray, formal Chilean Senate building to see Senator Volodie Teitelboim, who was "the" ideologue and thinker of the Communist Party, and I was astonished at what he told me. Teitelboim, who was a Communist but a realistic one, told me that Chile was such a traditional parliamentary democracy—and so deeply so—that it would have to continue as such for many years before becoming "socialist." It would need to continue to get aid from the United States. But Allende and the MIR were pushing things so much too fast that tragedy was approaching. If they continued things like the land takeovers in the South, which were enraging so many people, there would be a military coup that would destroy everything they were trying to do.

When would that coup be? Teitelboim, a little gnomelike man with heavy glasses, looked at me for a moment. "About eighteen months from now," he answered.

Later I looked back at my notes and found my breath catching. That was exactly when Allende was overthrown and committed suicide. And Teitelboim was one of the few to escape the new rightist tyranny—he was in Paris, showing again that realistic analysis knowledge is not only power but, often, survival!

Allende was overthrown by the Chilean military in September of 1973. As the Chilean bombers closed in on the palace, Allende shot himself and Augusto killed himself just afterward. When certain liberal commentators put forth the theory that Allende was some "innocent" overthrown by American imperialism and that his regime was neither Marxist nor flawed, I knew too much to take them seriously.

Journalists know what it is to mourn a country, and I mourned Chile as I have few others. Lebanon, Cambodia, Iran, El Salvador, all taught me firsthand and painfully that societies can die, that they can disintegrate, that they can fade. But Chile confronted me with the cruelest pairing of dream and nightmare—first with the extravagant hope that the terrible problems of a poor country could be solved in our lifetimes, then with the cruelest devastation of those hopes.

VII.

Che in Bolivia:
They Made Him the Stranger

"A new concept of guerrilla warfare has seen the
light . . . the cities are graveyards for revolutionary
individuals and resources. . . . Any individual, though
he be a comrade, who has lived his life in the city is
a bourgeois without realizing it in comparison to the
guerrilla fighter. . . . All modern American experience
confirms this disharmony and disagreement between
the mountain and the plains forces, giving it the
force of law."
—RÉGIS DEBRAY in *Revolution Within the Revolution?*

As luck would have it, I found myself in Russia for that
vast, closed land's brief opening to the world—the celebration of the
fiftieth anniversary of its revolution—when something of transcendental importance occurred across the globe in the world of revolution in which I had become so deeply involved.

The legendary Che Guevara was dead, killed in Bolivia after one
of the more bizarre "adventures" (it could, in fairness, be called
nothing other than that) of modern times. That is the way things
happen. If I were to gain any solace from history, it would be from
Vincent Sheean's classic of journalism, *Personal History*. Sheean, in
China for its great revolutionary upheaval, had waited and planned
for months to travel with the great Russian ideologue, Michael
Borodin, back to Russia when he was expelled by Chiang Kai-shek's
forces. When the time came, Sheean was out in the countryside, and
Borodin made his way dramatically across China, Inner Mongolia,

116

Outer Mongolia and Siberia and Russia . . . alone! I was impressed in his book with how unembittered Sheean was. I did not have the same gracious feelings about missing Che's denouement. Besides, all my friends were there for it.

In March of 1968, fully six months after his death on October 8, 1967, I took off for Bolivia in a second-best mood with no particular plan. Soon I became deeply involved in what appeared to be the one last really substantial effort to understand what had happened: the battle to get the diary that Che had kept through those strange, lost months.

As soon as I checked into the old Sucre Palace in ethereal La Paz, there appeared Andrew St. George, a free spirit seeking company. Charming, hand-kissing, Hungarian-born, and the type to do everything in as difficult a manner as possible, Andrew was a person I immediately warmed to. "Look," he whispered, for he always whispered, "we are going to get the diary. You can be in on it." Andrew had put together a consortium representing several European publishers and *Parade* magazine. The Bolivian generals had the diary, however, and with their particular mixture of Indian cunning, sloe-eyed innocence, and market sense, they naturally treated the diary as war booty. We were in it for five thousand dollars, and we were fully aware that the generals would very probably pocket the money.

Down the Prado, eyeing St. George jealously was Daniel James, a suave, Mexican-based American representing other interests. Then in came the delightful Don Schanche of Magnum, and a group of Maoists who kept wringing their hands over paying "blood money." There also duly arrived the French writer-adventurer, Michele Ray, who was soon being swept around the country by the president, René Barrientos. Barrientos was to remark dryly when she left, "Miss Ray had such a good time here I doubt she had time to do any investigations."

We should have known that nobody was ever going to get the diary. Perhaps we can blame our foolishness on the fourteen-thousand foot altitude. There was the night, at a birthday for one of the generals, that Andrew arrived out of a taxi from one side balancing

117

a huge cake that read *"Felicidades."* At the precise same moment James appeared from the other direction with a little band of musicians. That night they decided to set aside the rivalry for a night and retired to a striptease together.

The Bolivians, meanwhile, were not in the slightest hurry. As an observer ungallantly put it, "The whole problem is that this is the first time that the Bolivians have had anything to sell." When the whole thing fell apart, a Bolivian journalist, after noting what fools all of us had made of ourselves, noted laconically, "What none of them realized, neither Che nor the generals, is that nothing ever really works in Bolivia."

When it became obvious, after hanging around La Paz for a couple of weeks, that this could go on and on and on, out of desperation I began to search out other things to do. Finally I determined to retrace the footsteps of Che, to talk to those still alive and to try to tell any untold parts of his story that I might find. My first stop was the handsome modern house of René Barrientos, in search of permission to visit the imprisoned Régis Debray.

"I'll give you the permission to go," said Barrientos, a square-jawed, highly Americanized general whose popularity and charisma with the Indians made him a good populist leader. "But we cannot force him to see you. So far, he has talked to no one." The next day I left for Camiri.

Camiri—another one of those Ends of the Earth. From the barren, windswept, fourteen-thousand-foot-high plain of La Paz, you take off from the most dramatic airport in the world. Winds blow and scream like banshees through the Andes, washing bare the jagged black peaks. Brilliant turquoise jewels of lakes are hidden in the hollows of the peaks and they flash like jewels when the sun hits them. On the Altiplano, where the mountains turn shades of purple and pink or sink into mist depending upon the time of day and wind, the Indians who have changed so little since the Conquest stand on small piles of rocks when the violent squalls sweep past; they are patiently waving palm leaves at the rain to drive it away.

The plane lifted up, up over the black, forbidding Andes, and down to the eastern slopes. Here, the sheer, razor-sharp peaks lower into friendlier mountains, filled first with green forests and then with omnipotent jungle which stretches out across the belly of the continent almost to the central escarpment of Brazil. Camiri was in the jungle, an outcast oil town that nestled uneasily in the curve of the rough mountains and in the sinuous arms of the muddy rivers. The town itself was a dusty conglomeration of Hollywood stage fronts. In the center was a pathetic raggle-taggle attempt at a park. Camiri's people were brown, poor, friendly, and unpretentious. Rather than hatred for the guerrillas they seemed to feel a certain touching pride in the sudden attention shown their region. The hotelkeeper kept insisting that most of the Camiri girls were "madly in love" with Debray. And one bank clerk remarked of Debray, "He is very intelligent." He paused. "I think he's too intelligent," he added with insight.

The colonel on duty at the military "base" told me to go ahead and try. "Just one thing," he warned me. "We can't make him talk. He's very temperamental. Sometimes he throws his dishes on the floor if he doesn't like the food." The colonel shrugged; it wasn't every day he had an international prima donna as a prisoner.

The military club, where Debray was "imprisoned" in a regular bedroom, was a square stucco building, pleasant enough, with a large sunny patio and rooms opening onto it from all sides. I waited for a minute in the sunlight, and Debray came out of his comfortable "cell." Unshaven and slim to the point of looking gaunt, Debray nevertheless had not lost his air of being the French aristocrat-intellectual inexplicably lost among the savages. When my glance traveled from him to the stout, dark-skinned Bolivian officers, the feeling of unreality grew even sharper. It was as if a peacock had been set down in a watering place for buffalo.

We sat at a little table, the sun pouring in from the patio. He looked at me with a look that was both surly and beseeching, as if he almost wanted to tell me something.

"I live well," he began, sitting in a sunny corner and leaning against a scabrous old wall. "My days are like the days of any prisoner

119

in the world. I get up, eat, read, go to the patio and sleep. It is agreeable here, not really a prison."

Indeed it was not. While the hapless Bolivians who fought for Che were *really* in prison, Debray lived here in relative freedom, getting his meals from the local hotel and having unlimited access to books and papers. In his book, which actually had been dictated to him by Castro in Havana, he had argued the new Castro philosophy of revolution. In guerrilla wars political power should not be in the old-style Communist parties (the Soviet idea) but in the guerrillas' military leadership. What it did was to read the Soviets right out of the revolutionary movements in Latin America. What, then, had gone wrong?

"Was Bolivia a good place to start?" I began.

His thin young face, coated with a few days' beard, broke out into a big smile. "Apparently not," he said, glancing about his "jail." "But only apparently," he quickly interjected. "Failures sometimes show the need for a change of tactic."

During this, our first talk, he switched back and forth constantly —from puppylike friendliness to chary reserve to brooding hostility and then back again. He was, after all, only twenty-eight. But eventually he talked openly. The movement had failed because (several million people could have told them this before) they had underestimated Bolivian nationalism against the "foreign invaders." They simply had not recognized—despite the historic fact that Che had actually *been* in Bolivia in 1952 when they had their revolution, the second in modern Latin America—that Bolivia was already postrevolution. Now he had time to think about it.

"They put me in an untenable position," he said. "This thing of nationalism is very important. You can't rise above these feelings of nationalism."

I asked him if his ideas about the Latin armies—the kind his sort so loved to call "gorillas"—had changed.

He looked startled for a moment, as if he hadn't quite thought this through, then said soberly, "Yes, they have. The armies in Latin America are the major obstacle to revolution. It is the institution as

120

such you have to destroy because it is in the hands of Yankee imperialism." But—he paused—"the Bolivian army has several peculiarities. When you get closer to it, you see there was a revolution here. One sees there are revolutionary officers. One notes that the social makeup of the army is very different than in Peru, Argentina, or Brazil." The young man who only a year before had looked at the entire Bolivian military as a fruit so spoiled it could be squeezed to pulp with the first touch, had at last learned. For Che to learn it was too late—but then he had not come to learn.

"I have not changed the idea that the political power lies in the military leaders," he said, "but you have to say much more. It is one thing to say that all political power is centered in the military chief and another to say that he is the maximum leader." What then was he concentrating on? On "What is internationalism?" On "What is the political apparatus?" On "What is the value of that which is not purely military?"

Then he paused and said, "The Bolivian government was very intelligent. They posited the Bolivian nation against strangers. *They made me the stranger.*"

After my first session with Debray I walked slowly through the oppressive heat back to the little, waterless Hotel Marietta, where the redoubtable Madame Farfari, wife of the former Italian fascist officer who escaped here to open a hotel, liked to reminisce of the guerrillas who had originally stayed here in disguise. "And Tania stood right there . . ." she would say. "And Pombo stood there by the stairs."

I sat that night eating baked lamb in the patio and thinking. I'd had a fine exclusive interview with this "revolutionary" idol of so many of the young. But the process—the part of journalism I perhaps love most of all—had just begun. It is a little like love or faith or making love. *You* begin it, then *it* carries *you* along like the river that Isaiah said would bring peace to Israel. You become caught up in it, you add to it, it forms you. It is a beautiful and invigorating process, even though it never brings peace. I decided then not to leave immediately, as I had planned, but to stay in Camiri for several

121

days. The next day I returned to the "club" and asked the officers to see the other, Bolivian, prisoners from Che's strange escapade. To my surprise they agreed.

Meanwhile I looked back over my notes from two years before in Cuba. I went over my '66 interviews with Fidel Castro in Havana, and suddenly, with a kind of chill passing through me, came across something Fidel had said in an apparently offhand manner about Bolivia. "But that is a revolution that has died," he had said, with an intensity that should have indicated something to me at the time.

"I think you're wrong, Fidel," I had said. "It has had trouble, but it is a revolution that still inspires the masses of Indians."

He shook his head. He wouldn't believe it. Then we mused together over the country's exotic beauty. "How I would love to go there," Castro said in an almost dreamy way, "but I would like to go as you go—anonymously." I nodded—being a journalist, moving everywhere without fanfare, to every corner of the earth, was far better than being a dictator, with all those tiresome powers and all those endless fears. Besides, we were anonymous; we blended in, we were at one with the universe, interpreting it and loving it, instead of confronting it always and fighting it.

At that precise moment, of course, Fidel knew that Che was already in Bolivia trying for the "continental revolution."

When I arrived at the casino the next morning, there was a ragged, scrawny lineup of poor chaps waiting for me in the sunlit courtyard—the officers had brought forth all of the Bolivians who had fought with Che. I had that marvelous feeling of excitement and curiosity that is journalism at its best. It was the first time they were to tell *their* story.

José Castillos "Paco" Chávez, a tall, gaunt Bolivian, was at first hesitant and distrustful. He sat on a simple wooden chair next to me. Then, under gentle questioning, for these men had been through too much for me to badger them, he opened up like a wounded but eager flower. "The Bolivian Communists offered me a trip to Cuba and I was very interested," Paco related. "Then they told me the Cuba

122

trip was off and instead we were going to the Soviet Union. So we left one night and I found myself up in the mountains at this farm. I soon came to realize what had happened. I was very resentful that they weren't honest with me, and told me they couldn't tell me more for security. Che told me he didn't believe my reasons for feeling resentful. He said that I wanted to leave because of cowardice."

It was, I thought but didn't say, the same thing he had said to Debray—and later *about* Debray in his diary.

A picture soon began forming in my mind: a grisly picture of an utter stupidity that was so profound that it had somehow to be deliberate. From the beginning it was clear that something was very, very wrong. Paco was not the only one. Others, too, the unemployed and the adventurous and the inspired and the desperate—all were lured from La Paz with a week's advance salary and promises of high adventure, only to find themselves in a run-down ranch, Nancahuazu, which Che bought with $1,250 on the empty eastern slopes of the Andes. Belatedly they discovered they were "guerrillas" fighting under autocratic Cuban leaders: men who wore beards (Indians do not have beards and distrust them ever since the Spanish Conquest) and men who did not even try to speak the Indian language, Quechua.

Moreover, the leaders had chosen a deeply forested, sparsely populated, isolated area on the eastern slopes of the Andes where they could hide but where they could do little else. It was a miserably difficult place, infested with strange bugs, and an area of steep mountains and debilitating heat. The tactics were to set up three fronts, one in the Andes, one in the north, and one in the center of the country. After the Cubans had "trained" the Bolivians, they would move on to another country. They fully expected Americans and Argentines to intervene and they reasoned this would inspire the nationalistic Bolivians to join up.

None of this happened. While "El Che" sat reading books in the camp, the disgruntled Bolivians began to desert. Two former miners left and told the police about the "strange ranch" in the mountains. And as the months crept by, the extraordinary mistakes of the

Guevara movement piled as high as the mountains from which they had expected to launch their attack on a continent.

My next Bolivian prisoner was Orlando "Camba" Bazan, a young man with a ragged goatee and eyes, now sad, that must once have danced. Camba told me a fascinating story—later confirmed to me by everyone, including Debray—which explained, on the most immediate gut level, why Che had failed.

It was New Year's Eve, 1966, out at the "strange ranch," and Che had inexplicably been idling his days away, as if the revolution could easily wait. That New Year's he had a special—an important—visitor, Mario Monje, general secretary of Bolivia's Soviet-line Communist Party. He had made his way through the high jungle for a clandestine rendezvous with Guevara. For two hours in the later afternoon Monje and Che had met privately in the camp near the house and discussed working together. The natural division was obvious—the guerrillas would rule the countryside; the party, the urban support movement. But behind the two men on that historic occasion was the same division—the same difference in dogma— that was to doom the movement and doom all of Castro's adventuring in the Latin Americas of the sixties and the seventies, until he turned to the much more malleable Africa and to Central America in the late seventies and the eighties.

The Soviet parties, born in the thirties and taking their cues from Moscow like a conditioned reflex, had since 1965 chosen a nonviolent line of working within the political processes. The line matched the Soviets' interest, in the second half of the twentieth century, in respectability, diplomatic relations, and trade treaties with Latin governments. For the Cubans this was anathema. Out to "revolutionize" Latin America, they were convinced it could be done only through violent overthrow of the present states.

As they sat there under the waning sun, as the year was about to turn so fatally, Monje laid down his demands. The Communist Party would take part if: (1) Bolivian Communists who followed the Peking line were not allowed to participate; (2) the military and political direction was in the hands of the Soviet-line party; and (3) Che

124

solicited the help of all the Communist parties of Latin America.

Che was furious. Why had Monje come at all? He was particularly enraged by party leadership demands. Che would never give up direction of the movement, never!

Before he left, never to return, Monje then met privately for two hours with the fifteen Bolivians fighting with the movement and told them what Che had said. Camba told me, as this tale spun itself out, "Che warned Monje that if the Communists would not enter the movement, they would accept other non-Communists. Monje could not accept that either. We thought he should enter under the guerrilla movement in order to seize the directorate later. But Monje said that even if they took part, they wouldn't be given political leadership. He always stressed the political must dominate the military. Che thought the other way."

Why had the Bolivians, most of them Communist Party members, stuck it out?

"*Bueno . . .*" Camba said. "Well . . . we wanted the revolution the fastest possible way. We didn't want to die for the old ideas but for something more radical. Now we realize the party was right. You can't get thirty men to fight in the front lines unless it's for political reasons."

These may seem esoteric arguments—theology debates—but they were crucially important: It was this bitter division that sealed Che's fate in Bolivia and sealed, in effect, Cuba's attempt to "revolutionize" a Latin America that was not so ripe or rotten a fruit after all.

In real terms it meant that without anyone in the cities to provide information, support, and supplies, the movement became isolated and lost in the vast green forests and mountains of Bolivia. At the end they literally lost each other among the trees in a strange and lethal minuet of the blind. The guerrillas had no representatives anywhere. A press release on their activities took more than a month to reach nearby Cochabamba. At one point Che wrote in his diary, "I receive everything [from Havana] by radio, but it is useless if you don't communicate simultaneously with La Paz." He had to communicate with La Paz through Havana!

125

This information I put together through Paco and Camba and Debray, as well as other sources elsewhere, but I also learned of the sense of hopelessness of the entire venture from someone else—Ciro Bustos, the Argentine Communist artist also captured with and held with Debray. As it happened, I was in the casino the second day interviewing the Bolivians when Bustos walked out of his room. He was a tall, sad-eyed, balding man who always wore a slightly desperate air about him. The Bolivians, kind as always, were letting him make extra money by allowing townspeople in for Bustos to draw their caricatures. I immediately asked permission for my caricature to be done, and permission was duly granted.

All of my interviews had been with the accompaniment of either an American Special Forces officer, or, if in Spanish, a Bolivian officer. This was my one chance to be totally alone—for long periods of time—with one of the principals. The first day Bustos worked on my caricature, which I still have, for two and a half hours. Every once in a while one of the officers came and looked in the window, smiling.

At that moment, of course, we were there unspeaking, I on a high stool, Bustos working assiduously behind the easel. All of the rest of the time . . . we talked feverishly.

At the end of the first day Bustos feigned artistic temperament, threw up his hands in the presence of the officer who had come to get me, gazed with darkened brows on his work, and crumpled it up in front of all of us.

"What are you doing?" I cried, like a benighted heroine of old, almost on cue.

"It is awful, awful," he cried out in answer. "We must do it over again." That meant three more hours of talk the next day.

As I sat there the next day on the high stool and he stood there wrinkling his brow and swiping at the paper with a piece of chalk, he talked freely. "Che did everything wrong," he began. "I myself couldn't understand it. After one attack, we stayed twelve days in the base camp, instead of moving. Twelve days! And then we returned to the place of the ambush." He paused and shook his head, as if in physical pain.

What, I probed, did Debray really think? "Debray agrees," he answered. "When I was in prison at the time of the death of Che and heard him saying that that wouldn't stop the revolution, I was bewildered. To me, it was the end. I was in total disagreement. Then I realized he was saying that for political reasons. There were many errors in everything. It was almost unbelievable. There were no political ties with the city. I said something to Che once about the political liaison, and he said ironically, 'Yes, we have three people.' He didn't seem to want it. There was no support at all."

But the biggest problem he outlined was the one I had already seen in my interview with Debray. "Because of Che's vision of the revolution as continental, because of this, he didn't see the weaknesses of choosing Bolivia," he said. "He underestimated Bolivia— the army, the will, the nationalism. He simply didn't expect them to resist the way they did. He didn't expect the army to fight the way it did. And then there were the Cubans. They were a drawback." He shook his head. "Too many Cubans." A lot of people in the world would come to echo those words.

Two days later I moved on, over the mountains by small plane to Santa Cruz, a bustling "new city" on the Bolivian edge of the vast flat Chaco that spreads out to Paraguay, Brazil, and Argentina. From Santa Cruz I moved up, by car, to my last stop, the mountain town of Vallegrande, where Che's body had been brought and laid out after he had been killed in the small town of La Higuera.

Vallegrande is no typical Indian town, with small plain buildings and colorfully dressed people. Nor is it a *mestizo* or *cholo* town, of mixed blood. Vallegrande is an almost pure Spanish town, with women with black shawls over their heads and a sad, desolate air about it. All pitted whitewash and restless dark shadows, Vallegrande seems to be a town in perpetual mourning.

I checked into one of the hotels, a simple little place with a large,

127

flowery patio. The room was tiny and we washed at the fountain in the patio. I soon discovered that the "legend of Che" had quite taken over this strange, anomalous backwater, fed by its dark Spanish curiosity and superstition. Picture postcards of Che in death, his eyes open, his bearded, handsome face closely resembling a drawing of Christ, were in every store window. I bought as many as I could find. The townspeople, with their dark Spanish heritage, perhaps understood much more than the rest of the world what had brought Che Guevara to Bolivia.

One night, for instance, I sat in the pleasant dining room of my little hotel with the wife of the owner. She wore her black shawl, with its echoes of Moorish times, around her head and shoulders. Why, I asked her—and myself, for the thousandth time—had Che come to Bolivia?

She fixed her dark olive eyes upon me. "They came looking for death," she said, unsmiling, unemotionally. "They killed many, and they found it."

The chill of those words remained with me as I went my rounds, talking to everyone from soldiers who had captured him to townspeople, to the doctor who had examined him. In trying to put together the story, I, too, had become obsessed with death.

At the end, without shoes (they were not even *that* well prepared) and in two groups totally out of contact with each other, Che's band, including an East German agent, Tania, with whom he was having a love affair, wandered aimlessly through the forest. The peasants, whom he himself had written must support any guerrilla movement or it would fail, had reacted only with empty stares and cryptic answers. Then, when the strange band, as strange with their beards as the Spanish Conquistadores had been to the Aztecs and Incas, had passed, the Indians informed *their* (Bolivian) army of the passing of the New Conquistadores.

"They are impenetrable as rocks," Che wrote finally in his diary. "When you talk to them it seems that, in the depths of their eyes, they are mocking you." Finally, too, he dropped all pretense of "inspiring" or "liberating" people, as do all totalitarians when they cannot have everything precisely their own way. By the end he was writing in his diary, "Until now, the peasants have not been mobilized, but through terrorism and intimidation, we will win them." That, I was to learn in Bolivia and many other places, is what revolution and "love of the masses" so often comes down to.

It all grew so desperate that when a peasant tried to enlist toward the end in a village of Alto Seco, Che told him bitterly, "Don't be crazy. Can't you see we're finished? We don't even know how to get out of the forest!"

Then, with the suddenness of one of the jungle storms, it was all over. The day of his capture, October 9, 1967, which was also his last day on earth, Che and seventeen guerrillas met Bolivian rangers at 1:30 P.M. in a narrow valley one mile from the remote village of La Higuera. Just before 3:00 P.M., Captain Gary Prado, tall, hawk-nosed leader of ninety rangers, suddenly found himself face to face with the "legendary" Che. Through interviews I was able to reconstruct the day:

"I am Che Guevara," the guerrilla said simply. By now he was wounded in the leg and barely able to walk.

"Show me your left hand," Captain Prado commanded, for Che had an identifying scar from the days in Cuba's Sierra Maestra. It was there.

"We did not know the rangers were going to be here," Che said, his voice wandering. "Everywhere we go, there are soldiers." Then, to Prado, "Don't worry, Captain, it's all over." Later Che recouped and said, "Don't be naive, my friend, the revolution does not have a chief. But very soon, Captain, these same soldiers that you now command are going to shoot against you."

This was more than Prado could stand. "We have a democratic army here," he told him. "We have had our own revolution. When I go out on the street at night, I go with my soldiers. They are my best friends. Why didn't you go to your own country, to Argentina. You need a revolution there."

"Maybe you're right," Che answered reflectively. The enigmatic, bittersweet smile again.

Meanwhile a Bolivian guerrilla named Willy muttered despondently, "We're just pieces of meat. They throw us here, they throw us there. Of what importance are we to anybody?" Like a Greek chorus.

Meanwhile Prado got into radio contact with the command in nearby Vallegrande. "Hello, hello," he kept repeating. "We have papa, we have papa."

"I'm papa?" Che asked, amused. "You call me papa?" For a moment the two adversaries smiled at each other.

But it was the last time he was to smile, because, unbeknownst to him, his friend, the "revolutionary" Régis Debray, was in actuality the one who had sealed Che's fate. First, when he was captured, it was he who had told the Bolivians that Che was there. Second, it was his trial, made into a worldwide spectacle for the Left, that had set the Bolivians, who after all had been invaded by these "strangers," wondering what they would do when they caught Che, whose trial could bring forth almost anything. It was decided that Bolivia could not risk bringing Che to trial—Che would be killed when captured. And he was.

The first story was that he was killed when captured, but there were too many observers for that story to last. The second story was that he was shot in the schoolhouse at La Higuera. But I heard a third story, which I believe to be true.

One of the many people I went to see in Vallegrande was the doctor who had examined Che when he was brought on a litter to Vallegrande and who had pronounced him dead. A slight, dark-haired, serious young man, he invited me to come to his house to see "something peculiar." It was one of those truly fortuitous moments that one comes across as a journalist.

One dark night in Vallegrande I went to his house on a side street. He lived upstairs in a barely furnished room: as austere as everything else in this strange "Spanish" world. Finally he brought out a rumpled shirt, a bloody shirt. "This was Che's shirt," he told me quietly. "I took it off of him." He spread it out on the floor. "Look at these rips." There were bullet holes, yes, but there were also long slashes.

130

He stared at me in the candlelight. I couldn't figure it out. "Che was not killed by bullets," he told me flatly, "he was killed by a bayonet to the back and by a machete." If true, it shed a grim light over the death of this obsessed man. Was it true?

I came to believe it was. First of all the doctor had nothing at all to gain from telling me this. I offered to buy the shirt—at an exorbitant sum—but he said he would never sell it for any amount. You could tell by the blood around some of the jagged rips and not around the others which gunshots and knife wounds had been made before death and after. But it was something I never could actually "prove."

Still curious, I began to make my own investigations into the deeper psychological "whys" of the whole Che adventure.

Most important—absolutely crucial to the entire thing—was the peculiar mental state of Che. It was a suicidal state which I sensed from the moment I read about his death so far away in Russia. People who deify revolutionaries—and this includes many journalists —miss these things because they see every motive as clean and pure and ideological.

In the thin, parched air of Bolivia that early spring I heard story after story of Che's will to failure. But it was a supposition that I really *knew* to be true only when I read Muhammad Hasanayn Haykal's book *The Cairo Documents,* published in 1971, and then talked to him in Cairo. Egypt's Haykal, Gamal Abdel Nasser's alter ego, had seen Che in the mid-sixties just as he was about to embark upon the first part of his "revolution" adventure in Africa, just before he "disappeared" from the face of the earth. It was, of course, when the African part—which took him to the Congo, to Brazzaville, and perhaps to other places—failed so miserably that he turned his eyes again to Latin America.

Both Nasser and Haykal were stunned by Che's mood. Well aware that he had failed miserably in Cuba as economic czar in the postrevolution days, when he bought totally useless factories in East Germany and transported them whole to a Cuban economy that had no use for them, Che kept talking about "dying," not as redemption, but, as it seems, a kind of compensation for his failures.

Nasser told him, according to Haykal's book, "If we had only the romance of the revolution without the necessary developments, it would be a catastrophe. If you don't do all those difficult and full tasks, then there will be no revolution."

Haykal writes: "Guevara replied, all his frustration showing, 'But after a revolution it is no longer the revolutionaries who do the job; it is the technocrats and the bureaucrats, and they are antirevolution.'"

At their last meeting Guevara told Nasser that the only thing he was searching for was "where to go, where to find a place to fight for the world revolution and to accept the challenge of death."

Nasser, Haykal relates, said to him, "Why do you always talk about death? You are a young man. If necessary, we should die for the revolution, but it would be much better if we could live for the revolution."

Che did not want to "live for the revolution." I talked with the elegant, ironic Haykal in his apartment over the Nile during the Cairo Conference of 1977 and he told me that, yes, the entire talk with Che had been along these morbid lines. Che wanted to die for the revolution. Or did he? Did he perhaps want to die for himself?

The Cubans—and one aristocratic Frenchman—went to Bolivia to prove their new ideas of the "continental revolution" and of the seat of political power within the military guerrilla forces. What they did was to *disprove* them.

The Cubans did not understand their own revolution. They believed it was waged by only a handful of courageous men in the mountains who mounted the fight against Batista. Indeed, they were the revolution's symbol. But the revolution was really waged in the cities—by the middle classes who came to despise Batista. Nor did the Cubans really care about Bolivia, that funny, beautiful little Indian country where all the tables have three legs. They looked at it in the way that the United States so often has looked upon little

132

throwaway countries—not as nations of intrinsic value, but strategically, manipulatively.

Bolivia was simply a stepping-stone to new, Bolivarian-Castroite glory. The first domino. Bolivia was a means and not an end to them, just as Vietnam was—at the same time—to the United States, and both paid a steep price for such dangerous oversights.

All of the Cuban leaders came from well-to-do families, in contrast to the Bolivian army and peasants. All were the kind of déclassé intellectual who fits in so well with the world-view New Left. In all of them revolution began in the cerebrum, not in the stomach, and so the most natural step was to theorize revolution to death—to be governed by ideas, rather than the more practical tyranny of need.

At the end Che was in a rage against the Bolivians for not obeying him; he was going to "force" them, to kill them for their independence and recalcitrance, even though they were just fulfilling his own death wish. The entire experience only reinforced what was coming to be my basic skepticism of revolutionaries and their motives and their concern for people. Being from the South Side of Chicago, where life was real, the romance of "revolution" and "liberation" never captured me.

In 1970 Castro adopted not only the Soviets' economic overseeing of his disastrous economy but also their ideological concepts. Now he backed their slow road to revolution and, in places like Chile, even warned Allende against moving too fast. The diary got to Cuba and was printed there. Debray eventually was released and faded into obscurity for a while before coming back in 1981 as an adviser to the new French Socialist government. A series of deaths of the Bolivians involved, including President Barrientos in a mysterious helicopter accident, added a last touch of drama to the saga.

The epitaph for this tale of revolution-in-our-time was told to me later by a Bolivian colonel. One day Debray received a Christmas card from a little French girl. "She said she was praying for him," the colonel related. "It was very sweet. I asked him to translate it and he threw it to the ground." The colonel shook his head. "How can you kill for the new generation and not care about that child?"

VIII.

USSR: The Well-Fed Wolf

"The well-fed wolf does not become a lamb."
—Old Russian proverb

By the spring of 1967, although still very much in love with Latin America, I was also ready for a change: ready to move on, geographically and professionally. I had lived in Latin America for three years and had covered the continent from Panama to Tierra del Fuego. As always I had to do my own planning, for editors everywhere seem perfectly happy for you to stay where you are.

I decided it was time to go to Russia, time to be completely (not, as in Cuba, peripherally) drawn into the dialectic of our era between democracy and totalitarianism.

The ostensible reason was the fiftieth anniversary of the Russian Revolution. The paper immediately agreed to the trip, and I began planning. This time—in contrast to what it would be when I went back in 1971—planning was relatively easy. The government wanted to impress foreigners and was even (unheard of!) working with foreign journalists, instead of against them. Novosti, the government's press agency, was willing to work with foreign journalists for a price and to arrange interviews. I set as my major task the investigation of Soviet youth. At this critical juncture in Soviet history I would attempt to see what the next fifty years would bring.

The trip there was filled with expectation. Years before I had

134

fallen in love with Russian history and literature, had cried over Turgenev's young and idealistic heroines, had dreamt of the barren vastness of the steppes and the wild darkness of the forests. Now it was all within my grasp. Henry Gill, the same fine photographer I had gone to Guatemala with, and I were planning an elaborate and seductive approach—from Japan by ship to Vladivostok's port of Nahodka, then across all of Siberia, down through Central Asia and up to Moscow and the cities of the north.

En route to Hawaii I arranged to stop in San Francisco to see Eric Hoffer, the famous longshoreman philosopher and author of *The True Believer*. I had written ahead of time and, among other things, told him how shamelessly I had "plagiarized" him. Apparently that caught his fancy because he invited me to dinner. His answering note consisted of four lines written in a small cramped hand, crowded up on the top of a piece of lined schoolbook paper. He wrote that he would be happy to see me and where should he call for me? Then, when I arrived at the hotel, there was a similar note saying, "Welcome to San Francisco. Please call and let us know you are here."

By five o'clock, the San Francisco fog was slipping down from the tops of the hills and then cowering in the valleys. Between these two layers, I saw a brown-gabled house with windows looking out from under eyebrows of sagging vines like great eyes. It was a gentle house —a kind house—and when I rang the bell there was a friendly bedlam.

"Come into the kitchen, we'll have some Scotch, we'll have a nice time, don't you like the kitchen best?" The kitchen, indeed, was one of the warmest and most hospitable I'd ever seen. As I looked at Hoffer, a big man, almost bald, he seemed to me like a person in whom all the good qualities of the workingman—the man whom he writes about and believes in—were personified. He was a warm and passionate man, nothing about him was quiet or restrained; his voice boomed; his laugh was proclamation. If we had Capitalist Realism statues, he would be our model of a workingman. Lily, his friend, was a beautiful woman of Italian descent, her dark hair falling

135

naturally into curls, her eyes silky and her mouth slow and sensuous. They were all big, vital people—bigger than life really, a lot like my own family. He, particularly, reminded me of my father.

Hoffer's book, *The True Believer*, had become a bible for many people, particularly in the fields of revolution I was working in. In it Hoffer had characterized, analyzed, and theologized about the "weak" of the earth—immigrants, women, workers, but people who worked out and through their weakness in the American, democratic mode instead of the Russian, totalitarian mode which I was soon to see firsthand.

He saw, in short, that America had been settled and peopled and given its peculiar character by the weak, by people who had been torn out of their communal European societies and tossed adrift— physically, psychologically, and emotionally. Later he would fashion his philosophy of the weak—the misfits, the outcasts—as the catalyst of history, and he would write:

"People torn out of communal societies become isolated and afraid unless they have abundant opportunities for self-realization. The only way to acquire confidence and self-esteem is to make individual existence bearable." But, he went on, the "shock of change"—to be successful in releasing vast human energies, like those of the uprooted immigrants who came to America—must occur simultaneously with a tradition of self-reliance and the opening up of abundant opportunities for action. These factors, however, are not present in much of the underdeveloped world. Hoffer saw weakness as corrupting if it did not have these "abundant opportunities," and wrote: "Weakness, too, corrupts. The resentment of the weak does not spring from any injustice done to them but from a sense of their own inadequacy and impotence."

For, he went on to contend, if the uprooted were not permitted to work off their desperate and lonely energies in unceasing activism, the only other answer to their gnawing insecurities was faith: absolute faith in which they could ease the burden of their suddenly freed selves and avoid the terrible consequences of freedom without purpose or form. How well this fit the Third World revolutionaries I'd known and particularly the Marxists I was constantly covering! "Every extreme attitude is a flight from the self. . . . The passionate state of mind is an expression of inner dissatisfaction." Such people, moreover, could easily switch from one passion to another, for what they really sought was not truth but faith. And so Communists could turn easily to become violent anti-Communists. Hoffer also had his own notion of what the uprooted of the world desired. This was generally thought of by Washington analysts as material things and economic development, to start with. No, said Hoffer, their needs were not primarily material, their needs were psychological. "Give the people pride and they'll live on bread and water, bless their exploiters and even die for them. You do not win the weak by sharing your wealth with them. It will but infect them with greed and resentment. You can win the weak only by sharing your pride, hope or hatred with them."

In that evening I spent with Hoffer and friends, it came through to me even more dramatically than in his books how much he believed that America was not only the quintessential, but the only country of the common man. Hoffer distrusted the intellectuals—they were too theoretical for him. He saw them as the true oppressors because when they came to power they demanded not only physical submission but mental submission as well. I could not have arranged a better briefing for my trip to Russia—where before the Marxist revolution the czar could own men's bodies but only God could own their souls.

Once during the evening Hoffer shouted—that is the only verb to use, for his voice was so resonant—"I will never leave America." How like Saul Alinsky, whose friend he had been!

Over a groaning dinner with roast pork, huge scoops of ice cream with walnuts, and glass after glass of red wine, he discussed the recent Berkeley riots, which was exactly the sort of event to disgust him. He saw this kind of student in the same light as the intellectual —wanting to tell the workingman, who after all produced all the wealth, what to do, wanting to make him respond like a Pavlovian dog.

137

"When I saw those riots," he said with an impish look, aimed particularly at me, the Latin Americanist, "I wrote down in my little book, 'The working men of the world are becoming Americanized, and the American intellectuals are becoming Latinized.' " As to the black firebrands then looting cities, he declared without equivocation: "They are not revolutionaries. Revolution is not stealing and burning." Stokely Carmichael was someone who "wants to be given power as if it comes in a can. The Negro needs pride in himself. He can't be given things." During this he continuously called intellectuals "scribes."

But he listened, too. I was able to tell him several things that backed up everything he had written—among them the fact that in Latin America "anti-Americanism" was the preserve of the intellectuals and the middle class and that, on the contrary, the workingmen are very pro-American. I told him that his ideas about the dependence of the weak upon the strong and the resentment it caused were particularly apt in Latin America where the weak (the Latins) resented the strong (the United States) not so much because of injustice but because of their own feelings of inadequacy.

Hoffer replied: "I knew it . . ." He cried out, then: "The workingmen of the world will all look to America. They will all understand America."

I remember the evening as though it were yesterday: the sheer human zest and passion, the wonderful talk, the belief in a future for mankind—but a *realistic* one.

Only days later, Henry and I stood on the deck of the Japanese ship as it approached through the gray mist the empty, dimly outlined coast of the eastern Soviet Union. Low, hilly, bleak. I was filled with a deep emotion, as though a long-held dream were about to be realized.

Soon it was all spreading out in front of my eyes, so close and yet, always, always, always so far. There, in Khabarovsk, where the men fought tigers with their bare hands. There in Bratsk, far north in the Siberian wilderness, one of the "new towns" where people went to escape. There in Samarkand and Bokhara, between the Red and the Black Sands in Central Asia, in the great blue and gold cities of Tamerlane. It was all within my grasp—and always and ever eluding my grasp.

Our days everywhere were similar. We were always housed in some utilitarian but acceptable (finicky male Henry didn't agree with that last word) hotel where nothing ran efficiently or smoothly, but instead with the utmost of bureaucracy, which is what the Russians substitute for efficiency. In each city we could contact the Novosti man and he would have arranged appointments. The appointments were always formal and utterly similar, as though we were dealing with well-informed and well-planned puppets. Every moment we were challenged; we were "the imperialists"—why were all capitalists so ugly, so inhuman? Facts, statistics, history: nothing moved them. Every night we came back to the hotel exhausted with that special exhaustion that no one can know who has not known Russia. We would stagger to the dining room, sometimes struggling for hours to catch the waiter's or waitress's eye. Deliberately, insouciantly, scornfully, sarcastically, they would ignore us. Sometimes it took three hours to get the simplest and always the most banal of dinners. Since in the Soviet Union any service occupation is looked down upon, they excuse themselves from serving other people by scorning them. It was enraging. Often we got around it by ordering caviar and champagne in our rooms. Eric Hoffer would have enjoyed the sight of us, here in the "workers' paradise," surviving by eating caviar and champagne!

How was I going to write about this shrouded land, this cloaked people with their souls hidden deep inside them? Where was I to go to discover their real selves? Were there even "real selves"? Was it all in the propaganda and in the harsh statements that the officials so avidly fed me? Was I wrong always to grope underneath the psyches presented me? What were the clues—and how would I even recognize them when I found them? Every night I went to bed with the same heavy and dull exhaustion that seemed to permeate all of Mother Russia.

Then I began—just began—to get clues, to have this strange secret world open up. As in so much of journalism you could not push it; you had to just be around, to hang around, and then suddenly people would reveal themselves, like actors waiting for their —never your—cue.

Once on a ship in the Black Sea, for instance, my guide and I were standing against the railing quietly watching the dramatic seacoast where Jason sought the Golden Fleece when suddenly he said, "The government explains it all by saying we can't leave because they need the work force." I didn't answer. The words had come out of nowhere and hung there like spiders spinning their own web. No Russian would admit that the government forbade them from leaving, you see; but suddenly, when you least expected it, it came out.

Then there was a night in Kiev, when I was talking with a charming young woman I shall call "Natasha." The conversation in the hotel dining room had started with the typical chauvinistic Russian remark that Russians could not create anywhere except in Russia. We moved on to Stalin and I mentioned, "Look at all the people killed. The top members of the party, the politburo. . . ."

"You know more than we," she said, now defensive but also sad. (How many times was I, for whom "knowing" was so important, to hear that from young Russians!)

"And they were the top members of the party," I went on, because I had a relentless intention then of *making* them see or at least hear the truth. "It's the Communists who should hate him."

"Maybe this is why the ordinary people do not hate him," she suggested tentatively. "You ask people today if they hate Stalin and you'll be surprised. . . ." Then her mood suddenly changed. She became very upset and tears rolled generously down her cheeks. And then she made the most extraordinary revelation for a Russian.

"After the death of Stalin," she started, "I was terribly upset." By now we were sitting on the darkened steps of the hotel, and perhaps that gave her a feeling of safety—that plus the wine. "It was a great disillusionment for me to hear about his crimes—I can't tell you how deep it was. I couldn't even go to the institute to study for two years. I lost all interest in everything. It wasn't until my marriage, when my husband began to explain things to me, that I began to feel again." By now she was crying very gently.

"Now . . ." Her voice suddenly became fierce. "Now I don't want to know things."

When I suggested to her that to be fully human you had to "know" things, she shook her head fiercely.

"Why?" she demanded. "I don't think it's at all necessary. So what if Stalin killed a million people, as you say? There are still two hundred million of us left!"

I was not in Russia during the "thaw" of Nikita Khrushchev, for that was largely over by the mid-sixties. But some of it lingered on. Stalin was long dead—and the society would not return to that mailed fist, to that "man of steel" and epoch of steel and blood. The United States was getting over the sickening death of John F. Kennedy and was full-blown in the war in Vietnam. Latin America, with such hope during the Kennedy period, now was pulling back; the democratic solutions offered in the early sixties were dying by the wayside, and Central America again was slipping toward the all-out civil war and guerrilla "solution" that later came back to haunt us in unspeakable nightmares. Africa still was freeing itself from colonial rule, and China remained in the Maoist grip.

But, Russia? What *was* Russia, this "world" that had been set up by history as our nemesis, our antagonist, our enemy? How could we deal with something we knew so little about? How could we reach it—and reach into it?

Gradually, as Russia unfolded before me, little insights and events piled up upon little insights and events and began to show me "how." One night in Irkutsk, a charming old Siberian city where the political exiles built churches and forts in challenge to the czar, I went over to talk to the Komsomol youth in the university. As Komsomolski they were or should have been the most totally indoc-

141

trinated of the lot; and they were. At one point the young woman leader and I were arguing about the U.S. Finally I pointed to a poster emblazoning the wall marked, "Kill the Yanqui gorillas in Latin America," the "gorillas" being the American-backed military.

"I don't think *that* is so friendly," I said with a distinctly miffed air.

I fully expected her to argue with me. Instead she went over to the offending poster, looked at it for a moment pensively, then took it down. Underneath it was one reading, "Release political prisoners in Greece!"

"There," she said soothingly, "we can all agree on that!"

In this and other situations I tried to watch for signs—of anxiety, of sudden interest, of whatever—that would show me what people really were wanting and thinking. In Novosibirsk at the Institute of Electrical Engineering, for instance, I sat all afternoon with fifty high school students. The usual questions were repeated hostilely and by rote: "How could you respect Steinbeck anymore when he came out in favor of the Vietnam War?" "Why did we go into Hungary?—Hungary fought against us in the great war. . . ." Etc., etc., etc.

Then suddenly the conversation shifted—and I could sense it shifting to the things that really interested them. Finally one boy stood up and said wearily, "That's enough of politics." Then they all began asking with great eagerness, "What do American students do at night? Where do they go? Do they worry about their futures? How do they get jobs?"

This curiosity for the "personal" later was reinforced and interpreted by Dr. Vladimir Lisovsky, the USSR's preeminent youth sociologist. I looked him up at the University of Leningrad and got to know him—and like him—as well as anyone I met. In his studies on youth, for instance, he found that they wanted, in this order: to get an interesting job, to receive a higher education, to visit foreign countries, to be well off, to have good housing conditions, to improve one's qualification (for work), to find loyal friends, to bring up children to be worthy people, to find one's true love, to build a family, to buy a car, to receive secondary education, and to move to a housing project under construction.

One afternoon I had Lisovsky, a totally genial man, and my two guides up to my room at the old Astoria Hotel in Leningrad for champagne and caviar, when another telling event occurred. Suddenly Lisovsky, such a charming and rational man, was sputtering at me inexplicably.

"You Americans . . . are always criticizing us," he was saying. "No hot water. No amenities. No . . ." By now all three sets of deep Russian forest eyes were glaring at me. Friendly only a moment before, the looks now were shrouded and angry.

"Now wait," I interjected as calmly but firmly as I could. "Think a minute. I've never criticized anything here. Nothing at all."

They all looked at me in utter astonishment. What I had said was true. But to their minds my very *being* there was a kind of built-in, implicit criticism.

That same afternoon, when we sat for hours eating and drinking, Lisovsky at one point asked me, "Now, tell me please, what do you not like about the Soviet Union?"

"Let me tell you first what I like," I said. And I outlined several areas—the egalitarianism, the respect for work, the quest for cultural values. "But there is one thing I could not abide, living here. That is the fact that your entire society is built upon dishonesty. You all live it every minute, you speak it, and sometimes even you yourselves don't know where honesty ends and dishonesty begins."

To my surprise these words were greeted with total silence. Lisovsky looked down at the table, stared at it. The two women looked away from me. No one would meet my eye.

It was also telling to talk (on those rare occasions when you could) with the officials, with the Soviet *"apparatchik,"* and to see the subtleties and complexities of their minds and utterances. One day in Moscow it was arranged for me to visit Ivan Tikhonovich Komov, a member of the Central Committee of the Komsomol, and a powerful force. Unblinking, gray, he received me sternly in his office.

"Perhaps this is not interesting to you," he started, "but we have a new program. We are trying to bring up a new generation in the experience of the former generation."

That struck me as a monstrously ungrateful task, but I restrained myself—and listened with considerable interest.

"We have now a new generation that has not experienced war and has not suffered the hardships of revolution," he said. "On the other hand, ideological subversion has increased. Some Western ideologists—they are actually propagandists—are trying to take youth away from the class struggle and from speaking of patriotism so they will not defend the country as they used to. Different sociologists of the West speak about the 'no-class society,' of societies divided only into good and bad. There is also the theory that capitalism and socialism are coming closer. That's why, in order to fight these ideas, we are trying to educate our young people in the spirit of 'Proletarian Internationalism.' "

Then he actually criticized Russian youth: "For example, the idea of free education—they take it for granted," he said somberly. "They do not know how it was achieved, at the cost of how many lives and how much labor. The younger generation must know these things. Among the young there is very often the idea that all the exploits are over. In peacetime what can they do? Our task is to give young people the idea there is still heroism."

Just hints, but real hints? Youth was not as patriotic as it should be—they were worried about it. Youth took too much for granted —youth was not grateful. Youth was, even, disloyal? That was what I got out of that—and that was an extraordinary revelation.

Despite everything, I was learning. I was learning how, in closed societies like this, you learn things. You learn, not by direct questions or comments, but by the inflections, by comparing innuendos with the types of innuendos the people used the last time. You learn what is real by pauses and coughs. You learn what is true through what people do not, will not, and above all psychologically cannot do or tell you.

Everywhere I went, the same journalistic and intellectual conundrum awaited me. You do not simply report on Russia: you can't. Here is a society where virtually everyone is living on a level of dishonesty, where interpretations are so different from ours as to be from a totally different world. How as a reporter do you deal with this? Do you look for any "window" or any slip and then grasp it —or is *that* dishonest? Do you take them at their word—that would *surely* be dishonest? You find yourself sifting every grain of talk and truth, trying to find out what is real, and in the end you wonder if you will ever know reality again, anywhere. Russia is a torment for an honest journalist, and the torment lasts long after one has closed the door on that isolated and strange land.

Henry, a fine photographer and friend, was also an anxious traveler. As we made our way across Russia that first month, he became more and more enraged by their idiosyncrasies and stupidities. "Tell me," he kept saying, sometimes almost desperate, "tell me that when we get to Moscow we'll go to a nightclub . . . and have a good meal . . . and dance. . . ." I soothed him, as women have always soothed men, and I told him we would—I was actually far from sure.

It was a Friday and late when we got to Moscow and (one of the things people do *not* expect from Russia) no one met us. We could have escaped into that sea of mystery, but instead we went and checked into the vast Rossiya hotel. The rooms were nice. They awoke you with chimes playing "Moscow Nights." Promising.

Saturday morning we raced around getting things, arriving back at the hotel at noon for lunch. While waiting for Henry in my room, I felt a considerable sense of satisfaction: we had made it all the way across Russia; we had good material (considering the situation) and now it would be easy. Now we would find the nightclub. I could not have been *more wrong*.

At noon, Henry came suddenly to my room with a look of stupefaction on his big, ruddy face. "They've stolen my cameras," he said as though he were sleepwalking. "I had them locked in the cupboard in my room and they've stolen my cameras." I told him it was impossible. We were in the workers' paradise where *there was no*

145

crime—was he perhaps imagining it? What would Hoffer say? What would Saul say? I grinned, despite myself.

Although my Russian was not good at the time, I went immediately, not to the grisly floor woman who ruled over everything, but to the maids on the floor.

"Who was the person who went into Mr. Gill's room earlier?" I asked.

The women looked startled, disturbed. They began chattering like magpies.

"There was no one but him," one said.

"At what time?" I asked.

"He came in, oh, about ten o'clock," another offered.

After I had got a full description, and only then, I told them that this man standing with me was Mr. Gill. It took a while to convince them and all the while they grew more and more distressed. They had clearly let in a man who was not *"Gospodin* Gill." This information was to save us when we had to face down Russian officialdom.

In the manager's office downstairs we got a first look at officialdom —and it was nasty. Henry, a big, square man, faced the woman manager, who was an almost equally big woman. She was unwilling to admit that the situation even existed. After all it was clearly "crime," and *there was no crime in the Soviet Union.*

"Maybe, Mr. Gill," she said at one point, "you took the cameras yourself!"

I intervened just before Henry could take a swat at her. We then sat in her office, in a state of unmitigated confrontation that would make the Israelis and the Libyans look like allies, until five o'clock that evening. At that moment Henry scored what may have been the eventual breakthrough.

"I am not leaving this country," said Henry, who could be very mean, "I am not leaving until either I get my cameras back or I am paid for them." I seem to recall seeing her flinch at this suggestion of having Mr. Gill on Russia's hands in a state of perpetual care. Later I became convinced that this "promise" turned the tide.

From there we went to eat, if you can call what you do at meal-

time in Russia eating. The Rossiya had an enormous—but enormous
—dining room with all the charm and intimacy of a roller rink in
The Bronx. It was exactly two blocks long. We entered at one end,
exhausted from the rather full day, only—naturally, for this is Russia
—to be placed at a table at the very other end of the hall and at the
only table where people were sitting. Unwilling to argue any further,
we sat down with the two others, who appeared to be workingmen,
only to witness another extraordinary scene.

The man next to me was drunker than anyone I have ever seen
(even in Chicago). He had his napkin in his shirt, like a baby, and
his eyes were closed. I blinked as I realized he was asleep at the table,
little lines of slaver trickling down both sides of his mouth.

Just then the other man took *his* napkin, spread it out on the
table, and gathered everything into it, including the uneaten
chicken, the bread and butter, the beer bottles, and the salt and
pepper shakers. Carefully, never looking at us as we sat there spell-
bound (I was afraid finicky Henry might vomit), he tied it up like
a bum's knapsack and staggered off through the front door. Just then
he remembered his friend. So he staggered back in, jammed the
friend in the ribs to wake him, and both staggered out.

That was the end of our first day in Moscow. The little episode
also confirmed the impression that we were all too ready to accept
that virtually the *only* pleasure people have here is drinking themselves into oblivion.

Henry was like a bulldog after the cameras. Daily he was atop the
manager's desk, sitting there and staring her down for hours. They
had detectives working, and it was clear that they were highly embarrassed not to find the cameras. Despite his threat Henry *was* going
to leave a week later and we didn't really know what more to do. The
afternoon of our departure he walked into my room with another
stunned look on his face.

"They just called me," he said, "and I went down. She handed
me five hundred rubles and said, 'Now, Mr. Gill, see what you can
do with these.' "

We tried to think how—legally—we could get rid of the rubles for dollars since any such money transactions were totally forbidden. And I could not use them. Suddenly it dawned on me. I called our friend, Henry Bradsher, the bureau chief for Associated Press.

"Sure," Henry said, "bring them over. I can exchange them with no trouble."

At the airport they were waiting for Henry. "Don't you have some rubles, Mr. Gill?" the woman at the money exchange desk asked him, leading up to the wonderful moment when she would then tell him she could not exchange them.

"No, I don't," Henry said, "but I do have a check on the Chase Manhattan Bank." And then he strode forward . . . out of Mother Russia.

Often, nights, after the interviews, after long days of fighting for every crumb and being constantly insulted by people who knew not the slightest thing about the outside world, I would retire gratefully to the foreign currency bars in the hotels, the only haven we had. These were places where foreign visitors like myself could buy drinks of all kinds, but only for foreign currency. It was a way to get the foreign exchange and to give all the foreigners a place to play— together and alone. In Leningrad one night the Hotel Astoria bar —in sharpest contrast to the tiresome order outside—had the mood of a city besieged, where anything goes. It was the last night of the world, a kind of Soviet Babylon. People were falling out of chairs and sprawling across tables. Buxom and braless girls shook frenetically on the dance floor, and at the bar men pawed the women like untethered wild animals. Otherwise sedate and proper Europeans I had seen earlier in the hallways of the hotel were behaving as though they were in the Berlin bunker the night Hitler's Reich was falling.

We all got quite desperate.

Some nights this wildness would come over me the way a wildness suddenly overcomes my cat, Pasha, when his ears go back and his eyes get black and you just know he can't stop himself from biting you. One night in Kiev, after sitting and drinking with some African students, who were always in varying stages of desperation in the

Soviet Union, I went out on the street and ran . . . and ran . . . and ran. I must have run for an hour, up and down hills, until finally I drained all the anger and frustration out of myself.

Another night, in Kiev the next trip in 1971, I met two young sculptors and their wives, all delightful people. One evening we got away from Nellie, my guide. They took me to an incredible party, one that could have come straight out of Dostoevsky, at the apartment of the famous Armenian movie director Sergei Paradjanov.

Here was a perfectly ordinary Soviet apartment: as boxlike and sterile as any other in the Soviet Union. But how they had transformed it! Paradjanov, a short stocky man with quizzical eyes, of tremendous personal assurance and a devilish beard, had made it into a lair of old Russia. I expected to see Rasputin any minute, stepping out, rolling his eyes, and licking his lips over some ripe peasant girl. In one room was a long, carved-wood banquet table, on which was spread every sort of fish, caviar, cold meat, and delicacy. Wine was served in hung animal skins. Icons, handwoven cloths, and scabrous old crosses filled the room, while the young men and women who lolled insouciantly against the tables with their curious feline smiles seemed to be escapees into some strange netherworld. One young woman artist immediately showed me her sketches of Dante's *Inferno* and they seemed somehow appropriate.

The party, which started about 8:00 P.M., was just beginning to pick up in spirit and passion when I had to leave. Nellie and I were catching a plane to Odessa, the beautiful old French-designed city on the Black Sea, at the uncivilized hour of 1:00 A.M.

As I hurried to leave at about eleven (Nellie had not the slightest idea where I was) Paradjanov went about the apartment and plucked things off the walls: a hoary old cross and a beautiful piece of Ukranian handwork for me, an embroidered jacket which he asked me to deliver to the novelist John Updike, etc. . . . He stuffed them all in a pillow slip and I went running out with all of this, like a furtive robber with a pack of treasures.

*   *   *

149

There *were* places to "have fun" . . . if you knew someone. Another night in a central Russian city, after dining with a high-level party official, I agreed to go dancing. We walked into a nondescript building with a public restaurant in the front, crossed through the dining room, and came into another building in back. He flashed his party card at the door and we entered a type of nightclub that was about as common in the Soviet Union as a stock exchange.

"Can anyone come here?" I asked as we sat down at a table in a discreetly lit room with candles and a large dance floor.

"Why, yes, of course," he said as he ordered some Scotch, which you would never find in a Russian restaurant. A floor show (!) came on after midnight; girls in skimpy Western nightclub costumes began dancing to the theme from *Dr. Zhivago* (!), and couples began doing a clumsy Russian version of the twist without anyone's coming over and telling them it was immoral.

At the end of the evening, slightly tipsy, I turned to my escort and whispered again, *"Who* can come here?"

He smiled knowingly. *"We* can," he whispered back.

On my second trip, in 1971, when I returned to finish research for my book on Soviet youth, I had to work out a much more complicated means of accomplishing this. On my first day in Moscow, Pavel Gevorkian, one of the Novosti chiefs and later identified in the U.S. as a major KGB man (which I had taken for granted), took me out to lunch. "I am sorry, Georgie," he said, "but Novosti cannot work with foreign correspondents anymore. The policy has been changed." I was speechless. I had depended upon this one aid. In effect I was on my own for two months, and to be on your own in Russia is to be almost helpless.

That afternoon I sat down in my elegant old room in the czarist-era Hotel National across from Red Square, threw down a couple of cognacs, and thought. I felt like lying there and whimpering, which is what I always did when sick and alone overseas. What I clearly needed, in this country of plans, was a plan.

First of all I analyzed the situation. Here I was, with two months

150

yawning ahead of me, in a totally closed totalitarian country where almost no one would want to risk talking to me. My timing could not have been worse, yet I was determined to get to people despite all the odds. Since the official route was closed, I had to develop new routes of my own. But where do you start in a country that does not even have a telephone book?

I took out a yellow pad. On it I wrote down the names of everybody I knew or could know in Moscow: embassy officials of all nationalities, journalists of all nationalities, the few Russians I already knew. I reasoned that in a country and in a situation like this, you couldn't ask too much of any one single person but you could ask a little of everybody before implacable resistance set in.

I decided to ask each person I knew to help me with one appropriate interview. I would ask a journalist for one phone number or to help me arrange to see someone he or she might particularly know. I would ask a diplomat to help me with one official he might know. In addition, with obvious, noncontroversial people, I would ask Nellie, my excellent Intourist guide, to help.

Then I wrote down the names of the people I wanted to see. This included everybody from Komsomol leaders to playwrights to women sociologists. Then I matched them up with my first list and systematically began to go about contacting people.

This time-consuming route proved quite amazingly successful. Correspondents who had lived there for years had not been able to see the people I saw, or really to see anyone. Also the fact that I was coming in quickly and leaving quickly—the fact that I would not be around to remind them of what they had said or not said—served in good stead. It is *not* a help to be around Russia too long!

One of the major new stars in the youth firmament, for instance, was Andrei Volkonsky, a famous pianist and a romantic figure to many Russians partly because he was the grandson and namesake of the immortal "Prince Andrei" of *War and Peace*. But—how to find him?

One foreign diplomat made the obvious suggestion that I go to performances and then use the acceptable custom of going back-

151

stage afterward to greet performers. This I did. I went to one of his performances, went backstage, stood in line, greeted him in Russian and—as this very sophisticated man literally gawked at the sheer brazenness of it—asked him for an interview. He agreed; and he met me at the hotel the very next day, his eyes still rather questioning.

I was particularly interested in Volkonsky—as tall, dark, handsome, and haunted-looking as one would rightly expect Prince Andrei's seed to be—because he was the center of a wildly popular revival of (of all things!) old church music. We sat for two hours, talking of this.

"I am a great-grandson of the Volkonsky of the Decembrist uprising," he started, as we sat in the restaurant overlooking the Kremlin, its gold onion domes gleaming in the sun. "We are related to the czars of the Romanoff family and also to Prince Vladimir of Kiev and to Alexander Nevsky."

I was properly breathless—all of the most romantic dreams of the historic Russia I so loved were unfolding right in front of me in this person. Then he said, with just the touch of an ironic smile, "They're just relatives. The family had its own czars and saints. But I have nothing to do with saints anymore." A pregnant pause, then an open, friendly smile. "Besides, I'm not a saint myself."

In 1965 Volkonsky began what six years later had become a wildly popular renaissance of early pre–Peter the Great (and thus pre-European influence) Orthodox church music.

"At the time of Peter, there were reforms in the church services," he explained, "and part of the reform was a kind of Europeanization of the service. The old type of music was forgotten. A new singing during the services was introduced that had nothing to do with the old music. I believe everyone must feel very sorry because the music today is poorer. It lost its Russian features."

Volkonsky had formed a performing group called the "Madrigals," which by 1971 was giving one hundred totally sold-out concerts a year all over the Soviet Union—but not before he personally had done the mammoth and intricate job of searching out and decoding the music, which lay untouched in old libraries and monasteries. "For thousands of people, particularly students, this ancient classical music replaces pop music," he summed up. "In a way, it's a kind of social experiment."

His "social experiment"—and, in particular, the tremendous success of it—seemed to me something of overwhelming importance.

In a country like the Soviet Union, where you cannot ask direct questions and where you cannot believe (in our sense) the answers people do give you, you have to learn to listen on many levels, to catch nuances, to watch for the continuation of themes people may be not at all aware they are revealing to you. Perhaps women, being naturally more empathic listeners, are better at this than men. At any rate, as I systematically and exhaustedly asked young people simple questions like, "What is your greatest passion in life?" or "What interests your generation most?" I was prepared for answers like, "Creating the new Communist man" or "Destroying the bourgeoisie throughout the world and establishing socialism."

But these questions were met with blank stares or quizzical, bemused smiles. Either they found my questioning curiously outdated or found me ripe for membership in the Central Committee.

What *did* come through? One answer, everywhere and always, even in young officialdom: "The spiritual life of man."

One of the most cogent and provocative answers came from a twenty-eight-year-old physicist-turned-psychologist at Kiev State University, Valerie Melko, to whom I was deliberately—which in itself was telling—sent by the youth section in Novosti. (One of their rare instances of assistance.) He seemed to incorporate in himself the searching both of objective science and of the inner self. By the time I met him, Valerie, brown haired, with unhurried eyes, a sharp mind, and utter honesty, had tired of pure, dehumanized science and was exploring psychology as an antidote to it.

"Even if you know how to do things, the problems of what for still remain," he told me as we sat in a small, drab study room of the university that cool October day, talking for nearly four hours. "For what do we use modern technical things? What do they give

153

to man? What do they give on a spiritual level? The world of things is known well. But what concerns man we know least because it is the most complex system. This tendency is quite unlike the Renaissance—which put man in the main spot, made man the most precious thing in the world." He smiled, shifted in his chair.

"The formation of the inner consciousness of man is not decided haphazardly, without order. We don't know on what it depends. We suppose it depends on social and economic conditions. But what? We don't know. We can only surmise. We hope that many features can be improved in man. But the first thing is to awaken a will in man to improve. To do this, we must know on what the will depends."

Most Americans would perhaps not recognize what a staggering thing he was saying, because most Americans no longer read history and understand the simple different cultural standards of other peoples. Thinking they are just like us and will react the same way, if treated right, is the utmost in contempt and egocentrism because it denies the other person's and people's own experience, own realm of being. One had to know history and Soviet thought—at least at its most simple level—to understand how amazing it was to hear a young Marxist, a man quite within the system and indeed a jewel of its intellectual world, saying that his generation did not trust social and economic advances to solve psychological problems. This was taking place in a society that had consistently claimed that men's psychological and personal problems were simply an outgrowth of the social imbalances that communism would solve!

It was Melko, too, who told me most brilliantly about the changes in ideology in regard to collectivism. "The ideology is changing somewhat," he reflected that day. "Such features as were ideal for one generation—collectivism—are changing to solidarity. But this still excludes individualism. It means that, when deciding the problems of all the people, we must pay special attention to the individual needs of everyone in the group. In addition, such features as discipline from outside now have become internal discipline."

*   *   *

154

So, yes, I did find the Soviet Union changing, but I was very, very cautious about making any dramatic predictions on that change—or allowing myself the luxury of believing either that they were at heart "just like us" (the liberal sentimental idea) or that they were outside of human history, anti-historical, monsters (the conservative version). I saw a totalitarian state with a history that created a mind-set which above all prized authority and obedience. It was the exact antithesis of the American ideas of individualism, human freedom as the predominant value in human life, and existential self-determination. It was no mystery that they therefore had been posited by history both conspicuously against us—and, in an odd way and on another level that Alexis de Tocqueville understood so brilliantly, very much with us. Both believed in enfranchising the average person, but in totally different ways: one in the equality of egalitarian horizontalism, one in the authoritarian equality of totalitarian verticalism.

So, when I looked at the youth, I saw, yes, a new generation striving for much more in terms of material goods and in terms of personal fulfillment; but I had to predict in my book, *The Young Russians*, that these desires would only nominally affect the leadership class, which would stay hard and tough and totalitarian.

Later I would cry and wring my hands over some people in the Carter administration, including most unfortunately the President himself, who really thought that the Russians were just like us, and would respond just like your neighbor in Iowa City if we didn't irk them too much. But I would then wring my hands just as much about the Reagan administration, which looked upon the Russians as almost anti-human. What the Russians wanted from us was for us to act as a credible deterrent—to stop them from doing certain things—but the U.S. in the seventies and eighties has not understood this.

The ideas and experiences and memories behind the mind-sets of the Russians and the Americans are totally and unequivocally different. Linguists have told me that the Vladivostok agreements are so different in the two languages that they could quite literally not be called into effect. Their ideas about information are totally different: the Russians see information not as the search for truth (they *have* truth) but as a means of furthering their objective, the spreading of socialism in the world.

All this points to a major lesson that I had to learn as a journalist. We cannot judge others by ourselves—that is the ultimate and the unforgivable egocentricity. We must go further than just good reporting, we must somehow incorporate into our writing an implicit understanding of the different truths that other cultures are living by—and dying by. When I was in Russia, Iran was still to come, but in trying to understand Russia and in all the agonies of working there, I learned once and for all of the different shadows in the wings of our histories, the different memories, the different howls in the night that each people hears and that we can ignore only at our deep peril.

Often "listening" brought glorious rewards. One gorgeous October morning, with yellow leaves falling on sidewalks still black from the night's rain, I walked into Czarina Katherine's beautiful blue and white palace outside Leningrad in Pushkintown. Reacting to the cold weather we had been having, I was wearing my heavy Russian fur coat on a day clearly much too warm for it.

Behind the coat-check counter stood a typical old *babushka*, looking like a gnome in her black cloth coat with scarf tied tight around her temples. When she saw me, she started, then clapped her fat, creased hands together as if to ward off a bad omen. "Oh," she said, her eyes wide and disturbed as she looked at my coat. "Oh, my, you're frightening summer." In Russia, one also found sometimes this tremulous beauty.

IX.

Man of Steel

"Do women have equal rights in America too?"
—An Uzbek farmer

As I worked my way deeper into Russian life, trying to unravel the mysteries, I was, as always, deeply interested in the women. I suppose it was a selfish search, for I was searching for myself in them and their "solutions." The Russian revolution, after all, had "freed" women. They were—in jobs, in education, and in recognized potential—equal. There was much to admire. But I soon found many contradictions, many conflicts, many conundrums.

One day in Moscow I was interviewing Ann Martinova, the crisp, dark-haired editor at _Literaturnaya Gazeta,_ and eventually I asked her about the "problem" of premarital sex relations. All of her carefully constructed manner of insouciance and sophistication dissolved immediately, and the blood rose in her pale white face, causing a distinct flush. Her lips became more set; then, "WE HAVE NO 'PROBLEM' OF PREMARITAL SEX RELATIONS," she snapped. "Our family life is very solid. This exists only in _your_ country."

How very interesting, I thought. Another example of Russians facing reality head-on. For everywhere I went, young people told me exactly the opposite. Premarital and extramarital sex among the young (and old) was so widespread, so common and so casual that

157

one could only come to the conclusion that most Russians take it, as the early Bolshevik and free love advocate, Madame Alexandra Kollontai, told Lenin, "like a drink of water." (And he, typically male, answered that he preferred "not to drink from a dirty glass.")

And Russian men . . . Russian men do not make "passes" (such a gingerly, Western, British word for what they do), they have home runs, or try to, the first moment they decide they want you. They do not approach, they lunge, they attack crudely. I very deliberately watched out for them. When I saw them drinking too much at a table where I was sitting, I often left, for nowhere in the world had I seen such aggressive, crude, and dangerous men as the Russian ones.

And when, as a woman, I tried to study the Russian women, I came up with some very interesting impressions. The image of Russian women outside is that they have arrived in some kind of nirvana of feminism. Nothing could be further from the truth. Women, yes, are equal, but they are "equal" to work outside the home and bring money home, to do all the housework and shopping, to bear the children and then give them up to child care—in effect, to do everything. And the men do not "mind" it; isn't that marvelous of them!

I was curious to see this "Russian syndrome" occurring just a little later in the U.S. But in 1971 surveys showed that Russian wives had half the amount of leisure their husbands had and one hour's less sleep a night. A Professor Kobalevsky, writing in *Molodaya Gvardia* or *Young Guard*, tabulated that in industrial districts working women had three hours less free time on workdays and nine to eleven hours less free time on Sundays and holidays. In consequence, he determined, "the woman slowly neglects herself, loses her former attractiveness, and the onetime love dies out."

"I came to our school one morning early last week," a teacher in Kiev told me, "and another teacher was sitting there with her head in her hands sobbing and saying, 'I wish I were back in czarist days. At least then I'd just have one thing to do—be a woman at home and have men flatter me and do certain things for me. It's just too much.' " She paused. "Yet we don't want to stay home. We consider that a kind of grave."

The Russian women were, very simply, conflicted beyond belief. They were overworked. The "macho" Russian men refused to do anything—anything—around the house. They were often drunk. They still beat women. But we have to understand this, too, within their specific historical context.

Russian women have always worked. They toiled in the hardest type of manual labor and they fought in the wars beside the men. Actually, historians have traced three strands in Russian women's history: the subordination of women, equality in hardship, and also creative equality. That last, which in the past existed only for the aristocratic classes of women, is still out of reach for most women in Russia, and elsewhere, today.

But the Russian women at that time were getting even in a very special way—they were not having children. The birthrate of one child per couple that was, by the 1970s, the norm among European Russians was obviously not going to reproduce the population, which requires 2.2 children per family. Moreover the Asiatic Soviets were reproducing at such a high rate that by the year 2000 they will constitute a majority of the population, thus changing the country's entire racial makeup. I found that the state was utterly terrified of this—it would mean that Great Russian control over the vast and scattered former "minorities" in the Soviet Union would be diluted and perhaps dead. My own feeling was that this fear had something to do with the invasion of Afghanistan—like the ancient Roman Empire, they needed an outlet for their minorities; they needed to give their minorities spheres of their own. And who had done this? The Russian women had done it, simply by refusing to give birth. If it was not a direct revolution, it was certainly a direct geopolitical threat to the empire.

Yet I do not want to intimate that Russian women have not gained a great deal, because, to be fair, they have. Attitudes, even in Central Asia, have changed dramatically. I remember one day, just outside of Tashkent, when we stopped in the Uzbek countryside on a little river. An outdoor teahouse, consisting of square piers which hung over the river, was filled with Uzbek men lounging and drinking tea and gossiping over a languid green river. Above were swaying willow trees, and an occasional oxcart trundled across an old bridge nearby.

Next to us on a nearby platform sat a group of seven Uzbek farmers from a nearby collective farm. In their traditional clothes they could have been out of a world of five hundred years ago, or even fifty years ago—when the emir still kept mistresses and each day threw the one he liked best an apple as she bathed in the pool. Before 1917 these Asian women went out only when completely veiled, and if a woman removed her veil, her husband had the right to bury her alive.

We sat down at one of the little piers and eventually the man who was the leader of the group next to us, a fifty-three-year-old farmer named Dadsmotov Hosneden, invited us to join them for pilaf, which we gratefully ate with our fingers.

"Do your wives work?" I asked him.

"Of course," he said. "If they have small children at home, they don't. But otherwise—of course. They are equal to men."

When he asked me how old I was and I said "Thirty-two," he exclaimed, "And you're not married yet?"

"I travel all the time," I answered. "Maybe in another year."

"But you should marry while you can enjoy your youth."

"I'm enjoying it now," I answered.

What was so striking was that all the men accepted that it was quite right and natural for a woman to travel about the world alone.

"Yes, it's true," Hosneden said. "When you're eighty, you'll have things to tell your grandchildren about the whole world." Then he paused and asked, "Do women have equal rights in America, too?"

The Soviet state of Georgia is a ferocious land: it is exquisitely beautiful, with dashing Caucasus rivers that swirl and crash down from the wild mountains, with a capital city, Tbilisi, that is as weathered and beautiful as its most celebrated son, Joseph Stalin, was cruel and evil. The Great Russians call Georgia and its ways "Asiatic." It is certainly different from central Russia, although perhaps only in degree—and what happened to me there is different only in degree from what happens to women everywhere and throughout history.

In Georgia I saw, firsthand, a less liberated side of male-female relations.

In my roamings and rummagings about the Soviet Union in 1971 I had planned to go to Mongolia as a "side trip" (to see the homeland of Genghis Khan), but at the last moment, not unexpectedly, the Russian authorities in their wisdom refused to let me go. I was heartbroken, for Outer Mongolia had a hauntingly romantic appeal for me. But what could I do? We included Georgia instead and I was pleased to have a few days rest in a fascinating and historic place.

The first afternoon in Tbilisi, just as I was beginning to relax after exhausting weeks of trying to work with the Soviet authorities, I went shopping on the main street. I felt at ease in "Russia" for a change, and there were lots of things to buy, Georgia being noted for its folklore and handwork. Tbilisi is also known for its arrogant, dark-haired, mustachioed men and I knew well enough to avoid and ignore them. Even in the hotel restaurants you could not sit down for two minutes at your table without the waiters bringing you note after note from men at surrounding tables, suggesting . . . everything. It was Latin America but with a distinctly dark side and sinister cast.

Very quickly a young Georgian—a broad-shouldered man with a handsome face and a witty manner—started walking beside me. I shooed him away, refused to talk to him, insulted him. He started jogging next to me to keep up, I was walking so fast.

"You should get to know us," he said, panting theatrically. "We're nice. The Russians don't like us because we're rich and they're jealous. They say when a Georgian goes to Moscow and goes to the checkroom to get his coat he puts down a twenty-ruble note and says, 'Never mind the coat.' "

Despite myself I smiled at this. But I still refused even to look at him. As we approached the new modern hotel, he was suddenly hailed by some friends, who soon surrounded me, laughing and joking. "But we're okay," one said in American-type English. "We're all journalists." At this they took out their journalists' cards —and they were indeed journalists. Finally they convinced me to stop in the hotel coffee shop, the most innocent of occupations in the Soviet Union, and we all had champagne and caviar. I was amused at the way they all joked about and jostled the young man I had first met on the street, whom I shall call Ivan. He was *the* television announcer on Georgian news.

"He's nice but too big," the other Georgian—a small man with bright black eyes, a look of continuous surprise and a devilishly pointed chin—said of Ivan. "You should see him on television—he's all head. That's all you can get on the little tube."

Ivan seemed to be unusually fair-minded, even for a Georgian, who are known for their avid anti-Russianism. He talked very emotionally about the two Soviet astronauts who had just been killed and then said, "But I felt the same when your astronauts were killed. We are all human beings—I do not feel any differently about our people or your people."

Another time he said about the Russians: "They are brutes. You hear them all the time making dirty jokes about their mothers. No Georgian would do this.

"I suppose I could go abroad now," he went on, "but I don't really want to, the way we have to go. You march around in a group and you sit in a bus and someone says, 'There on the left . . . and there on the right. . . .' I'd rather stay here."

When we walked back the couple of blocks to my hotel, Ivan waved off the rest and insisted we have dinner. I said, "No. No, no and no." He called me later. Again I said no. The next day I said no again. I was beginning to sound like a multiple American negative, but later it became very important to me that I had been firm and unyielding about saying no to something really quite innocent. Had I not felt so confident about my behavior—had there been even the slightest flirtation with him—God knows what my typical, traditional female psyche would have dredged up to torment me.

Two days later my Georgian guide, a nubile young woman with dark, guarded eyes, by the name of Ia, and the chauffeur and I gathered in the lobby of the hotel about 10:00 A.M. We were traveling out to Gori, Stalin's birthplace, to spend the day there. And who should appear, out of nowhere and thoroughly uninvited, but Ivan.

"I'll go with you," he said, for lack of confidence was surely not one of his traits. "I know a lot of people out there, and I can help."

I still strongly demurred, but now it was Ia, the prissy little puritan, who took me aside. "He's very well known here as a television commentator," she assured me. "A fine fellow."

All right. I nodded my head. And the day turned out to be splendid indeed. We traveled, singing and laughing, over golden, close-cropped mountains and valleys, carved by meandering streams. The villages were picturesque, the orchards heavy with every kind of ripe and robust fruit. After two hours' driving we came to Gori, a large, industrial "new town." And in the midst of a pretentiously long parkway that stretched out at least half a mile, with low pine trees forming a parade line on both sides, stood the tiny wooden hovel that was Joseph Dzhugashvili's birthplace. The hovel was covered by a second roof held up with Greek columns—quite extraordinary! When Stalin's wise old mother saw it, she is said to have uttered one vulgar but precise Georgian word and quickly returned to her simple home in Tbilisi.

We roamed around the strange monument. There were pictures of Stalin as a young man, when he was a seminary student, his natural fanaticism steeped in the passionate peasant religiosity of the Georgian Church. He was handsome, dark-eyed, terribly serious, this Joseph Dzhugashvili. It was later, during the revolution, that he abandoned his real name and took the name Stalin, which means in Russian "Man of Steel."

Knowing some Russian history, I could only look about me with total disbelief at the flagrant disregard for truth. Above one statue were engraved the words: "I have always been a student of Lenin's, and that is all I ever want to be."

But where in the museum—or in the Soviet psyche—was there

163

any acknowledgment of Lenin's final "testament," written in 1923 before his death, in which he recommended Stalin be brought down as head of the party. "Stalin is too rude," he wrote, "and this fault, entirely supportable in relation to us Communists, becomes unsupportable in the office of general secretary of the party. Therefore, I propose to the comrades to find a way to remove Stalin from that position."

As we left the museum, I must have fallen silent, for even Ia, who had been so proper and pristine-pure, suddenly volunteered something. (This, I found, often happened—you could never push people to talk in Russia, but they suddenly would when you least expected it.) "We think he did more good than bad," she said suddenly, as though I had asked or criticized something. I simply looked away.

Then Ivan sprang to life. "Let's go to the country," he said. "Let me take us to dinner. . . ." I hesitated, but then he added, "It's my friend. I'm the godfather of their child. He is chairman of a *kolhoz* and they'll be happy to have us for dinner."

The farmhouse turned out to be large, perfectly square, and made of plain brick and wood. Inside, the furniture was heavy and nondescript, but what was so memorable was the fact that the walls were painted a very bright red. Over every one hung the omnipresent picture and the hard black eyes of Joseph Dzhugashvili.

Dinners like this in Russia take on a peculiar rhythm of their own. There is a point-counterpoint of eat and toast and drink and joke and eat and toast and drink that leads on to an ever higher level of joviality, before it catapults into oblivion. But it was always forced joviality, and it was always forced drinking.

After the dinner had started, the husband, a husky, swarthy farmer, raised a toast of homemade wine "to the friendship between Stalin and Roosevelt." "They greatly respected each other," he said, and "that shows the Americans and the Georgians are friends." He raised the two-foot-long animal's horn that Georgians adore drinking from, filled it with homemade wine, and passed it to me.

I felt more like vomiting. Stalin had killed up to twenty million Russians alone. But what exactly was one supposed to say at a moment like this? "It would make me sick," I said, only. And I pointed to the end of the table. "Please, the small horn," I said.

And I remembered then what the great writer, a liberal, Victor Rozov had said to me in Moscow: "I think to this day people are still seeking new ways of development after the death of Stalin. This is still under way. Some people, especially in the West, thought after the death of Stalin that everything would change magically, but, to be serious, it will be very long. I personally do not believe in magic."

Even then the workers—the Russian "hard hats"—yearned for the days of Stalin, when there was "order" and when the "intellectuals" were not allowed to "raise hell." To the common people Stalin was their *vozhd,* their Russian *"Führer."* He was the direct emotional successor of the czar, their Communist "little father," who would save them from error, protect them in war, punish them for their own good, and take care of them just as the czar had . . . and just as the czar had *not.*

Who would not then resent and even hate someone like Khrushchev, who destroyed the security of fealty to the *vozhd,* who demanded the rigors of knowing the truth, and who tore away the comforting curtains of the past, even if to Westerners, with our ideas of freedom, they seemed more like shrouds. Discarding Stalin meant having to grow up into thinking, individualized, self-regulating human beings. As I thought about this, in Russia, I thought about *machismo* in Latin America, about Saul Alinsky with his insights into power and its mechanisms, about Eric Hoffer and his, about dictators and free people, the totalitarian mind and the free mind —everywhere. It was very saddening.

We reached the hotel about 10:00 P.M. and they dropped me off, everyone still feeling quite jovial, at the hotel. Ivan walked me to the door, said he would phone the next morning to go swimming, and left. He could not have been more polite and I found myself chiding myself for my inordinate suspicion. I *should* have gone to dinner with him, how stupid and silly of me! What a puritan you are, Gee Gee! My phone was not working, so I strolled down the hall to the floor woman's desk to make a phone call to Nellie, my Moscow guide, who had not felt good and thus had not gone with us. Then I returned to my room.

At ten thirty there was a knock on the door. I thought it must be Nellie. I called out, "Who is it?" but no one answered. When I opened the door a crack to see who was there, there stood Ivan. He pushed the door inward, violently, pinning me behind it.

"*Nyet, nyet,*" I cried out angrily.

But within seconds he had locked the door behind him and stood facing me.

The most astonishing thing—what had it been, thirty minutes, forty at the most?—was the extraordinary change in his appearance. When he left me at the door, he had been tastefully dressed, a perfectly decent young man of twenty-eight with impeccable manners who seemed totally in control of himself and blessed with a rather fey sense of humor.

And now . . . now his face was grotesquely contorted. His skin was flushed. His jacket was slightly askew, and his tie and the top of his shirt were open. His eyes had taken on a strangely savage look, and his mouth was set in a cruel expression that was so different from the slightly bemused and tolerant expression it had had all day that I wondered if I were seeing the same man.

Later I would remember the words of an anti-Nazi Austrian officer, who said of this kind of Slav: "They're like that. Suddenly something snaps and they become raging beasts. During the war they were very kind to children, they never fired into children, as the Nazis did. But they were terribly brutal with women."

He held me tightly by the left wrist, staring at me with those strange, feral eyes. I had never been nervous, much less hysterical, but now I felt the hysteria rising inside me. Was this a political setup? I must admit that, ironically, that was the *first* thought that went through me, for the Soviets were so adept at that. Or was he going to rape me? Kill me?

I had always thought, when I allowed myself to think of it, that I would rather be raped than murdered, and occasionally I had

wondered what exactly I would do. Now there was no more wondering, and my reaction surprised even me.

"No," he said with a quiet determination behind the crazy eyes.
"No, I have come to stay." Then he raised his large hand and ripped
my nightgown down the front.

Questions flew through my mind. How had he gotten in, with all
those guards and floor women? Could the floor woman hear me?
Could I get to the open window? Could I jump two stories? Could
I get from him the bottle of liqueur the farm family had given me?
I knew the reason behind the last question—and it rather frightened
me—and it was because I was going to kill him with it if I could.

Then, instinctively, I began screaming. I screamed loud. And I
saw the rage rise in his face. The first blow was so stunning that I
spun against the desk and lay there, while with his other hand he
still held my wrist. When I came to and could look up again, I could
feel the excitement rising in him. He liked this. Perhaps it was *this*
that he had come for.

"I want a drink," I said. I wanted the bottle, and I was as calm
as death about it.

"Oh, no, oh, no," he shouted. "I'll get it for you." He wouldn't
let me anywhere near the bottle.

I screamed again. He hit me again, this time nearly knocking me
unconscious. I hit him back, again and again. He laughed at this
presumption and struck me again. I remember only my body hitting
furniture, over and over, until I was almost unconscious. He was
more and more enraged at my resistance and started screaming,
"Pig," in English and then *"Schweinehund,"* in German (which he
purported to speak, poorly I can assure you).

"Tomorrow the police, tomorrow the police," I kept repeating.

"What police?" he shouted, laughing a nasty laugh. "I'm with the
television!"

I started to scream again, perhaps because it was the only way I
could assert my humanity, my response, any control. His response
was to keep slapping me, and all I remember was spinning off more

167

sides of furniture until I could barely see anything but his ugly face, with his teeth bared and his eyes heavily dilated.

"This," he shouted, now brandishing a fist that could easily break open my skull if he hit me with it.

Now I was desperate. Should I let him stay—in effect, let him rape me and then try to call the police? Should I let him rape me and just try to get him out? By now I was far more desperate about staying alive. But just as I was about to sink into some oblivion of conscience and consciousness, one of the stranger things of my life occurred.

Suddenly his eyes started to get groggy and his head began—just began—to sag. I could feel just the slightest letup of the viselike grip on my arm, the first tremulous feeling of blood flowing back to my hand. He forced me to sit down on the bed, but he didn't touch me. I sat as far away from him as possible. Strangely, he said in Russian, almost appealing, "You want me."

"I don't want you, I don't want you," I spat out.

Then, almost defensively, he asked, "Why not?"

For a moment he seemed to be thinking. His demeanor was growing more and more groggy, remote, strange. Finally he said, almost sleepily, almost as if his feelings were hurt, "If you don't want me, I'm going to go."

"I don't want you," I said softly in order not to break the mood.

To my continued amazement, now he stood up and pulled me up by the wrist. "I'll go if you promise me two things," he said, as if we had been having a cocktail party conversation.

"Of course, anything," I murmured.

"If I come to the United States, you'll sleep with me? And tomorrow we'll go swimming?"

"Of course," I said, scarcely able to believe what was happening. "Things are much different in Chicago, much different than here."

"You promise?" His eyes were growing heavier and heavier.

"Yes, of course. Tomorrow at three."

"Tomorrow at three." He repeated it like a parrot. Then he let

168

go of my wrist for the first time in perhaps forty minutes. He stepped to the door, opened it, and, without another word, left.

Unbelieving, I stared at the door. Then I ran to it, sprang upon the key, and locked it. I ran to the window, and though it was on the second floor, I locked *it*. For a few seconds I sat on the bed, trying to draw my breath again, trying to figure out what in God's name had really happened. Within minutes I went down to Nellie's room and told her the whole story. A wonderful Russian-Jewish woman from Moscow, Nellie had been with me for weeks—she knew what kind of woman I was.

"Tomorrow morning we'll decide what to do," she said finally, veritably choking on her fury. "We'll get this man's job—that's the least thing."

I lay there all night, awake and terrified, waiting desperately for the dawn. And as I lay there, I became aware of a pain in my leg that got worse and worse and worse. By the first lights of dawn I was in agony. I couldn't wait for seven, when I had told Nellie I would call her, so I got up at six and stumbled downstairs. I couldn't put any weight on my left leg and the pain was almost unbearable. It had also turned black overnight and I was convinced it was broken.

At 7:30 A.M. exactly Nellie came into the dining room looking frantic, her eyes wild. "Oh, my God, I thought you had gone somewhere," she said.

Nellie made the rounds of the hotel and came back looking utterly disconsolate. "He bribed everyone in the hotel," she said, a strange thing for a Russian Intourist guide to admit.

I told her we had to "do" something. She said it was the same for women everywhere—they would "only make it look bad for you." I told her it wasn't that way in America. She said angrily that it was. And she was more right than wrong.

Ia appeared and sat in the room with "I told you so" eyes and her pursed virgin's lips, even though, I reminded her, it was *she* who had "known" him, who had praised him. "I'm sure he is sorry," she said coolly to me, her eyes still veiled and accusing. To Nellie, on the side,

169

she said, "She deserved it, she brought it on." Though I hadn't *done* anything, barely talked to him, I had allowed him to buy food for me by taking me to the dinner. *"Buy food for me?"* In Georgia, she said, that means a woman has "agreed." So when he came to my room expecting payment for the coffee, sugar, bread, and sausage, he had every reason to be angry. And to act as he did? "Yes."

Beating women, of course, is an old and revered custom—in Russia even more than most places. Why, after all, are the poets Andrei Voznesensky and Yevgeny Yevtushenko always writing poems about wife-beating? It's an old custom, even more fun if the woman is not your wife, and one of the few that have survived with no modifications into the Soviet period.

Nor did Ivan himself appear to think he had done anything even untoward. The next afternoon he duly telephoned at 3:00 P.M. on the dot, as I lay there in agonizing pain. He wanted to know if I wanted to go swimming.

But what came to be most interesting about the entire situation —and in many ways most horrible—was not what he had done to me but what I saw, first, in people around me and, second, in myself.

Back in Moscow I immediately phoned my "friends" in the American embassy and went over there, as difficult as that was since any pressure on my left leg left me with extreme pain. I will never forget sitting in the office with these men I considered my friends and having them say, their eyes all too eager for every telling detail, "And then what happened?" First I blushed crimson, the whole situation was so frightful to me. Then I blushed out of sheer anger. At the end they did not really want to do anything about it. As one put it, "Do you really want people to *know* this?" I hobbled out of the embassy with a new, colder anger.

But far worse than anything were my own feelings that I had to face. Why, when I talked from Moscow to Nick Shuman, my editor in Chicago and a wonderful friend, did I not tell him about it? I told myself I was afraid the Russians would hear and that I wanted to spend my last ten days there interviewing dissidents and not get thrown out, but this was specious. It was because I began to feel myself somehow guilty—guilty because I was a woman and reasonably attractive and thus the source and chalice of Evil.

What stayed with me was not only the terror of that evening in Tbilisi, which came so unexpectedly that ever after that I believed that anything could happen anywhere, that any man could change from normal person to brute, but also the slow realization and concretization of my situation as a woman—and the situation of all women, internally and externally.

When I got to Vienna, I wrote out the entire situation to Nick in a letter. I could not bear to tell him on the phone—I was too ashamed, yes, still feeling too guilty simply for existing. I went from there to Egypt to get the first interview that Mrs. Anwar Sadat, new as first lady, had ever given. And when I arrived home in Chicago two weeks later, I walked into the office expecting them to say something, to do something, even to write something. As Mike Royko, one of the few angry men around there, later put it, "What if a Russian woman journalist had been beaten up in this country? It would be around the world in five minutes!"

I waited. Nothing happened. No one said anything, although innuendos drifted back to me: "A girl like Gee Gee has to expect things like that. . . ." "She probably brought it on herself. . . ." Even my mother said, "Dear, I'm surprised it hasn't happened to you sooner."

I was beside myself. I couldn't speak of it. In my own mind, somewhere deep in that feminine psyche, I had been coded like other women to believe that *I* was wrong: that I, by simply being, was evil. As impossible as it might seem, particularly for a "woman of the world" like me, the fact is that I spent a full year still reenacting the horror, still having nightmares, still believing that any man could change anytime as Ivan had. During this time I said nothing to the office, but I brooded. At times I hated them for not standing up for me, for not "protecting" me against that world out there (little girls should be protected by men) and for accusing *me*

171

of evoking it. Yet at the same time, I was accusing myself, so how could I realistically or fairly blame *them?*

And since finally I would have to react, I did it in the most clumsy and absurd manner possible, just as I had done when I wanted to go to Santo Domingo. Unable to speak of the Georgian experience, when I wrote a memo a *year* later about going to the Middle East to our respected editor, Daryle Feldmeier, I inserted deep in the middle of the memo a bitter paragraph. "Yet," I wrote, "if you are all to let me down as you did after my attack in Russia, I do not expect you to. . . ." I am embarrassed to include the rest.

Daryle, a dear friend, was staggered. He had given orders that anything I wanted done when I returned be done—but I had asked for nothing.

It was an emotional confrontation. I began to cry. Nick had tears in his eyes, as did Daryle. They had been wrong, yes, but so had I been wrong. Programmed as are we all, I had been done in by the old female "genes." Despite everything that had been put into me to change me, despite all the education and opportunities, despite all the experience in the world, I was still a walking dictionary of all the old female beliefs, and fears, and traumas.

But I learned in Russia—and in the eerie aftermath—something that was as simple and as sure as my childhood beliefs: If men could do this to women, and if other decent and intelligent men could think there was nothing wrong with it and really rather like it, and if I, with all the blessings and benefits that had been poured into me, could still act in the absurd and agonized way I did, there is something deeply and darkly violent and destructive between the sexes —along with that which is creative and loving and transcendent. No theories of economic deprivation can ever begin to explain this. But I had had so many of the loving and transcendent relations with men, too—as family, as lovers, as fellow seekers, as colleagues—that dark events like this marked me but never defeated me.

X.

Men of Iron

"When the pope came here, we could see our Polish masses all around us. Before, it was pretty clear who they were. Now we saw who we were."
—JANUSZ ONYSZKIEWICZ, Solidarity national spokesman

Not by accident, much of my early professional life had been passionately dedicated to studying and understanding Latin America, and in particular Central America and the Caribbean. There was reason and purpose in this: I loved Latin America, yes, but I also knew that one can know most about a nation if one studies how it treats its neighbors—just as one can know most about a man by knowing how he treats his wife. So, later, when I went to Russia, and then ten years later, in 1981, to Poland, it was very much a part of this never-ending and fascinating study.

What does one learn about the Soviet Union through its satellites? What kinds of mechanisms had the Poles hammered out consciously or worked out subconsciously to deal with their powerful neighbors? Was it the love-hate relationship that the Latins had for us? Was it similar to the Finns, who had arrived at a _modus operandi_ with their neighboring Soviets by which they would keep their freedom by never, ever criticizing the Soviet Union publicly? It was neither; the Poles dealt with the Russians, as with their other powerful neighbor, the Germans, through a kind of suicidal romanticism that allowed them spasmodically throughout history to rise to great,

173

brief heights of heroism as a slap at fate—and then to sink back again until the next shining "moment."

Yet, after the dramatic "August 1980," it had seemed that this pattern was over, that there was indeed something new in Poland.

It was a wintry Sunday when my Lufthansa jet took off from Frankfurt's bustling and commercially Dionysian airport and headed east: east to where the harsh borders of Russia and the Orient meet. And as we sped toward Poland, the skies thickened into a great, gray curtain hanging in the sky beneath us. Occasionally this fog would part and fleetingly we could see the snow-covered landscape. Eventually we landed in Warsaw in a rain so thick it could have been raindrops frozen in the sky.

Since it was my first visit, I had really very little idea of what to expect. Poland, that hot and tumultuous and glorious August of 1980, had erupted. Communist Party control of the country was not only broken by the extraordinary phenomenon of the Solidarity free trade unions; it virtually collapsed of its own outer corruption, inner inertia, and squalid arrogance. The Eastern bloc of totalitarians ruled over by Mother Russia had never seen anything like it, and even the Russians did not know what to do with this new type of child. But now it was winter, and the Russians knew very well how to wait in winter, always their cruel but real and proven friend.

What would I find? How would I operate, how insert myself into this new type of society, half free and half still totalitarian? I had not the faintest idea, for I had not had time even to plan this trip. No one in Warsaw knew I was coming (which at times, of course, can also be a great advantage).

A young German businessman and I made our way into the city, our taxi cutting the thick gray blanket that enveloped it—symbolic of the entire Eastern bloc—like a slowly moving dull knife. Dull, dull —everything was dull, gray and dull, smothering, in the gray, rainy surface of this city with its granite gray facade.

But soon I found that I was privileged to be present at the moment when a window to gray Poland—to this closed, totalitarian, shrouded, silent society—had momentarily opened. And inside there was a shining, shimmering, new reality that for eleven days I could hold in my hands like some precious but oh-so-breakable blown glass treasure. After twenty years as a journalist I could still feel poignantly and totally the fresh excitement of a new land and a new historic experience. To hear these voices—no longer shrouded, true, open, honest—was indeed like hearing the voice of God.

The "Polish revolution," if that is what we can or should call it —different as it was from all the other revolutions I had covered— was probably intellectually the most stimulating story I had ever covered. Part of it was that the Poles are indeed a highly intellectualizing and inward-turning people. Part of it was the fact that I found myself in the middle of a political society that was turning itself inside out—and in which everybody had his own distinct ideas about how to save it. Every morning I awoke and arose filled with excitement about the conversations I was to have, the ideas and schemes for salvation I was to hear. For this was a society in which people were rationally and cautiously but systematically (and often against their own historic romantic and suicidal natures) involved in the desperately intricate business of freeing themselves.

In this country, which only months before had been held tight in the straitjacket of the Soviet Union, on the second night, I sat in the Interpress office at 6:00 P.M. in the early winter darkness, with the great Warsaw Opera House etched across the sky outside. I was listening to Andrzej Wroblewski, the deputy editor of the party newspaper, *Polityka,* a writer and self-described "romantic socialist." "I regret to say that people are fed up with the system," Wroblewski was saying. "If there were a poll on whether people wanted socialism today, most would say, 'No.' "

Wroblewski, who was strikingly handsome, then went on to analyze the generational problem. "I think that my generation was committed to a sentimental or romantic version of socialism—*egalité, fraternité,* all of that," he said thoughtfully. "The younger people today have nothing to do with ideas. They assess things as they are. Being unsentimental or brutal in their assessment, they

175

analyze it for what it gives to them. Does it give the prospect of a better life? I would rather blame our generation. It was too idealistic, inclined to forgive too much of our system. . . ."

There were several ways in which, as the days rushed by and as I went from interview to interview, walking often ten miles a day in the absence of ready taxicabs, I began to analyze this totally fractured and disintegrating society—and it was one of the most difficult analyses I have ever had to make. For, when I asked Marek Brunne, the spokesman for Solidarity, one turbulent afternoon, "Who is in control in Poland?" this frantic man answered, with total honesty, "Nobody is in control! Really! Nobody!"

First I tried to analyze the "Polish revolution" in terms of sociology—it was clear that this time, in contrast to former "uprisings" in 1968 and 1976, the workers and the intellectuals were together. It was this solid ground swell that was so shattering to the system and so uniting to the often divided Polish people.

Then I began to analyze the role of the Catholic Church and, in particular, the role of the Polish pope, John Paul II. I posed my questions about the Church phenomenon carefully. I did not ask, "Did the Church play a role in the Polish revolution?" I asked, "Could the revolution have happened without the pope?" And I got interesting answers.

Sitting in the busy Solidarity headquarters in Warsaw one afternoon, I asked this of Janusz Onyszkiewicz, the national Solidarity spokesman. "When the pope came here, we could see our Polish masses all around us," he answered. "Before, it was pretty clear who they were. Now we saw who we were." I was deeply moved by those simple yet eloquent words describing how a people had suddenly been pulled together by a spiritual unity that they had not known existed among them before.

Then I journeyed to Cracow, the aristocratic city in the south whose graceful old buildings from the medieval times were left untouched by World War II, and there I learned even more about the pope's interesting and crucial role.

There are scenes and moments I deeply treasure, and this was one of them. Interpress, at my request, took me up to the extraordinary Catholic newspaper, *Tygodnik Powszechy,* and to its editor, Jerzy Turowicz, an old gentleman of obviously fine tastes and cultured mien. In the warm old room there were many informal and glowing photos of Pope John Paul II, during the thirty years he worked and wrote as a young priest in Cracow. Books and shelves filled with old file covers lined the walls, adding to the atmosphere of the room. I felt in the midst of a loving embrace.

Turowicz first told me how his beloved paper ("exceptional in this part of Europe," he said modestly) had wondrously survived, even through the Stalin days. And how much things had changed since "August." "Censorship is ten times more liberal," he said with a certain sense of wonder. "Every week we publish things that a year ago we couldn't have imagined. Every week we get closer to reality. . . ."

But could it have happened without the pope? (I am always single-minded and obstinate about getting certain questions answered.) "No," Turowicz said thoughtfully. "When he was first elected, people were depressed and resigned. His being chosen gave to the people some partly irrational and some partly rational hope. He was a moral authority who came from our experience. He changed the whole psychological atmosphere in Poland, especially his visit. We saw ourselves as a real country, able to manifest and express ourselves quite fully. And nobody could impede us. For the first time we saw ourselves all united, even the party members."

I was utterly fascinated by this—but how, indeed, do you express these spiritual and abstract ideas in the very hard language of journalism? How do you insert them into the genre? And if you do not, are you really telling your readers what is going on? I certainly think not.

Trying to put together the entire Polish picture was, for a journalist, a constantly complex and engrossing but an endlessly difficult job. Who was where? What was really happening? How could you find out? How would you be treated at any minute? *What in all hell was really going on inside this magnificent gray land?* No one knew. You lived from moment to moment, but the sheer richness of the intellectual analysis and stimuli was enough to excite you and keep you at it.

Lech Walesa, for instance—one just had to see Lech Walesa, the "Man of Iron" who had led the working men and women of Poland from a kind of totalitarian slavery to the beginnings of a representative form of government. But Walesa was not in Gdansk, nee Danzig, he was in Warsaw for the negotiating talks with the government. This was bad because it meant that neither the Gdansk Solidarity nor the Solidarity chapters could reach him.

My "man" at Interpress and I sat in the Interpress coffee shop overlooking the square in Warsaw and talked it over.

"There's only one solution," he said. "They always stay at the Solec Hotel when they're here. It's kind of the Solidarity headquarters. Why don't you just go on over there?"

I did. I walked over to the Inter-Continental Hotel, which was one of the few places you could get a cab with any ease, and took off for the Solec. There I found another of the anomalies of Poland: a modern, Swedish-built hotel that reminded one of, say, Grand Rapids. It was neat, clean, clean-cut, and utilitarian in that special Scandinavian way. It didn't look any more like the old fluted and romantic and gray Old Warsaw that I had imagined than it looked like the Bangkok riverways. I had, once again, to readjust my thinking. Here I was, in a "Communist" country, watching a free trade union organization meet to discuss its negotiations on restructuring that "Communist" country, in a modern, Swedish-built hotel, with labor leaders who looked like they belonged in Detroit.

Behind some glass doors, in a spare little room, I found Walesa and his men. Walesa, wearing a dark blue corduroy jacket, with his rakish mustache and his sensuous eyes, was obviously exhausted. But the discussion among them was by turns serious, animated, and deadly serious. Walesa cajoled, he laughed, he wrung his hands; and when he came running out (he always seemed to run, not walk), it struck me for some reason with surprise that he was very short. I was (and am, I suppose) five feet six inches—he must have been five feet

178

three. He reminded me, in his size and in his perpetual motion, of a kind of hyperactive bantam rooster.

I never did quite catch him, I have to admit it; for he dashed away then to Gdansk, then back to Warsaw, then back to Gdansk. We kept missing each other.

I tried to work my way into knowing Solidarity better, and I did have a splendid talk with Janusz Onyszkiewicz, a charming young blond man who spoke philosophically about the whole situation, which was indeed deteriorating. Was Solidarity having serious divisions? "No question about it," this pleasant young man with the Norseman's face said. "Until recently our program was pretty negative. It criticized the government and everyone was unified. Now we are forced to take a positive attitude to get out of that. If you want to make a positive program, you must choose between values because one value limits the choices. From a moral point of view, things are not quite clear."

Then he went on to say, again thoughtfully, "We can ask people to make sacrifices if we can tell them that we are on a definite path. The problem is timing—that's the main game. What comes first? To do so, we must say we are on the path, that the institutions are established, that they operate, that future development is secured. . . ."

And Poland didn't have that—that was the problem. There was no assured path as yet, no new institutions. In fact the country was in total chaos. Theories and new terminology abounded. It was a "self-limiting" revolution. There was a dangerous "paralysis of authority." Events were creating "a real socialization of economy, an anarchization of life." In spite of all this it was still a wholly unprecedented attempt to build into a totalitarian society, from within and nonviolently, pluralism and checks and balances and the mechanisms of people's control.

But I soon came to see, too, the all-too-real and new potential danger. The Polish revolution also could become a "zero-sum game," in effect a situation in which all the forces canceled the other ones out. That was the real danger of Poland's winter, which always comes after every August no matter what in life you do, and that was what the Soviets cunningly were watching, were banking on and planning around.

Next to the question of what the romantic, sad-eyed, dramatic, suicidal, wonderful Poles were doing, lay the question of what the Russians were doing with the Poles—and, most of all, why they hadn't done anything after months and months of the once-unimaginable "Polish revolution."

I finally filed the following column about the Russian policy in Poland. I was and am convinced that it was an entirely different and new policy that we were seeing, and that we were missing it at our own loss:

> Warsaw, Poland—In these last 16 months of the "Polish revolution," not one Western embassy reported from Warsaw that there would ever be a Soviet invasion. Yet almost every one of their home capitals nevertheless insisted there would be. Therein lie some crucial and unanswered questions:
>
> Where are you Russkis? Why haven't you come yet, despite all of Washington's public warnings not to (and many, too many cynical private hopes there that you would)? Are you too busy in Afghanistan and Aden? What the devil are you doing?
>
> The grand and potentially tragic situation in Poland is not something to joke about; but the predictions from Washington, coming almost exactly every three months, that Moscow was about to invade have become a truly bad joke here.
>
> Poles returning from trips to Washington are uniformly angered by American hopes that the Russians will invade and thus "show the world what they really are." One now-out American official, General Bobby Schweitzer, last August even predicted the invasion date: Sept. 22.
>
> This is not only naturally deeply offensive to the Poles, it has also turned out to be a superficial and dangerous misreading of Russian actions and intent in Poland.
>
> For the Soviets have used a wholly new tactic in Poland from their all-out invasions of the past. Basically, the new policy is one of tolerating inner reforms in Poland so long as they do not affect the Soviet

Union's system of alliances or strategic communications across Poland and—less certain to observers here—the predominance of the Communist Party.

On its more subtle and sophisticated and cynical level, I call it the Russians' "Wait for winter" policy. For centuries the Russians have been absorbing everyone from Napoleon to Hitler to the Golden Hordes in their vastnesses and in their murderously debilitating winters. Now they are applying that same policy of patient absorption to the Poles' gallant experiment; and if it destroys itself from lack of internal cohesion and degenerates into Civil War, well then nobody in the world will really blame the Russians for invading.

As unknowable as the Kremlin remains, there are a number of indicators to back up this analysis:

—In his recent and unusual interview with the German magazine, *Der Stern*, Soviet Chairman Leonid Brezhnev, asked about the preservation of peace in Europe, very pointedly said, "And I would add, the place of socialist Poland in Europe."

This shows that detente—the relations between East and West pushed since the early '70s and now abandoned by President Reagan—was the policy that really opened up Poland and gave it the possibility of changing. But it also shows that the Soviets want Eastern-isolated Poland to play a new role in linking both East and West.

—Well-informed participants here like government spokesman Jerzy Urban stress that in the last 16 months, the Soviets "never expressed any negative attitudes toward the reforms going on here. The Soviet Union never said we were not to have an independent trade union in Poland, but only that we should never attack the system."

Is this a new and different response? "Yes, entirely," Urban went on. "And it might be that the prospectus toward Poland could indicate a crucial change in Soviet attitudes toward all of Eastern Europe. The future of the political experiments going on in these socialist countries depends upon Solidarity's (temperate) responses."

—Solidarity leaders tend to agree with this. Janusz Onyszkiewicz, Solidarity national spokesman, pointed out that the Hungarian trade unions actually answered Solidarity's recent letter to them urging cooperation. "Two of three sentences were important," he said,

181

"those in which they indicated we should talk. We were not totally rejected—and that answer had to be approved by the Soviets."

—On Nov. 21, for the first time, open questions such as "Does Poland lose or win in commercial contacts with the Soviet Union?" have been asked publicly. These were posed, even more extraordinary, in the government paper, *Polityka.*

While all of this is going on, then, for the United States to talk about the desirability of a Soviet invasion is not only cynical in the extreme, it is completely missing the major new points here. Instead of only a singular policy of obsessively trying to embarrass the Soviets (and condemning the Poles to a new hell), we should be working to help the Poles truly develop the first pluralistic society within the Eastern bloc. Without question, that—and not the freezing of the bloc that would follow a civil war and an invasion—is the most effective and even apocalyptic way to change that bloc.

Now, as anyone familiar at all with the Russian policy and intentions toward Eastern Europe could see, there was a very new and far more sophisticated policy emerging here. Months passed, and yet the Soviets—despite all the dire predictions from Washington—did not invade.

The problem for me was how, in the midst of all that mystery and alchemy and dissimulation, to get enough information to make this interpretation believable to others. How did I satisfy myself that my analysis was correct? When you are dealing with will-o'-the-wisps and with lightning bugs, where do you as a journalist begin to start catching them?

Fortunately I had a long background of working in and studying of the Soviet Union. My Russian, though rusty, could still be called upon. Without this—for Russian policies are a little like reading Sanskrit—I could never have told what had changed; could never have recognized the new signals and realities; could never do what journalists in these situations must do, which is taking all the signals and putting them gradually together.

But I was doing about others only what the Poles were doing about themselves: they were turning inward in the most moving way

182

to discover their own history. It was the history that I had seen in the catacombs of Wawel Castle one Saturday morning in Cracow, where I found the tombs of archbishops and generals all lying together. After World War II the Russians had attempted to wipe out Polish history. It was not taught in the schools; its great heroes were not publicly mentioned. And yet now, thirty years later, after all those years of silence they were rediscovering themselves; or perhaps not so much rediscovering themselves as revealing publicly for the first time in three decades what they had always known inside. And they were doing this in different ways. Small intellectual and university salons studied Polish history, filling in the blanks the Russians had created with their historic lobotomy on the Poles. Solidarity ran history programs. On anniversaries they marched to the formerly unknown graves of national military heroes. Youth groups like the Democratic Youth in Cracow sought out war heroes and graves. I was seeing before me the kind of shining reawakening not only of nationality and of faith but of what I dealt in and lived for—true information—that alone keeps people sane in this world.

Just before I left, I had an appointment with Jerzy Urban, a former popular commentator turned government spokesman. He was a small, round man with an almost all-bald pate and he looked very much like the hard line incarnate. But like so much else in Poland then, he wasn't quite what he appeared. Within ten minutes I found myself again deeply involved in one of those Polish paradoxes. For there I was, speaking to the *official government spokesman* for an hour and a half—rationally, systematically, analytically —about why communism had failed in Poland!

"The reasons were both political and economic," Urban said as we sat in the little room that was colored in the historic Polish colors of dark green and a dark, deep rose. "The Polish economy in the seventies was based on very expensive imports from the Western economy. But we could never produce exports for hard currency. Polish society simply consumed too much of the credits. So the fault with our politicians was that power was exercised in a very arbitrary way and by very few people. There was no control over them, and they got rich at the cost of the people. They became divided from the people. Arrogant. The problem, in one sentence, was that we didn't introduce slow political reforms."

As to the "Why?" of the new Soviet response, Urban gave three other fascinating reasons: "(1) You could really feel the social struggle behind the changes occurring. They were obviously not performed by small groups. (2) Events in Poland occurred gradually. It was not a sudden uprising endangering the balance of forces in Europe. (3) The Polish character was always different. There was always private property. And the Church. The Soviet Union got used to our differences. It was impossible to change us."

I remember walking out of the big, ponderous, gray government central building that early evening in the rain and suddenly catching myself up and shaking my head. I had been listening for an hour and a half as though it were the most normal thing in the world to have the Polish national spokesman telling me why communism had failed. Suddenly the fact hit me with all its resonances—it was, simply, extraordinary!

We journalists were, once again, privileged. We were there at the window the moment the curtain opened, and we were the only ones allowed to step inside—into this wonderland we had suspected, but did not know, existed. Only we were allowed in to seek out the little (in this case, not so little) truths of the great historical saga that had so suddenly revealed itself to the world—and that could just as suddenly close.

No matter what happened, I knew inside myself that Poland would never again be the same. One of the brightest men at Interpress told me, "We have three crises in Poland—economic, political, and moral. The moral is at the base of the political. And in the moral, we have to first have the clarification in terminology. Until now we have used different terms for the same phenomena. It is the first time that we have different viewpoints but don't feel offended at different viewpoints. We treat it as natural that we differ in viewpoints."

Again—the importance of "terminology" or of "information." Again—the purifying aspects of my profession are calling.

Still, as intellectually and morally exciting as it was, Poland was in a dangerous situation of collapse. The forces—the Communist Party and government, Solidarity, the army and the Church—could not hammer out the new form of government. And they could not call upon the people to make sacrifices if they could not tell them what the new institutional form that would save them would be. That was the danger. It was not unlike the disintegration I had seen elsewhere, an "ideological Lebanon."

You could often feel and see it collapsing as you made your rainy rounds and observed it. The Polish zloty, at the regular rate, was thirty-three to the dollar. But the black market rate was four hundred to the dollar!

The first night, reacting to the regular rate, I ate carefully in the hotel dining room. After changing the money the second day, I had smoked salmon, creamed mushrooms, chateaubriand, and a good bottle of red wine—every night. The dinner cost about two dollars.

Did I not feel guilty about sitting there in that relatively nice atmosphere and eating so well, while the Poles were lined up outside every day for hours and hours waiting for the most paltry of food rations? Yes, as as matter of fact, I did. But I did it. I rationalized that I was walking ten miles a day, which was true, and that I needed nourishment. And basically, I knew that whether or not I ate an elaborate dinner didn't matter.

Some nights the dining room reminded me a great deal of the foreign currency bars in Russia; waiters were changing money in every known currency at every table. One night, in a fit of final madness, I attempted even to include in my feast the Russian caviar that was on the menu.

"No caviar," the waiter said impassively. Then he whispered loudly, "You like to buy some in dollars?"

I asked to see it, and he brought it out barely covered with a pink napkin, which he elegantly lifted to display the precious little black cargo. But he was greedy—he wanted eighty dollars, which after all was what it cost in Washington—and I said, "Absolutely not!"

Another day I was wheeling around Warsaw in the rain with my big, burly cabdriver, who was also my money changer. We would "change" between the seats as we traveled through the city. This day, I said, with rather exaggerated politeness for the situation, "Do you speak English?"

"Nah, nah," he said ebulliently, "Chust money. . . . Change. . . . Changea money. . . ."

Then, for some reason, I went on to ask him, *"Sprechen sie Deutsch?"* or, "Do you speak German?"

He started the most eerie singsong. "Nah, nah, chust *Geld.* . . . *Wechseln.* . . . *Wechseln Geld.* . . ." Then he proceeded with this strange singsong, in five different languages in which this man of the street and man of our times used only—only—words that had to do with "changing money." It became a kind of interchangeable singsong, and as we spun through the streets, I found myself understanding Bertolt Brecht.

Despite these amusing scenes, I knew that what I was seeing was a society falling apart, disintegrating, dying, where some were suffering a greed for freedom and knowledge and others were still indulging their greed for untrammeled power and for *"Geld."*

Exactly two weeks after I left Warsaw that gray, rainy November of 1981, the Polish army declared martial law—and virtually destroyed the "Polish revolution"—for the moment. Those of us who had "been there"—the foreign correspondents, the Western diplomats on the spot, the other analysts—all said, as had the American embassy, that it would not be a Soviet invasion, that it would be a Polish military takeover. Yet, far away in Washington, ideologues who refused to be governed by "knowing" the intrinsic qualities of a situation again misanalyzed and mispredicted what would come. When martial law was declared, they were still predicting a Soviet takeover and therefore were unprepared to respond to the real situation that occurred.

Again the people who "didn't have to be there" but were . . . were the ones who were right. They "knew."

XI.
Entering the World of International Terrorism

"The base of the lighthouse is dark."
—Old Japanese proverb

In 1969 I entered the world of international terrorism. I entered as a journalist, which meant an even more intricate balancing act among the dangers than it did for a participant. Journalists are in danger not only for what they might do, but for what they might think, for what they might write, or even for what might be interpreted as their intent or beliefs.

This entire business was full of questions with few answers. How do you analyze guerrilla or terrorist movements? How do you tell the difference between them? What standards do you use; in an area in which no journalistic—or other—standards have been hammered out? How do you separate necessity from brutality? How far should you go out of the way to try to balance any imbalance of the general media, such as we certainly had in the Middle East? Finally, how much do you forgive and how do you survive?

I was one of the first journalists thrown into this murderous and maniacal milieu, and one of the very first women, so I was working out guidelines and principles as I went along. The first task, as always and everywhere, was to get to know the people you were writing about, to fathom their cause and problems and correctly to judge their insecurities and insincerities. And this was, of course, made

187

more complicated (to say the very least) when a movement was basically underground and afraid.

Oddly enough, when my foreign editor and friend, Nick Shuman, sent me to the Middle East in the fall of 1969, I had little or no interest in the area, in the Arabs, and particularly in the Palestinians. I had long been extremely pro-Israeli and the "Palestinian question" frankly drew a blank for me. But soon after I was there, I began to realize that this "situation" was not at all what I had been led to believe. I had seen many situations where the reality little resembled what one had been led to expect beforehand—but never had I seen such a chasm of misunderstanding as this one.

At that time the monarchy of Jordan's legendary King Hussein was largely ruled by the regulars and irregulars of the Palestine Liberation Organization. Indeed, as I drove into Amman by cab from the airport that first night, open jeeps of PLO men in full uniform careened around the streets of that lovely city with its villas of gold-colored stone. It was all too obvious that they were taking it over from the king; an air of imminent civil war hung about the entire place.

In the evenings on the outdoor terrace of the Hotel Intercontinental, the guerrillas of Fatah, As Saiqa, or the Popular Front, or a score of other movements, would walk around with macabre "politeness" asking for donations. The silent machine guns they carried lent the requests a certain urgency and clarity. When you donated to any one group, that group would put a yellow or a red or a green slip of paper on your table—you would not be bothered by *them* again.

One of the most exciting efforts I have undertaken has been to penetrate these organizations. They are madly suspicious, and being an American certainly did not help. They can turn on you at any moment and their important functions are, for the most part, underground.

Only in the beginning, in dealing with this strange shadow world, does it seem odd that these "underground" movements have "information offices." Then your mind adapts and you become just as crazy as everyone else and it seems perfectly natural to go along with the often sinister drama.

So the first thing I did was to go to the Fatah Information Office, where I first met Zudhi Terrazzi, the fiftyish scion of an old crusader family from Jerusalem. They spelled his name "Terzi" on his visa application, so he turned out as "Terzi" at the UN. Then sleeping on a cot in the office, Zudhi was later to become the PLO's first ambassador to the UN. A cultured, calculating man who was utterly dedicated to the cause, Zudhi started me on the little journeys necessary for a journalist's work.

The first thing for a journalist to do in such a situation is to create trust, which takes time. One way to do this is to "make the rounds." Dutifully, day after day, I trooped out of the Jordan Intercontinental, sometimes with a group and sometimes alone, to see the training camps, to see the little Palestinian boys training, to see the wounded in the hospitals, in effect to go through the whole ritual.

In order more fully to understand, I spent a night in the Marka refugee camp with a refugee family. We drove out that day to the Marka camp just outside of Amman, and I settled in with the Abdel Khader family, originally from a village named Jemsu in what was now Israel. The first little "crisis" came when, despite the fact that I had (I thought) worn a very conservative black dress, as I sat on a low stool my knees showed slightly.

There was a flurry of whispers. But everything was solved when the manager of the camp himself appeared with a towel which he demurely draped over my knees. It was my first encounter with the fact that elbows and knees drove Arab men quite mad.

Later that evening I had put on a heavy long nightgown of the wife's (apparently just fine to wear in front of the men) and when it was time to sleep they all piled their thin mattresses up one on another and I found myself sleeping several feet above the rest of the family!

But it was in the Marka camp I began to see, firsthand, the real problem of the three million Palestinians and, even more so, the dangerous unreality of our ideas about them. I could see with this family, who talked endlessly about the day when they would return to their old village of Jemsu (as though it were still as it was when they left), how the poor Palestinians had made out. One million of them remained in camps, mostly without citizenship and without work, having been driven from or having left voluntarily what had been Palestine and what was now Israel. But there were also other Palestinians—neither hungry nor in refugee camps.

Soon I was in Beirut with these others—the vast body of business-men and intellectuals and educated people that also made up the Palestinians. One day there, Walid Khalidi, a brilliant man who refuses to indulge in "vulgarizations about his Jewish cousins," was explaining to me why it was that of all the refugees in the modern world it was only these Palestinian refugees who kept on with this insane insistence upon a return.

"It was the wholeness," he explained, "the wholeness of every-body being put across a frontier . . . and not on a time scale to allow the Great Healer time to do his work. You woke up and you said, 'Am I not in Jaffa? Of course, I must be.' Then, compounding injustice, plus insult, there was the closeness of standing in Jerusalem and seeing a Jewish family washing clothes on your balcony. And at the same time, there was the din of applause for your persecutors ringing constantly in your ears."

I was beginning to put the Palestinian "problem" into some perspective, and I realized that there was a new theme just lying there and waiting to be sung—the truth that the Palestinians were only secondarily the Abdel Khaders in the camps. With 100,000 college graduates or more, they are the most developed people in the Arab world and *the* major catalyst for change. In November 1970 I wrote in *The New Republic:*

The Palestinian Arabs—those ultimately fanaticized people who just masterfully sabotaged the Middle East peace plan—are not what they seem to be. They are not, as they have widely been pictured, poor. They are not, by and large, uneducated. They are not a people without hope and their cause is not a cause born primarily of depredation and poverty. . . .

It is nearly impossible, among the 30,000 to 50,000 commandos or "fedayeen" (the Arabic word for "those who sacrifice") to find a leader or sub-leader who is not a doctor, lawyer or literary person. And in this apparent contradiction, almost unnoticed in the plethora of news coverage of this obstreperous revolutionary movement, lies the fascination of this curious people. They are a revolutionary force in the world today not because they are poor and without hope but rather because they are the most advanced people in the Arab world.

I was trying to get to the "base of the lighthouse," which was indeed always dark even as the lighthouse shone its light across a darkened sea. It was very much the same job as a psychiatrist's: to listen and to understand, to get at the trauma and let it speak. Terrorism was the symptom of breakdown, and I knew I was dealing first-hand with one of the epi-themes of our era.

After going through the "rounds" of getting to know the PLO and its strange and often dark ways, and thus building confidence, my next step was to try to get to know the leadership—not, then, an easy move.

Despite my feeling that interviewing leaders is actually one of the more tiresome of life's concerns, from the first time I went to Beirut in 1969, I started working on interviewing Yasser Arafat, chairman of the Palestine Liberation Organization and, to many, the number one terrorist in the world. For an amazing number of years, eight actually, nothing happened. I applied through the information offices (never the way to get to the top men) and I reapplied in all sorts of ways.

I saw others, but I didn't see him. I met Abu Jihad, the head of the PLO military wing, in Damascus, and he and his wife inexplicably gave a Thanksgiving dinner for me. Since he was even harder to see than Arafat, that was extremely nice—but he wasn't Arafat. I interviewed Abu Iyad, who really *is* head of the terrorist wing, and

I was held in an Arab embassy where we talked for an hour until he returned to wherever it is shadowy figures such as he return to—or I would have been held responsible for anything that happened to him. But he wasn't Arafat either.

Finally, in the spring of 1977, an interview was arranged through a mutual friend, a Palestinian doctor, and I arrived in the broken city of Beirut on a Saturday evening that was my birthday. It was heart-rending, seeing those piles of blackened bricks where once the beautiful white city on the sea had been, and the next night I crossed over to the Fakhani section to meet Arafat. The meeting took place in the impeccable, bourgeois apartment of his secretary, a plump and buxom woman who bustled about bringing piles of food to everyone.

Actually Arafat surprised me, as I was often to be surprised in these interviews I now seemed destined to do.

For one thing he was far less harsh in person than in his pictures. He smiled and laughed easily, his face expressive and his odd, poppish eyes cushioned by the pouches that lay underneath them. There was, of course, the heavyset body, the head scarf or *kaffiyeh,* and the self-conscious khakis. He looked like a cross between GI Joe and the Buddha.

I was expecting the worst. I knew that interviews with him (with any "revolutionary" leader) were often filled with nonproductive rhetoric. So my relief grew when I soon saw it becoming something quite different.

"We are embarking upon a new program," he said with intensity, "a program of international legitimacy." Here is where you have to be able to read the hieroglyphics—the Rosetta stones of the liberation fronts—in order to figure out what is really being said. And what he was saying, this April of 1977, was that whereas before the PLO program had recognized no course of action except "armed struggle," now it would work through the UN and other respectable bodies.

"Do you understand the importance of what I am saying?" he asked me at one point, his eyes narrowed. "This is a very important signal."

The "international bandits" of the world were embarking upon an all-out program of diplomacy, to gain respectability in preparation for the formation of a "Palestinian state."

And now he talked about that state, something he had always denied before. He said there could indeed be federation or confederation with Jordan, but only after an independent state had come into being. He vehemently denied that what he was saying was only "tactical."

When I pressed him on recognition and guarantees for Israel, he said that "the formation of a Palestinian state will solve (our problems with Israel) for the next twenty years."

"Why twenty years?" I pressed him, suspicious.

"From your questions," he answered, smiling a patient-impatient, oddly avuncular smile, "I can understand that you are asking for guarantees for Israel. I only say twenty years because by that time I will be dead. Others will have to work out the future." He then went on to renounce terrorism and to approve enthusiastically the new contacts between PLO representatives and "any Israelis or Jews who recognize the Palestinian people."

We started at 10:00 P.M. and we ended at 2:00 A.M. In between we finished off platefuls of typical Arab food. Just before 2:00 A.M. he said that of course he could not *fully recognize Israel at this time*, throwing up his hands and saying, "You are asking from the victim everything."

Yet I knew that he had in fact given to me in this curious interview an *implicit recognition*. On the side, his people told me they were thinking about de facto recognition of Israel in the first stage of settlement, with de jure recognition coming in the final stage.

And as I left him that strange early morning in that grotesquely wounded city that I had loved so much, this man that many saw as the new Attila the Hun smiled broadly and said, "I am optimistic, yes, I am optimistic."

As I got to know these Palestinians better—but never, believe me, as an outsider, really to *know* them—I kept searching for the secret to Arafat's leadership. What was his "genius," this chubby man with the stubble of beard? As I talked with his people, I began to see him as a kind of moderate, a juggler of passions who let a thousand flowers bloom in order to hold his then-disparate movement together. His were the welcoming arms that closed around every Palestinian, no matter what that man had done, or what horror he had committed, and tried to lead him back to the fold.

Indeed it was only half a year later that I saw him again—but now in a totally different manner. Now it was December of 1977, immediately after Anwar Sadat's stunning trip to Jerusalem. Now all of the hopes of Arafat, expressed to me only that last spring, were dead. This time, after the glory and drama of the Cairo Conference where Israelis and Egyptians met for the first time, he agreed to see me but only on the basis that it would be all off the record. Unhappy about it, I nevertheless agreed. And I found quite a different man.

It was as though he were drained of all energy. He spoke from the heart. His words, which I can here only paraphrase, were really cries of anguish. He had been in Cairo with Sadat. They had been talking about the new initiatives in the UN. He, Arafat, had left by plane to go to Libya to try to patch things up with Qaddafi for Sadat. In midair the plane was called back by Sadat: something urgent. Then Arafat was taken to the front rows of the meeting of the Arab Socialist Union, where Sadat had called an extraordinary session; he was even placed in a front-row seat. Sadat then proceeded to inform the population that he was going to try to make a breakthrough by going to Jerusalem. Arafat sat there, stunned, incredulous, unbelieving, and, above all, deeply and deliberately humiliated.

"Georgie Anne," he told me, "we were both sitting on a high platform, Sadat and me. Then he pushed me off. He—he is still up there. But I—I am down. I am finished." It was a strange, dread cry for help that I cannot easily forget.

I saw Arafat twice after that. Once in 1978, he had been sick—the flu it was—and I waited several days (what nonjournalists never really understand is that it is the ability to wait and outwait, not

194

perception, or aggressiveness, or intelligence, or penetrating questions, that mark the good journalist!) and so I waited. Finally, on a
Saturday, I recall, they said he was better. I trotted up to the
apartment again and there saw Yasser Arafat—the scourge of the
world, to many—sitting in bed in his blue starched pajamas with
blue flowered sheets and a white chenille bedspread. He and Mah-
moud Labadi, his excellent press man, and I sat there eating candied
apricots . . . and talking.

The last time I saw him, in March of 1980, he was, again, a
different man. Now he had just come back from Teheran and was
foolishly ecstatic. He had thrown the PLO's lot with Khomeini
(even at the time, I thought this quite mad) and was trying to help
negotiate the hostages' freedom. . . .

During these years the correspondent's role was changing. Diplomats could not get to these revolutionaries, for the revolutionaries
blamed them for their problems. We had become the new diplomats
—the new intermediaries in the world—the surrogates for nations.
And the diplomats—the good ones—were jealous. One American,
seasoned and experienced, remarked to me with unmistakable yearning, after I had been smuggled into Syria on a PLO "visa," "If only
I could once do that!" But they couldn't. That was left to us—the
intermediaries, the in-between people, the people who didn't have
to be there.

Interestingly enough, I have found that guerrillas . . . terrorists
. . . freedom fighters . . . whatever you choose to call them, understood us and our role perfectly—in many ways they understood it
better than many Americans. Only once, for instance, was I ever
accused by any of them, anywhere, at any time, of being a CIA
agent, and that was for a reason.

One of the leading PLO diplomats one night at dinner kept
accusing me of being CIA, until I quite lost my cool and snarled at
him something about how they really didn't deserve anything because they were so hopeless and never could analyze anything correctly, etc., etc.

After a hurt silence he finally looked at me and said, "I'm sorry. You see, we needed a contact with the CIA and we were just hoping you could be it."

Dealing with the Palestinians also had its most awful days and nights of terror for us as well.

Bob Allison, CBS correspondent, and I were sitting in the Sheraton dining room one night in Cairo, gazing from our privileges out over the massed humans and dusty dreams and sobering squalor that was Cairo. Suddenly Bob got a phone call from his office, and when he came back to the table, he was shaking his head.

"You won't believe this," he said as he sat down, wearing now that special, exhausted look of the correspondent who has been called away on one too many 2:00 A.M. flights to nowhere. "Some Palestinian terrorists in Khartoum have taken a group of diplomats and are holding them." He paused. "The American ambassador is among them."

By 2:00 A.M., arrangements all behind us, we were sitting on the single Sudanese Airways night flight to Khartoum, south from Egypt, down into the endless northern deserts of Africa.

As dawn was breaking over the vast desert city of Khartoum, where Chinese Gordon had fought off the Mahdi's dervishes in the 1890s, only to have his head end on one of the Mahdi's spikes and the British Empire in this part of Africa fall apart, we landed. After checking into a small downtown hotel at 6:00 A.M., we were off immediately by taxi and by foot to the sprawling residential area where the Palestinians were holding the diplomats in the Saudi embassy. It was a grim story. . . .

A typical diplomatic party had been held the night before at the Saudi embassy, a big, four-storied modern stucco villa that was as utilitarian as it was tasteless. Into the midst of the proper and dutiful crowd, representing all the establishments and structures of the world, suddenly had swept a band of Palestinians, faces ghoulishly masked with black ski masks and hands holding the ever-present Kalashnikovs. They took five guests: American Ambassador Cleo

Noel, the American chargé Curt Moore, a Jordanian, and two other Arabs.

When I heard this, my sorrow increased. Curt Moore I had met on a previous trip through Khartoum. A tall, bespectacled man, he was one of the finest officers I knew. Ironically, Curt was a splendid Arabist; he understood the Arab complaints. It shows, again, how little it mattered what we personally thought—or did—in terms of the world's "causes."

On foot, I reconnoitered the area. The streets around the embassy were now closed to the public by the police. But journalists could get right in front of the Saudi embassy and see the terrorists pacing the balconies in their grotesque black masks.

I was walking back and forth, wondering exactly what to do, when, catty-cornered from the Saudi embassy, I saw some people on a balcony soberly surveying the situation. They looked like Americans.

"May I come up?" I yelled, taking a chance.

"Come on," they answered.

I had happened upon what turned out to be the American command house, which was the only building in the immediate area still occupied. From the balcony upstairs we could look across a span of several hundred feet, onto the balconies of the Saudi embassy, and virtually into the masked eyes of the madmen.

From different places and voices we got bits and pieces of information. The terrorists wanted some of their fellows released from prison. If they did not get that, they would kill the diplomats. My mind was filled with the picture of Curt Moore again, the last time I saw him, sitting in his office at the back of the embassy and telling me with such intelligent, informed sympathy about the very things that were driving these terrorists to such insanity.

I left the area once in order to file quickly at the government information office and then to return. And, of course, filing in a situation like this is a special horror. The government had set up several telex machines in a jerry-built office. Most of the time things either did not get through or were endlessly delayed. I was lucky— I just handed in my copy and left and it got through.

197

The morning had seen a mood of busyness and purposeful activity. The police had smartly cordoned off the area. Even the gawking onlookers were quiet and orderly. Journalists came and went. Negotiations of every possible sort were started behind the scenes. But as the desert sun smote us with its merciless heat, tempers began to fray. Nothing was progressing—nothing. As evening approached, a new mood—one of desperation—began to set in.

Then suddenly the terrorists grew more violent and more impatient. They set a deadline of 8:00 P.M. for killing the men. People rushed about now, faces grim—time was not money but lives.

Meanwhile, in the American command house, I waited with the U.S. AID couple, two charming and generous Americans. The U.S. Marine guards were there, and the political officer, and the CIA station chief. The telephone line was kept open to the embassy so information could be relayed back and forth. I was the only journalist. President Nixon was sending an envoy on a special plane. But Nixon had also said at three o'clock that under no circumstances would he negotiate.

Somehow nothing worked. The special plane was delayed somewhere in Egypt. The demands were not being met.

A new mood seized us. It was as though the horror were palpable, as though it were sitting there, in black robes, with its eye sockets empty and staring at us. By 7:30 P.M., as a strange hooded sun was dropping over the spectral villas of Khartoum, we stood on the upstairs balcony staring at the stark silence of the Saudi embassy. The worst sign of all was the fact that now no one could be seen. I kept looking at my watch. The hand was creeping inexorably toward eight o'clock.

Five to eight: I could feel myself freezing inside. Four . . . three. I almost felt my throat close totally.

"They'll put it off, they'll give more time," the young marine lying on the roof above us with his machine gun murmured. The rest of us stood on the upstairs balcony, in utter, stark, deathly silence.

At eight o'clock I looked at my watch, as though pleading with it not to continue its march. And then, at eight o'clock, something so incredible happened that when I looked up from the watch, I thought perhaps I was going quite mad.

Before my eyes at *precisely 8:00 P.M.* there passed a perfect vertical wave of sand. Then that wave passed and we were in the middle of a blinding sandstorm, one of the worst Khartoum had ever had.

Inside the house, where we now barricaded ourselves trying to close up every crevice lest we be drowned in the pounding golden waves, the sand seeped in with persistence. The minute the storm started, the now-desperate Sudanese began to send tanks and soldiers in. Now, no one could *see,* even in outline, the Saudi embassy. The drama had entered still another form.

The tanks rumbled past us in the sand. From time to time we would take turns running outside to stand by the gate in the storm and then running back into the house to report. Sudanese soldiers were following the tanks, running from side to side for protection. Now there was the new fear—that the terrorists would try to escape in the storm, perhaps with their captives.

By 9:15, with the storm at its wild height and with increasing feelings of lostness and hopelessness, I stood on the upstairs balcony, only slightly protected from the driving waves of sand. I looked at my watch. We had again begun to hope. But the next moment the waiting was over.

Through the sand, we could see nothing. But we could hear. Volley after volley after volley of shots rang out in the night.

"I think," the young marine murmured, tears in his eyes, "that they just zapped my boss."

I knew in my heart they were dead, but tried not to know. All night long we huddled in the house. Over the open phone came some hope: It had been shots in the night. At 2:00 A.M. some Americans came. They tried to pretend. . . . But by morning we knew. The two Americans were dead. The Jordanian and the two Arabs had been spared.

The weirdness of the night outside, as the storm continued to bombard the hapless city, paralleled the weirdness of the night within. Nothing in the world will ever convince me that the two

199

events were not linked, or that *we* were not linked in some metaphysical whirlpool in which nature took upon itself to symbolize the horrors of men.

At 5:00 A.M., as a pallid sun began to throw a strange light over the city, I got up and slipped out—to file and hopefully to sleep. I walked out of the cordoned-off zone, and I can still remember and taste the sand hanging soundlessly in the air.

Saturday morning very early was the latest time I could file for our Saturday-night paper. So after filing I was free until Monday morning. Bob Allison and I went to the restaurant at the new modern hotel on the Blue Nile and sat for hours, drinking Scotch after Scotch. Certainly now at least I would sleep!

Instead it was the only time in my life that I went five days and five nights without any sleep at all. It was simply impossible. On the surface I was calm and I had performed as expected. But underneath that performance I was in a state of inner shock. The Khartoum story tormented me. I carried it in my heart and gut. I was torn between wanting to kill the terrorists and wanting to change the world so young men would not commit such atrocities.

When I was in Saudi Arabia that summer, I decided to stop off at Khartoum on the way back and see what had happened in the aftermath.

The Sudanese were holding the nine terrorists, and it was becoming a cause célèbre in the Arab world. Moreover, the Palestinians, while denying officially that they had done it, had sent a young observer to work there. I immediately went out to see him at his villa and found a pleasant, red-haired young man who invited me to lunch the next day. Since that happened to be the day I was leaving for the airport to fly to Cairo, I thought out loud in his office. "Maybe I will bring my bags here and leave them while I go to the airport," I said. "Of course," he said.

When I got back to the hotel, I realized the madness of what I had done. Go to lunch and leave my bags at the office of people whose whole life is devoted to putting bombs, grenades, electrical devices, letter bombs, and detonators in other people's bags? I was enraged at my own stupidity. And when I did indeed come for lunch the next day, Abu Khaled (for that was his name) eyed me with a gimlet eye (or so I presumed) and asked, "Where are your bags?"

I lied, and hardly convincingly. "I didn't have time to pack," I said. "I'll have to return to the hotel before going." A half-smile lingered on his lips.

At lunch I berated him bitterly for what they had done. "It's crazy —crazy," I said impassionedly.

Then he voiced words I shall never forget. "After all we've been through," he said, staring expressionlessly at me, "don't you think we would be a little crazy?"

The men were convicted and spent a few months in jail. Then they were sent to Cairo, where they lived in a villa under house arrest until they quietly disappeared into the murderous shadows of the Middle East.

How did one work in this terrorist world?

I controlled these shadowy, clandestine, ultimately lethal situations by never, ever giving terrorist leaders any reason to suspect me —and by giving them every possible reason in the world to trust me. And so, as in so many other areas, I devised my own little set of rules to operate by and live by:

(1) I neither flattered them nor insulted them. Unless they proved otherwise, I treated them as I treated all people: with respect.

(2) I never, ever had anything romantically to do with anyone in or around any movement. Indeed, my effectiveness rested upon my being a kind of "third sex," here as elsewhere in the Third World. If there were any problem at all with any of the men, I would have reported it immediately to their higher-ups. As a matter of fact, I like to think that because of my behavior and attitudes, there was none.

(3) I was quite open about what I was doing—I never pretended I did not go to Israel or did not sympathize greatly with Israel. At the same time, there was a line beyond which I did not want to go.

201

I never, for instance, wanted to meet the real "crazies," like the murderous Abu Nidal in Baghdad or even some of the more extremist elements in Beirut. There is simply such a thing as knowing too much about people like them.

Those, in short, were my rules for dealing with guerrillas. They are not perhaps the kinds of rules that most young women of similar education and background find themselves drawing up as rules for living as they move through life, but then life seldom turns out exactly as we would have planned.

In this work in the Middle East, as in Guatemala, there were advantages to being a woman. Guerrilla or "liberation" or terrorist movements—those dark children of the twentieth century—were generally Marxists of one form or another. So almost all of them hated American men, seeing in them the representatives of the imperial power, of the metropole, of everything that they themselves were not . . . and probably never would be. At the same time, they envied them, resented them, wanted to be like them. They could feel more at ease with a woman. Despite their ideologies I always felt that few could actually in their guts accept women as equal. Thus we could never really be a threat. Yet they were quite modern enough and quite aware enough of modern communications to know that I could, as a woman, get them what they needed. There may also have been the added thrill of dealing with the woman of the conquerors, with showing me (if they could never convince *them*) how powerful, how potent, how chivalrous, how courageous—and how dangerous—they were.

These "advantages," however, did not always help.

I had been in Baghdad in April 1973 when I received the news of the death of Kemal Nasser, the poet who was the spokesman for the PLO, during the Israeli raid on Beirut, and whose story will come later. I was deeply saddened, for I had been genuinely fond of Kemal. And as it happened, I was returning to Beirut from Baghdad the morning of the funeral for Kemal and the other two Palestinian leaders who were killed.

202

At the airport which I had then crossed and crisscrossed so many familiar times, I picked up the papers, skimmed them lifelessly, and only noticed in passing the blazing stories: ISRAELI BLOND WOMAN LEADS COMMANDOS, BEAUTIFUL ISRAELI BLONDE SOUGHT. Below were stories from neighbors of Kemal describing the "beautiful blonde."

After checking into the St. George's Hotel, I walked hurriedly over to the Fatah Information Office to get my press pass—something that I had done dozens of times and something that was indispensable to do in a situation like this—only to be confronted by three very young, very nervous, very inexperienced Palestinians. They had been searching the city, if only in their contorted minds, for the "Israeli blonde"—and I was soon it. Within minutes I realized that I was being surrounded. A uniformed man with a gun came in and wordlessly trained his machine gun on me. I was a prisoner.

I suppose most people think that scenes like this are tremendously dramatic—and frightening—and even grand. Well, they can be tremendously frightening but otherwise there is a kind of absurdity about them. What scared me most, I suppose, was how ignorant and now nervous *they* were. (I have always preferred pros; it is the amateurs who threaten the world.)

There we sat, for hours, in this small back room. One chap trained his machine gun on me, when he wasn't twirling and playing with it. A young skinny one with glasses (the interrogator) went through my purse and looked over everything, half-assedly.

He picked out an old picture of me with a friend in Macao and got very excited. It was a rather worn picture with the two of us standing in front of a mountain. It could have been anywhere. "That's in my village in Galilee," he kept saying.

Finally he said to me, "You call the American embassy and tell Mr. Oakley to come down here to identify you." (Bob Oakley, a fine diplomat married to my college friend, Phyllis Eliot.)

No doubt because I am blond and from the Midwest, I appear kind of Blondie-dumb to many people. My young captors obviously shared this opinion.

203

"There is *no way in the world that I am going to call the American embassy,*" I told him, staring calmly and speaking very deliberately and slowly.

Odd, it always works. People, even of other cultures, recognize when you have reached your outer limit. But you cannot pretend, you have to mean it. This does not apply, of course, to the brutes of the world; if they want to torture you, they can probably get anything from you they want. But in most situations like this one you are dealing with people whose business is bluff.

They brought me tea. When I tried to lift it to my mouth, the boy said coldly and suspiciously, "You're trembling."

"Of course I'm trembling," I said with not at all disguised anger. "You're frightening me to death." Then I sat back and glared at him.

After a while they picked up somebody else, *The New York Times*'s Juan de Onis, who had been the top Latin America correspondent for years and a good colleague. So now there were two of us. But eventually it ended, and it ended almost at the exact moment the funeral ended.

Soon people like Clovis Maksuud, a journalist who later became Arab League ambassador to the U.S., and other friends discovered my "captivity" and phoned. Now those same hostile boys became the soul of Arab hospitality and attentiveness. Did I want tea? I did. Did I want to go home? I did not, goddamn it. "Look," I said, "you brought me here. You've half scared the life out of me and you've made me miss the funeral of a friend. Now sit down and let me interview you."

They did. They were like puppy dogs. And during the next few days I was to stay in Beirut they came over daily with bits of information. One's information networks are not always planned ahead.

But the story of my "captivity," brief but nevertheless real and frightening, did not end there. From Beirut I moved through Cyprus and on to Israel and soon found myself being interviewed by Israeli television. As it happened it was on Friday, on the eve of

Sabbat, so most everybody saw it. Soon I was getting flowers from unnamed people and people would recognize me on the street. The Sheraton Hotel in Tel Aviv, always jammed, was telling me, "Anytime you want to come back, we have a room for you," and they gave me a duplex suite the next time I did come.

Finally I asked *Daily News* correspondent Jay Bushinsky what was going on. "You don't seem to understand," he said. "They are not sure you *aren't* the Israeli blonde who led the raid on Beirut."

Later my friend Yehoshophat Harkabi, the foremost Arabist in Israel and the man who was intelligence chief during the Six-Day War, explained what I had been caught up in. "There was an 'Israeli blonde,' " he said, "but it was a man in a blond wig. We never send women on these raids. And there was a reason." He paused. "In ancient times there are many stories about blond Jewish women commanders against Arab armies—Judith, for instance. It is a bit of psychological warfare."

Yes, I thought wryly as I left, a bit of psychological warfare that might have killed me!

But the whole saga was not yet to end. As I was leaving Tel Aviv for Jerusalem one day, I picked up my mail at the embassy and was rewarded with a copy of the story I had written after my "capture." Across the front page of the *Daily News* was emblazoned, OUR GIRL HELD BY GUERRILLAS. There was my smiling picture and the story, which had been completely rewritten into a caricature of sensationalism. As Nick von Hoffman always told me, "You are their white virgin in the jungle." Here, I surely was. And it was I and not those nameless editors who would have to live with this.

I called Jay, shaking with rage.

"What shall I do?" I asked. I could actually feel the blood rising and swelling in my veins.

Jay, always practical and usually right, said, "Don't do anything. No, don't call. No, by *all* means, don't write. Wait twenty-four hours before you do *anything.*" And so I did. I waited twenty-four hours. During those twenty-four hours my originally watershed level of fury grew to flood proportions. At 4:00 P.M. the next day I called the paper from Jerusalem and exploded. I kept my friend and editor Nick Shuman on the phone for one and a half hours, knowing that the spending of money was always a far more sensitive issue than any editorial.

Every time he would say, "We'll talk about this when you come home," I told him—quite honestly, "If you don't talk now, I'm not coming home. In fact, I'm quitting." It worked quite neatly, but only because I thoroughly meant it.

In the end I demanded and got two rounds of apologies from every editor involved, but it was small consolation. I was the one, not they, who would always be "Ms. Terror Filled the Room," as one of their better lines put it. Sometimes it seemed easier to deal with male guerrillas than my clear and "rational" colleagues in Chicago.

XII.

A Western Woman in Islam

"Avoid the cliché of your time."
—VLADIMIR NABOKOV

"You will never be able to work as a woman in the Moslem world," I was told over and over when I went to the Middle East for the first time in the fall of 1969. It was just more of what I had heard all my professional life: the litany of "You can'ts." But this time I almost believed them. After all, Moslem women were as oppressed as any on the face of the globe. Besides, the Middle East was a violent place, far more violent than Latin America.

As I have mentioned, however, I found that I became a kind of "third sex" to the Arabs. It was all explained to me several years later when an Egyptian male journalist said to me, "We restrict our own women because they have been raised under Islamic precepts. But you are a Western woman and a Christian—you are not expected to live by our beliefs." In addition, as with the various guerrilla movements, I was the Western female creature: the woman of the men they hated, for their power and for their success, but now also a woman in their very own realm who was fascinated by them and would gladly spend hours listening to them. Again I was appreciated not for what I could accomplish but for how _they_ saw me and for what _they_ read into me. But I did not have to go the Middle East to learn that.

207

In the Arab world I lived and behaved like the Virgin Mary. This was crucial, for they watched me carefully. One night in Amman, Jordan, the hotel clerk said to me, really in a pleasant and well-meaning way, "Miss Geyer, when we need the men correspondents, we look in two places: the telex room and the bar. With you, we only look in the telex room." That was a great compliment—it was also my protection.

In Cairo that first night I sat in my room in the Nile Hilton, drinking in the sight of the great river with its glorious pinks and golds. Where would I start? The next morning I called—cold—an Egyptian newspaper critic whose name had come to me from someone, I don't really remember who. He was cordial. "Come on over," he said, and I did. He asked me to go to a luncheon with him; and at that luncheon in a beautiful villa near the pyramids I met remarkable people. Clovis Maksuud sat next to me. . . . From then on I got to know just about everybody in Cairo. Soon I found that as a Western woman I was having exceptional luck in a most unlikely area: interviewing leaders—ironically, leaders whose own women were often kept in purdah.

I think I have mentioned before that I do not particularly like leader interviews. I find "leaders" boring. With only a few exceptions like Eduardo Frei of Chile and Gerald Ford of the U.S., they tend to be egomaniacs; they issue tiresome pronouncements about what "the people" want when they are talking about what they want; I would much rather talk to a Jorge Luis Borges or an Archbishop Oscar Romero of El Salvador—those are the real *menshen*. But you do it. You do it (1) because it is an important part of the profession of journalism, since we have to know what our "leaders" are thinking, if anything; (2) because it may help you know more about his people and his reign; and (3) because it makes you famous.

If I am to be truthful, let me admit right off that I would like to be like Oriana Fallaci. I would like to spin in on them, crashing the door behind me, and say, "All right, Anwar, why don't you wipe out Qaddafi . . . ?" But I would not be capable of acting that way even if I were high on hashish. I work, rather, in what I call the "absorptive" style. I go into "His" office and sit there. I am sympathetic. I may well look a little pathetic. I present "Him" with a vacuum and he virtually always fills it. I do present questions—and I can present them very directively indeed if need be—but 95 percent of the time I have found that that is not necessary. Men tend to open up and reveal themselves if you present them with the proper psychological presence, particularly a female one.

I almost forgot that there is certainly at least one other major reason for doing the "leader interview." This is because they are so goddamned hard to arrange that if you love the game and the chase, there is nothing quite so invigorating!

An exception to all the above was my first interview with Jihan Sadat, wife of the then-new Egyptian president. It was in 1971 and was the first interview she ever gave to a Westerner. At their beautiful seaside home in Alexandria she sat in the swing, wearing a beautiful flowered dress that made her look very much like the romantic heroine she is. She was lovely, with dark, liquid eyes and a spiritual manner, and I liked her immediately.

When she and Anwar were first married, she told me, and their fortunes were at their lowest ebb, they had spent their last few coins at a fortune-teller's. The woman told them, "You will be the first lady of Egypt," which sent them into spasms of laughter. She was obviously deeply and, even then, still passionately in love with her husband, who was physically and emotionally worthy of that passion. But at the same time what was most touching to me was the degree to which she truly cared about women and about women's rights— on the deepest and most rational level, as I liked to think I did. She believed, given the bitterly retrogressive qualities of Moslem life, that women must, like the peace process in the Middle East, move "step by step." She believed in "showing people" what women could do, instead of telling them. She was not a preacher, except by example—the opposite of me.

But by the time I saw her again in 1974, she was deeply disappointed; she had not been able even as the president's wife to get the most simple legislation on women's rights through the parliament of old sheikhs. Then, she was quite desperate, talking of sterilization in exchange for a water buffalo for the *fellahin* families who were destroying any hope for Egyptian development with their wanton population growth.

By the time Anwar Sadat was killed by the assassins' bullets in those dark days of October 1981, Jihan Sadat was extremely unpopular in her own country. Never mind her graciousness and charm! Never mind the wonderful impression she made for Egypt wherever she went in the world! Never mind her conservative dress! Jihan Sadat had tried not to be free or independent in our sense, but only to give women the most basic of rights, like requiring that divorces started by their husbands be heard before a judge. The treatment of Jihan Sadat gave me great cause for concern as to whether women were really progressing in the world.

For several years I also worked on seeing President Sadat, trying always to do it in the straight and official way. But nothing worked, despite my many contacts and friends. By the fall of 1974 it had all made me so angry that I picked up my phone in the Nile Hilton and phoned Mrs. Sadat's secretary and explained my plight. By the following day Mrs. Sadat had intervened and even had the precise date for the interview set.

In the four hours I spent with Anwar Sadat at their home up the Nile at The Barrages, a sensuous spot with the arms of the Nile delta stretching out into the sun and reflecting gold in all directions, I found one of the few charming men in power that I have met. His chocolate-colored face was beautiful, with its black olive eyes. We sat at two ends of a formal, gilded couch in his ballroom of an office, and he talked and I laughed. The more funny and witty he became, the more I laughed, which pleased him just as much as it does all men.

This was just weeks after the famous Rabat conference, where the Palestine Liberation Organization had been named the "sole representative" of the Palestinian people and where the PLO second in command, Salah Kahlef, or Abu Iyad, had tried again to assassinate King Hussein of Jordan. Naturally, I asked Sadat about this.

"I had him here last week," he said, beginning sternly enough. "He was sitting right where you are. And I told him, 'Abu Iyad, if you try to assassinate King Hussein one . . . more . . . time. . . .'" We both laughed. Then I asked him if he were not afraid that they would try to assassinate him. Now the levity dropped. "Of course not," he said. "They know my family."

I thought of that seven years later when I was analyzing the Moslem fundamentalist groups who had assassinated him.

Knowing a little about Sadat's personality and about his sense of apocalyptic mission in the world, I did not find myself in the least surprised when he went to Jerusalem three years later. This is one of the obvious advantages of the "leader interview."

But by the time I saw him again, in 1980, he was a deeply different man. Now he sat in the luxuriant garden of The Barrages, a haggard, lined, aged replica of himself. He had also grown quite desperate, for the full peace with Israel which he knew he had to have (and this had to include a real Palestinian solution to the West Bank, which the Israelis were busily annexing) was being totally stalled by the Israelis. He had always known that his peace was a gallant gamble, but a gamble. It needed movement; it required phasing and timing; and that just wasn't happening.

He rambled that day, his eyes flashed. And when I asked him about the infamous "Law of Shame" which he had just put through and which allowed him in effect to imprison any of his enemies (or friends, for that matter) who criticized him, he looked at me, a strange glitter in his eyes. He proceeded to give a most preposterous explanation, which came out of his love for movies.

"Did you see the film on the love affair between Clark Gable and Carole Lombard?" he asked me. By chance, yes, I had. "Well, you remember in that film how, because they were not married, Hollywood prosecuted them under this morals law and they could not perform in Hollywood." I nodded. "That is what I have in mind," he said. When I heard that, I knew that something was indeed wrong with our hero, Anwar Sadat.

And when he was killed that October a year and a half later, Sadat was probably killed because he had rounded up, indiscriminately, sixteen hundred of his real and imagined enemies. A certain paranoia and desperation had overtaken him. Was this the destiny of peacemakers?

As I roamed around the Middle East in those years, I had better and better luck with "leader interviews." And there was always something interesting, or quirky, or odd, or funny, about them even when I quietly made a fool of myself. In 1969, when I interviewed President Gaafer Nimiery of the Sudan, it was my first year in the area and he was so new to power that we had not even been shown any pictures of him.

The day of the interview two of us waited outside, and finally Nimiery's secretary came out and said, "I am very sorry, but the president will not be able to see you today." We sighed, again, at the ways of the world. "But the head of the cabinet will see you," he went on.

In a while we were ushered into an enormous office and at the end there sat an attractive, copper-skinned man sitting at an imposing desk. We began asking questions, and I would say, "Does President Nimiery think that . . . ?"

And he would invariably answer, "President Nimiery thinks that . . ."

After several exchanges of this caliber and genre, the other journalist with me punched me not so carefully in the ribs, and whispered loudly, "That is Nimiery." How was I to know? I ask you. Besides, I suspect from his demeanor that he rather liked the idea of referring to himself in the third person and thought it quite an appropriate term of reference.

Then in the spring of 1973 I applied in Cairo for a visa to Iraq. Since this country of Nebuchadnezzar and the doomed ancient cities of Babylon and Ur and the great empires of the past was the most closed in the Middle East—and indeed probably in the world —I did not have any extravagant hopes. But I always exercised a kind of "scorched earth" policy regarding getting visas and attempting to

212

cover whole areas. To my amazement the visa came through and I found myself approaching Baghdad from Beirut.

The first morning I was there, I did not rush over to the Ministry of Information, for I was well aware that letting them know you were there only gave them a head start on getting the bodyguards out to follow you. I did stroll in about eleven, knowing that by then they would be looking for me anyway. To my amazement three heads bounced to attention in the little office, and one gentleman said, with obvious and even ominous joy, "You're here."

Those few journalists who had ever gotten in in the past had never seen anybody and had constantly been harassed by the oppressive, clandestine, brutal Iraqi Ba'athist regime. To my surprise, that very first day I had four interviews, and all with important people like the head of the Communist Party. While not knowing exactly what was going on, I naturally soon became enchanted with the entrée I was getting.

That Friday, while using the Moslem sabbath to visit the ruins of Babylon, I suggested innocently, "Why don't we stop at Kerbela on the way back from Babylon?"

The young man in the ministry, who had been so helpful up until then, turned several colors and gulped several gulps. "You don't really want to see Kerbela?" he declared hopefully.

I nodded. "Why not?" I said. "I understand it's very pretty."

Then, to show how shame falls by the wayside when a journalist gets even the suggestion of a go-ahead, I added, "And I'd like to see Saddam Hussein, too."

I thought the poor man would sink into spasms.

Saddam Hussein, the mysterious underground strongman of Iraq, was someone whom no one ever saw. He was the toughest of the tough, the most brutal of the brutal, also the best economic developer and the single most mysterious and unknown leader in the Middle East, in the most closed and unknown land. To my surprise my guide said only, "Let's see. . . ." The wonderful hesitation hung pregnantly in the air.

At that time I was mercifully ignorant of the fact that the Shi'a

213

Moslem shrine at Kerbala, the home of the Shi'a Moslems and the place where the brutal and sanguinary ceremonies of self-flagellation take place every year during the exotic holy days of Muharram, is like Mecca. It is closed—but utterly closed—to non-Moslems and to Westerners. In my ignorance I had asked to visit the very symbol of religious and cultural paranoia and hatred of the "other." And the amazing thing was that it worked!

The next day they informed me that, yes, I could go to Kerbala, if I would wear the long black *abaya* of the Arab woman. I would. And it was not until my guide and I stood inside the giant mosque, with its tiny pieces of mirrors sparkling like a thousand candles and the gold trimming everywhere shimmering like sea waves in the sunlight, that I suddenly realized we were not supposed to "be there." Luckily, the Iraqis had sent with us the Kerbala police chief, an enormous man who must have weighed approximately three hundred pounds! The pilgrims, showing in their slanted eyes or golden skin their homelands as far away as Mongolia or Pakistan, looked at me with unbridled hostility as I tried to hide the shock of blond hair on top with my *abaya*. That sunny afternoon in the Great Mosque of Kerbala I saw the real roots of Arab unity, for these people had come from everywhere in Central Asia, all to worship together.

Five days later I also saw Saddam Hussein, and without my *abaya*. Indeed, I became the first American ever to lay eyes on this important man—afterward the American diplomats were dying to hear what the world's great terrorist leader was like!

No man in khakis, no Arafat in Arab headdress and olive drabs, Saddam Hussein was tall, dark, and erect, with beautiful black hair, a neat mustache, and eyes that were hooded much like the Arab falcons. He was as properly dressed as a French count at court. Indeed, he was wearing a perfectly tailored pin-striped suit, a white silk shirt, and a silk tie. He came forward toward me, his hand outstretched. Against the background of the gilded rooms of the palace of the kings, the last one of which was dragged through the streets until he died when the revolution occurred in 1958, the

214

image was perfect. But it was certainly not that of the underground terrorist, which was the image he wanted to leave behind and which was what this interview was all about!

We talked for a full four hours, an odd pair, this man whom the Western world had never seen and the foreign correspondent from the South Side of Chicago. He kept looking at me and repeating, "Don't hesitate, ask me anything you want."

So I asked him about his years as a terrorist for the Ba'athist Party before it came to power under him in 1962. He answered, "Sometimes you have to do things for your party that you would not do yourself."

He was trying so hard to be, or to appear, open and frank. But all of my questions evoked only hooded responses—as hooded as those handsome but chilled eyes. After several hours, out of desperation I fished about in my mind for still another question. "When did you join the Ba'athist Party?" I asked, thinking to myself, "What a foolish question."

And now his entire demeanor and mien changed. All the friendliness, so carefully constructed to go with the gilded room, dropped away. He looked at me now with open and unmasked hostility. "I don't remember," he said.

He didn't remember the watershed event of his life? I puzzled over this for a long time. Why should that utterly innocuous question have affected him when nothing else did? Years later a knowing psychiatrist said to me, "But of course—that was the moment he became a terrorist."

Before I left, I found out what it was that had provided me with these great strokes of luck. Iraq, that spring of 1973, had reached a turning point. Only weeks before, they had finally settled their old problem over the British-owned petroleum; they in effect nationalized it, but in agreement with the British. Saddam in those days wanted to turn toward the West, or at least to be open to it. My presence and newspapers presented a small vehicle that could serve that purpose—and it was only by chance that the timing served mine.

*   *   *

We all have our favorite political-leader interviews, and countries, and historic experiences, and I have to admit that mine was with a perhaps unlikely leader, Sulton Qabus, in the remote and exotic sultanate of Oman, at the bottom of Saudi Arabia where the shimmering turquoise blue of the Indian Ocean meets the strategic opening to the Persian Gulf.

In truth my romantic imagination had been fed by Oman— "Muscat and Oman," they called it historically—for many years. Until 1970 Oman had been the most backward country in the world. Ruled by the old sultan, a cruel curmudgeon who still kept slaves, who shot people for being outside the city walls after seven o'clock at night, and who forbade not only smoking and drinking but even sunglasses and bicycles, Oman was disintegrating. The most able young men were joining the Dhofar liberation movement, inspired by Marxists from nearby South Yemen. Moreover, the old sultan had kept his only son, the handsome, intelligent, languid-eyed Qabus, locked in a tower in the old mud palace in Salālah in the south for seven years! All this because Qabus had returned from Sandhurst with outrageous ideas about developing the country, which then had twelve miles of roads and no schools.

With the help of progressive Omanis and the British officers who advised the old sultan, Qabus moved in 1970 to overthrow his father: a dramatic and disturbing kind of political regicide. The cunning and ignorant old man went into exile, dying at Claridge's in London, where supposedly he might have discovered late in life that modern comforts are not so evil after all.

I kept hearing about what the young sultan was doing in Oman, but I couldn't get there—they had to want you and invite you. Finally, through the help of some British advisers, I was invited in 1978. What I found was so much in tune with the values that I held dear, in terms of political leadership and rational development: tolerance, rationality, dignity.

By then the little jewel cities of Muscat, Muttra, and Ruwi, which are strung along a beautiful rocky coastline, were fairy-tale cities, with the finest architecture in the entire Middle East. Seven hundred Omanis were studying in universities overseas and virtually all the children were in school, including the girls. Modern roads and communication spanned the entire country. The sultan was moving slowly but appropriately toward the representation of all the people in bodies like a consultative council.

The second time I visited, in 1979, I actually met and interviewed the young sultan. Dressed in magnificent white and beige robes with the silver Omani khanjar dagger at his waist and a handsome turban on his head, the sultan seemed almost too perfect to believe. But he was most believable, most modest and charming, and most effective and open. I could even ask him about the ouster of his father, an event that deeply affected the sensitive young sultan. An imprint of sadness lingers about him even today.

"In the beginning," he told me as we sat in his handsome crimson office in his palace at Seeb, "it never entered my mind that I would eventually have to do what I did in the end. All the time I was thinking about how to go about it. I had thought about it carefully. Then, in 1969, the time suddenly came. It was the time when I saw no opportunity of my being asked to help—and things were not going well at all. People were fed up. The country was emptying out as people went abroad. There was the war against us from South Yemen. It came very suddenly to my mind that I had to do something to save the situation."

It was very moving to me. But even more moving was the way he had led his little country, a seafaring empire two centuries ago, to the Omani "renaissance." Qabus's reign is rational and not ideological. It is concerned with helping the people rather than satisfying the leader. Most important perhaps, Oman is a country that builds upon its own ancient, tolerant traditions: an example to others in this increasingly intolerant, nationalistic, and xenophobic world.

Speaking, for instance, of the intolerant "Islamic revolution" about him, Qabus said to me, "We have thousands of years of history, and we are sure of ourselves. There are certain groups in our area that use religion today for other purposes which have nothing

217

to do with religion. They use religion to get into a position from which they can play a destructive political role. Here? Oh, no, no. One of the blessed things is that from the beginning we did not mix things." He meant politics and religion; and indeed the predominant Ibadhi form of Islam in Oman was very tolerant and open and dramatically opposed to the fanatical "Shi'ite" form of Khomeini and Iran.

Oman, of course, strategically placed as it is, is of enormous importance to the West as well as to Europe and Japan, for it controls by its territory the opening to the Persian Gulf. And here we had a fine, rational, dedicated leader who was doing things for his own people and for the West. Indeed, he told me first, in my interview of 1979, how much he wanted the American presence and aid, though he wanted the troops only "on the horizon."

He was also unusually fair-minded about women. When I saw him in 1979, I had just observed the strikingly lovely National Day celebrations. Among many things I was impressed with the manner in which the littler girls had taken part, faces uncovered, in the dances and in some restrained exercises in the dignified public extravaganzas in the stadium.

"There was only one thing, your Majesty," I said, referring to the races. "The little boys ran. The little girls didn't run."

He thought for a moment. Then he smiled and said to one of his British advisers, "She is right. Take a note. Next year . . . the girls will run."

But the most difficult interview of all to arrange was one that occurred in the summer of 1973—this time, with Libya's mercurial, eccentric dictator, Colonel Muammar Qaddafi. Again, as it happened, a friend in Cairo played the intermediary. "You should interview Qaddafi," he said. I threw up my hands.

Interview Qaddafi? First of all there was the little fact that the Libyans had passed a law by which Americans had to have all the data in their passports written into the passport in Arabic. What this law successfully accomplished was to keep Americans out of Libya since that legally constituted defacing your passport, and would cause you to lose it. Second, Qaddafi didn't want to see any journalists at all, and particularly not American ones.

"Why don't you send me?" the Egyptian said finally, as we sat in his pleasant garden in Cairo. "It won't cost you any more than if you go on an exploratory trip, and I have the contacts there—I can find out for you. . . ."

I thought it over for about two minutes and told him to go ahead. If it worked, I would put it on my expense account openly. If it did not work, it would be there but piecemeal. I never cheated the paper, but in cases like this I did what had to be done.

I understood fully that he had his own reasons for wanting to go to Libya, perhaps a Libyan lover he wanted to see or some bit of mysterious political business he wanted to attend to. But you soon learn in this business that unless there is something illegal or unethical or something that impinges upon your work, you are better off not asking. Amazingly, the plan worked! He came back and told me (1) that Qaddafi would give me the interview, (2) that they had invited me as a "state guest," which meant not that they were paying for me but that this way they could forget the writing in the passport. My friend then left Cairo, and it took me a full week to convince the Libyan ambassador that I was indeed their "state guest."

But my real problems began only once I was in Tripoli, that hot, blindingly white city on the sea. I reported immediately to the Ministry of Information, only to discover that they were in the midst of Qaddafi's "cultural revolution" and that nobody—nobody—was in the offices. Everybody was "out with the people," which could mean at home or on the beach or any number of other curious things.

A charming and beautiful Swedish correspondent, Birgitta Edlund, and I began working together, dismaying our male colleagues because they just hated to see that not only could women be good friends but that professional women could even work together in such fun and harmony. One day we decided to go direct to the top

219

and assault the Revolutionary Command Council, where Qaddafi was surely hiding from his blasted "cultural revolution." So we walked boldly up to the gate, explained who we were, and began to try to talk most convincingly of having to get in. . . .

To our surprise they were just delighted to see us. They could not have been more gracious or courteous; they ushered us in! They were showing us around when, as we reached the fourth floor, we said we thought we should see Colonel Qaddafi. The men looked at one another in bewilderment. "But Colonel Qaddafi is not here," one finally said. "This is the tobacco company."

When we finally did find the Command Council, we managed to get Qaddafi's office on the phone at the gate. I was watching Birgitta talking to them in French when suddenly a look of utter incredulity crept over her.

"That was the French television crew," she said as she hung up, dazed. "They are sitting in Colonel Qaddafi's office waiting for him!"

Finally our driver got on the phone in Arabic and told us afterward that, no, they wouldn't see us. As we drove away, I thought to ask him what he had told Qaddafi's office.

"That two foreign ladies wanted to see him," he answered calmly.

"Two foreign ladies!" Birgitta and I exploded in unison. "Goddamn it, we are not ladies! . . ."

Such was life in Libya in the good old days when Qaddafi was just a crazy young colonel and before he became the scourge of the Western world. Every day was rather mad, but wonderful. There was a Swiss journalist who ventured out of the city one day to visit an agricultural center, only to be "captured" by Libyans in the Bengasi airport as a "spy." (Having passed on from the "cultural revolution," Libya was then in the throes of one of its many "spy crazes.")

When the Swiss called me from the Tripoli airport after his release to tell me in mild hysteria what had happened, he said with a little cry of hurt, "And—me, the head of the Swiss–Libyan friendship society!"

Birgitta and I were the only ones who finally did see Qaddafi, for the men correspondents fell off day after day. We did it through an odd ploy. Knowing Arabs as both of us did—and understanding their deep and real sense of honor—we somehow spontaneously hit upon a successful tactic. We kept telling the men close to Qaddafi that they had "given their word" to us that we would see him, as indeed they had, and that we had believed them because "an Arab never breaks his word."

That Saturday night, at midnight, at the last possible moment, Birgitta and I were ushered into the presence of the "crazy" young colonel. Birgitta for the last two weeks had worn tight jeans and a blouse open almost to her waist, as we tooled around Tripoli on our madcap jaunts. Now she wore a flowing overblouse and loose pants. Trying to be respectful, I had for two weeks worn what I called my "Saudi dress." It was a dark cotton dress, with a long full skirt, a high neck and three-quarter sleeves; it was the kind of thing to wear not to offend the Saudi's sensibilities, and it was so ugly that not even the European men in the hotel dining room looked at me.

But Qaddafi of course did not know this. He did not know what a gorgeous spectacle Birgitta had made of herself for two weeks— or how modest I had been to all pure Islamic eyes around me. He only saw us now. He looked at me disapprovingly, then looked at her and said, "Now *that's* the way I like to see a woman dressed!"

I would like to say that I found Qaddafi interesting, but in truth I did not. I would like to say I found him handsome, but in truth I did not. His pictures flatter him. Actually his forehead is unusually broad and his eyes unusually deep set—which gives him an oddly asymmetrical look. His eyes were the eyes of the Baptist preachers of my youth who did not believe in going to the movies or to dances or (presumably) to motels, even with Baptist boys. They were tight, fanatic eyes.

He had just nationalized some oil firms and we got the exclusive story that he was going to nationalize more. But the only interesting thing came, again, when I could think of no more questions and asked him another "nothing" question. "How do you see Libya's place in the world?"

His tight eyes tightened still more, until they were virtually cold slits. "We are in a jungle surrounded by howling wolves," he whispered heavily.

"Howling wolves?" I repeated, startled. "Do you mean the European countries?"

"No," he said, "I mean the Arab countries."

This was long before he broke with Sadat and other Arab leaders, so it was a telling emotional revelation.

The next time I saw him, at an Arab-American dialogue conference in the fall of 1978 in Tripoli, he came before the group dressed in a tailored Italianate jacket and ascot, and introduced himself by saying, "Now you are hearing it from Qaddafi, the madman, Qaddafi, the crazy man. . . ."

Everybody wanted me to write that Qaddafi was "crazy," that he was "mad." I refused to do it. That would have made it easy: pat, clear, and woefully incomplete. Yes, Qaddafi sent terrorists out (I had no question about that and abhorred it), but he was also one of these Third World anti-imperialist leaders who could discourse at length about how the real "imperialists" were the Americans, who were frightening him with their Seventh Fleet in the Mediterranean. Once a man stopped me on the street in Chicago and asked me why, on television, I had described Qaddafi as a "young colonel who goes to the desert to meditate." He would have preferred to keep the image of a mad terrorist leader. I told him that Qaddafi was that, too, and that if we did not see these leaders in their entireties, then we missed the reality and could fatally misjudge them.

And the "reality" out there was always different, and often utterly bizarre. In the fall of 1978, after the ill-fated conference in Tripoli, Judith Miller of *The New York Times* and I flew with Najeeb Halaby, the prominent Syrian-American businessman whose daughter became Queen Noor of Jordan, from Tripoli to Amman in his small private plane. We had left Tripoli, where we had been drearily observing the "dry" laws, at about noon, determined to make Rhodes by evening and have a wonderful, fun-filled Greek evening. I fell asleep in the back of the plane and awoke a full four hours later.

Since we were approaching a city, I asked brightly, "Is that Rhodes?"

Two dark-visaged faces turned to me, growling, "It is Bengasi," Najeeb spat out. Bengasi—the city right down the coast from Tripoli? The Libyans had routed us so far south when we left Tripoli that we were almost over Chad, probably to avoid our seeing Soviet-supported military installations. (Qaddafi's Libya had indeed become "the" friend of the Soviets in the Middle East by the late seventies.) Since it was sunset, we had no choice but to land in Bengasi, even though we were officially checked out of the country.

To our amazement and curiosity we landed at an empty airport. There was no one around, even to refuel us. More, twenty-eight Soviet MIG-23 jets sat on the airport runways, unguarded and unwatched. We could easily have blown them up, had we been of such an unworthy mind. Instead, even more amazingly, we just locked up the airplane, caught a taxi into town, checked into the main hotel, had dinner, and checked out again in the morning.

Nobody bothered us for anything—except the landing fee, which we dutifully paid. Nobody asked to see our passports. Anyone could have landed there and done whatever he wanted and left. That, too, is this part of the world.

One always has to watch carefully and empathically to see a leader in three dimensions, and perhaps women do this better than men.

For instance, in October of 1978, soon after the Camp David accords and the drama of the peacemaking, I was in Jordan talking with the man who is probably my favorite Middle Eastern leader, King Hussein: always charming, gracious, intelligent, rational.

But during this interview, in sharp contrast to my others with him, I kept getting vibes of a new kind. He was deeply troubled by the peace treaty, deeply angered because he had been kept out of it, and even insulted by the various parties who nevertheless wanted and expected him to "come in." It became clear to me in our hour's talk that he wasn't going to come in at all: a dramatic revelation. But how could one tell? Again it is not through words.

223

The king, sitting in his handsome dark wood office, with the pictures of his legendary family, kept returning, almost melancholically, to the words "threat to the Arab identity."

"It concerns me deeply," he said at one point. "We must not lose our identity, our ties to the past—all that may be in jeopardy." At first I couldn't exactly figure out what he was talking about. Then at the end I asked another silly question. "Your Majesty," I asked, "why did you decide to grow a beard?" It was meant to be a light question, but the heaviness of his response showed me that he was deeply serious about the symbolism of it. "My grandfather told me when *I* was no longer young always to observe my inheritance," he said quietly.

I was getting a kind of shorthand that can be deciphered only if you understand the area, its history, and its culture, and then add intuition and empathy as well. I sensed that he was so disturbed by what he considered the terrible insults to the Arab history involved in all of this that he wasn't going to come into the Camp David accords.

When I saw our ambassador there, I asked him, "Am I crazy, or is there a 'new Hussein'?"

"No," he answered, "you're right. We've just become aware of it."

The "old Hussein," the favorite of the West, was now turning away, hurt and snubbed, and this was utterly crucial to the future of peace.

Gradually I learned to predict the unpredictable.

The late Chicago psychoanalyst, Heinz Kohut, one of the great men of our time and a respected friend, called the work of psychoanalysis "empathic immersion." By this he meant immersing yourself in the world of patients, listening to them as they are speaking of themselves and not only as you might be superficially hearing them, and then extracting truths from what you hear. As a journalist, and particularly as a woman journalist who used what are thought of as "feminine" abilities and principles, I "listened" to what people were telling me; I cared about them, and I immersed myself in their perceptions. With many male correspondents interviews become a "pissing match," as one irreverent but correct observer put it. Most men could never have "heard" what King Hussein was telling me that day, for there would have been too much competition between them.

Psychoanalysts and journalists both develop a "trained instinct"; they hear and see events and know, by something about them, that they represent things far beyond themselves. And there are always small telling signs. When I mentioned on *Washington Week in Review* that something terrible was going to happen in Afghanistan only weeks before the Russian invasion, it was more than a premonition. One day that fall the Afghan regime posted a list on the prison with the names of *nine thousand political prisoners* who had been killed in prison. The news was so outrageous that I knew it must represent a wholly new era. In Lebanon in 1974 the discovery of the first SAM-7 missiles in the northern Tripoli *souk* was a signal that all-out war was coming. In Egypt in 1973 the Egyptians were saying things like, "It would be better to be destroyed in war and rebuild —at least we would be doing something." There was an unmistakable air of desperation in Cairo, and it was too bad so few of us were "listening" to see the war coming.

Women journalists on the spot are also often aware of the way in which our own positions and feelings closely parallel situations within countries and peoples. Once in Riyadh, for instance, a young American woman, Martha, who was teaching in the girls' college, and I had a long talk about the "shame" aspects of the Saudi culture —and how those attitudes affected us. Martha was wearing floor-length skirts, long sleeves, and shawls. She admitted that she instinctively lowered her eyes when she saw Saudi men. I admitted that I, too, felt an overwhelming sense of shame when in these cultures.

"Would we respond with this demureness and guilt unless it responded to something inside us that said, 'Yes, that is basically right'?" I asked. We agreed that it reawakened certain shame aspects of our own background—which I found a disturbing but totally female thought and reality.

225

Indeed, I discovered over and over again that these odd kinds of "exchanges" flowed back and forth between women correspondents and the men and women of the countries we covered and worked in—and even, in an odd but real sense, between us and the countries themselves. Men, particularly in countries that were in traumatic stages of development, often spoke far more openly and emotionally to me than to male correspondents.

In the fall of 1974 in Saudi Arabia, for instance, I was quite accidentally sent to interview a young Saudi planner. The tempter was "How would you like to interview the first Saudi Bedouin boy to get his doctorate in the United States?" Since no one could turn down an offer like that, I soon found myself sitting with this slim, pleasant, intense young man with blazing black eyes who had just returned home.

At one point I happened to say to him, "You must be very proud of yourself. And your family must be very proud of you." To my amazement Faisal Bashir almost burst into tears. His dark face clouded even darker. "Proud?" he said, almost jeering at himself. "I'm not proud. I'm very ashamed. My mother needs me. They are with the herds somewhere up in Iraq now. I should be with her. Instead, I am here."

Before I left, I asked Faisal Bashir if he minded if I wrote about him, quoting his anguish, and he said to go ahead. In fact when I did write about this, he sent me a kind letter of thanks. Somehow I was never able quite to put aside the memory of that haunted young man, such a quintessential type in today's troubled and inexact world of development: a man so troubled, so conflicted, so haunted, in spite of the fact that he was doing great good for his people.

Then, when I returned in 1980, suddenly I got a message to call "Faisal Bashir, deputy minister of planning." Though I had remembered him, I had forgotten his name, so I was delighted. "You must come over and see my office," he said on the telephone, effusive and excited.

What a pleasure it was to see him! He was still slim, still darkly intense, but quite a man of the world now. He had moved into an elegant, wood-paneled office in the marble-halled Ministry of Planning, and was outgoing and all charm.

"Here I am, deputy minister of planning of Saudi Arabia, trying to implement the policy that will destroy the life that made me," he told me, a certain wistfulness and at the same time wonder in his voice. And the destruction of the old way of life that he had suffered over so much in 1974? "It was inevitable," he said now. "From the human element, it's true that I am working against the forces that created me. One more generation and it will end. Give us ten years, two more plans, and then Saudi Arabia will reach the stage of maturity in economic life."

Suddenly a small smile played on his lips. He got out the new issue of *National Geographic* magazine. The story of Saudi Arabia starts out with quotes from him. He was also a star on the TV special, *The Saudis.* They described him as "electronic magic." His American wife "advises" him. We both smiled.

I was happy, really happy, to see Faisal Bashir again. I was happy to see a balanced, immensely creative, and productive person at the core of a developing country. And perhaps I understood him because, on another level, I, too, had been "first"—as a woman in so many areas—and had hammered out so many of the same traumas. There was one big difference: his planning budget was $236 billion!

Again I found, in Saudi Arabia, that men in positions of power talked differently to me. They spoke honestly and, ironically, seemingly without hesitation and without embarrassment. They spoke of their traumas about their own women and they spoke of their own traumas vis-à-vis the United States; most of the new leaders had been the first generation to be educated, and almost all of them were educated in the United States. They had an inordinate love for the United States. Yet they felt that the U.S., in large part because of its support for Israel and its despising of the Arab world, did not appreciate them: a dangerous equation for our policy.

I wrote this—and I spoke about it. One day in Chicago I was speaking about it to the prestigious Chicago Committee of the

Chicago Council on Foreign Relations, and I happened to be sitting next to the president of one of the big oil companies. There I was, a girl from the South Side, telling this immensely powerful man about the Saudis' real feelings—and he was sensitive enough to listen and, I am convinced, to understand. It was an interesting role: Again, the woman as the interpreter of man to man, yet on a new level.

In contrast to what appears, Saudi Arabia is a country haunted by women. On the surface—on the streets and in the public places—it is a society quite simply without women. In the universities, even, women "see" their own professors, if they are male, only on television screens.

And yet the Saudis admit that they are "in turmoil" over women. Women are the terrible underground obsession, an obsession, moreover, that could ultimately destroy what they are trying to build. They talk about women "working," yes, for how can they keep the intelligent and ambitious educated Saudi women down? So they plan for them to work in all-female offices, schools, hospitals, and banks. One man suggested using computers at home. The number one development goal of the new development plan of Faisal Bashir, for instance, is to get over the need for foreign workers—but they cannot do this unless they utilize women's skills.

A further irony lies in the fact that when women there remain in their most dramatically traditional and primitive "place," that "place" could actually destroy the society men are trying to build. Thus arises the obsession, and somewhere way in the background are the whispers telling the Saudi men, who so need totally to control, that it is actually they who are being controlled.

On that same trip, in 1980, I had a strange reaction that was so spontaneous—and so intense and angry—that I knew it must represent something more. When I was leaving Riyadh to go home, I was seated in the Saudi plane near a window. All the other seats around me were free. A Saudi woman, completely covered with that ugly black veil, came up and started to sit down next to me. I was suddenly so repulsed by the veil that I waved her off (not at all my usual way) with an angry, "Why don't you take the free seats?" She fluttered away like a smitten black moth, and I sat there sulking, troubled by the knowledge that she had wanted to sit next to me for safety, because women in these areas cannot sit next to men on planes. But I did not want to be contaminated by a woman who had accepted this fate—if I threatened her, she also threatened me.

When anybody tells me that I am imagining the things that still tie and imprison women, I tell them two stories:

Once, about to take off on an assignment, I needed a prescription for the Pill as well as the usual shots. Chicago is filled with Catholic doctors: to be avoided under such circumstances at all costs. So, I got out the Yellow Pages and went down the list of doctors, finding a fine Dr. Shapiro right in the neighborhood. A Jewish doctor—that was what I needed. Off I went.

Dr. Shapiro was a fine sort, but I must admit that he seemed a little surprised to have me, known to him after all from the papers, suddenly drop in on him. Where had I heard about him? Why had I come to him? What could I tell him? Because he was Jewish and this was my day to avoid Catholics who might lecture me on birth control, and increase my guilt?

I started out—indirection in such matters has always been my way —by asking him for the necessary shots. Then, finally, I stammered out, "And doctor, I would like to get the Pill."

This pleasant, friendly man suddenly dropped all pretense of friendliness and became the righteously angry father. "And are you married?" he demanded. I shook my head. "And you want me to give you the Pill . . . ?" He went on and on. Finally, he had his son, a charming young man, come in from the adjoining office—and he gave me the Pill, and apologized for his "old-fashioned" father.

Dr. Shapiro, you see, was a professor at Loyola Medical School, the largest Catholic medical school in the area!

Thinking back on this, I don't know whether to laugh or cry. That I should have accepted such treatment . . . that I should have had put inside me such feelings about myself in the beginning and still have had them at thirty-three . . . certainly shows clearly the cruel absurdities heaped upon women of my generation and all those before. How really extraordinary, when you think about such things. How really sad.

Then, early in the 1970s, when I was covering the Middle East, I started to find myself growing physically weaker and weaker. Once, in Iran in the spring of 1973, I actually collapsed on the Teheran airport floor and had to be on intravenous feeding for three days. When one doctor could not tell me what was wrong, I went to others. In fact I went to twelve doctors in twelve countries.

Each one gave a different—but similar—diagnosis: they all placed the "stomach problem," for that was what it was, right squarely in my little female mind. The Israeli doctor told me peremptorily and pedantically, "If you would get married and have children and settle down, you wouldn't have these emotional problems." The American doctor suggested that it was due to the fact that I stayed with my mother when I was in Chicago. . . . Finally, irritated and impatient, I asked, "Doctor, why don't you do the stool test?" Something none of them had done.

The next day the doctor phoned me and said, "Gee Gee, I think you'd better sit down." I was prepared for the worst: He was going to tell me that there was nothing wrong with me. "You have a very bad case of amoebic dysentery," he said. "You must have had it for two years, for you have what we call a carrier case or a chronic case. It is quite serious."

To his consternation I began to laugh uproariously. It took only a few days, with the right medicine, for me to feel enormously better. In five weeks I was cured. For two years all those male doctors had only presided at my misery; clucking like "old wives," they made fun over what could have meant death. As a woman I was at the mercy (or lack of it) of male doctors who still looked at a woman in 1973

—a woman who had obviously been traveling constantly through infectious areas—and saw only what Freud had seen fifty years earlier in woman: hysteria.

By then I was indeed hysterical, hysterical with rage over their ignorance and over the disdain and hatred for women that sustained it.

XIII.

Avida and Kemal

"The Jews and Arabs of Jerusalem cannot afford to
get to know each other because, if they did, they would
have to acknowledge to themselves that part of what
the other side says is right."
—MERON BENVINISTI, Israeli scholar and former
deputy mayor of Jerusalem

The Moslem Arab world was supposed to be a difficult,
even impossible assignment—it wasn't. Israel, on the other hand, a
country I long had idealized, a country whose people I admired
enormously, a country with citizens far more similar to mine, was
supposed to be easy, a cinch—it wasn't, either. This again only
confirmed the rule that a journalist has to "be there," because
nothing is ever what we expect it to be. Indeed, Israel presented me
with the greatest and the most profound moral quandary of all, with
a sort of professional and personal wandering in the wilderness.

I had first gone to Israel in the fall of 1969 as an admirer of the
Jewish people and of their phoenixlike rising in their new-old state
out of terrible historic suffering. I would have liked to go to Israel
long before. But since we had a fine correspondent stationed perma-
nently in Tel Aviv, the _Daily News_ editors naturally sent me first to
the Arab world, where in its vast entireties of desert and garden we
had no one.

Still, my first day in Tel Aviv, when I walked into Beit Sokolov,
the government news agency, the officer in charge looked at me.
"We've been watching you as you went around the Arab world. You
certainly are an Arab lover."

232

I was stunned. Didn't a person have the right to go to the Arab world? Shouldn't the Arab world be covered by the press? For the moment I put it aside, but they would not let me be; I was already dubbed an "Arab lover" only because I had written objectively about the Arab countries. It resounded deep in my soul, along with the "Jew lover" and "nigger lover" from my youth. But, no, I did not believe that this kind of prejudice existed in Israel. Certainly not.

Then I began to read the history and found more surprises. Not even half of the very basic "history" that Israel and its friends had so carefully propagated throughout the world, and in particular the United States, was true. I believed—and fervently believe today— that the Jewish people have a total right to their state and to its security. But what about the five million Kurds, the scattered Armenians, and the four million Palestinians displaced by the Israeli state?

When I looked into history, I found that in 1918 there had been about sixty-five thousand Jews in what was then Palestine, up from only two hundred families in 1883. The Arab population, which had lived there for thirteen hundred years (long enough, one would think, to accrue some rights) was roughly six times that many. By 1948, when the UN divided Palestine into a Jewish and an Arab state, the Jewish population had risen to 600,000, compared with 1,200,000 Arabs. Then, in the Palestine wars of 1947–48, all but 200,000 of the Arabs fled Israel proper in the ensuing war started by the neighboring Arab states against the Israelis. They were later moved a second time, from the West Bank and other areas. And here is where the conundrum begins.

What is true is this: Part of the Arab population fled out of terror of the fighting; part of it fled in response to the calls by Arab leaders to flee in order to return once the war was over; and enormous numbers also fled because they were brutally murdered and driven out by Jewish groups like the terrorist Irgun Zvai Leumi of Prime Minister Menachem Begin or the Stern Gang of Foreign Minister Yitzhak Shamir. They were never allowed to return, and their properties, which were substantial—for Palestine was not at all a poor

233

area—were simply taken over by Israeli Jews. All of this is very important, for the Israelis' claim to total purity and their claim to having no responsibility for the "Palestine question" rests on whether or not they drove the Palestinians out. They did.

From the beginning I was torn by the Israeli-Palestinian conflict, seeing good and bad, guilt and innocence, suffering and overcoming, very balanced on both sides. But in the Middle East you were not permitted by either side to see both sides. This bothered me more in Israel than in the Arab world simply because they lay claim to moral superiority as the basis of their national life and our extravagant support is based on that. When you do this, then you must accept being judged by your own standards.

I came to the Middle East as I come to most areas, in a basically nonideological frame of mind. I have always felt that sentimentality is the graveyard of the journalist, who has to know and always remember that today's guerrilla or victim can well be tomorrow's totalitarian. There are not—or should not be—any final chapters in the journalist's life, not if she believes (as she should) that life is process.

What's more, most stands against oppression are all too fashionably late. Journalists and others must not be always fighting the last moral war but the new one. (Avoid the cliché of your time.)

Retroactive guilt—a dangerous thing. It is so very easy to say you will never again let happen something that already has happened, and that you cannot do anything about, and that will never happen again. In effect we were being asked to live for and write against "the Holocaust," and ignore the present sufferings of the Palestinian Arabs, who were the new oppressed people: the "New Jews."

As I went through this torment, I kept asking myself, "Is it enough to hate the evil done forty years ago and not have to do anything about the evil going on now?" I had always abhorred racism, sexism, ethnicism, tribalism—everything that cut person off from person—so how could I in conscience avoid writing about the Palestinian question?

234

But that came to mean criticizing Israel's policies, which were to ignore the Palestinians and to do anything necessary to keep them down on the West Bank. And that meant constant and bitter accusations of "anti-Semite." I truly loved and believed in Israel, and the Arabs were quite capable of doing any number of stupid and feral things. But as the years went by and I continued to cover the Middle East, I could only come to agree with the early Zionist Theodore Herzl, who said, "We have one right against another right."

Most of my friends in the Labor Party agreed with this, for that party was based on the idea of the two peoples living together and also of the "normalization" of the Jewish people. But it soon became clear that the Israel of Menachem Begin, the old super-terrorist, would have no truck with such rational solutions. Rather the Begin people looked upon the Arabs in much the same way, as a despised people and "vassal state," that the Germans and the Poles and the Russians had looked upon the Jews.

As the seventies passed and I visited Israel regularly and saw the changes occurring, I grew sadder and sadder about what was happening to this once idealistic and revered state. One night, for instance, I sat in the cozy apartment of Eliah Ariev, one of the founding fathers of Israel, the former powerful secretary-general of the Labor Party under Ben-Gurion and Golda Meir, and one of the finest total human beings I have known anywhere. We were talking with a friend of his, Yigal Elam, a young professor of history at Tel Aviv University.

Yigal cared deeply, as did "Lova" Ariev, about the original universalist vision of Zionism as the Jewish idea of justice for all, and he was deeply troubled. For as he went around to the kibbutzes to lecture on the origins of the movement, he found deep changes.

"It is obvious," he told me soberly, "that the early kibbutzim were idealists. But today when I say this, even in some of the socialistic kibbutzes, I always find some of the elders shouting something at me like, 'You dare to tell us it was not for the security and boundaries of Israel?' " He shook his head sadly. "Even the elders have forgot-

235

ten," he went on. "I always bring old documents showing what the original concept was, and I always win the argument. But they never forgive me."

What I was finding in Israel during the seventies was a country that had totally changed—and I started to analyze it. By 1978, for instance, it was clear that the "new Israel" of Begin was annexing the West Bank, thus driving the Palestinian Arabs out of still another part of their land (most families already had been driven out two or three times, first from parts of Israel, then from other parts of the West Bank). I wrote:

> Approximately one-third of all the land in the formerly Jordanian West Bank, occupied by Israel in 1967, is already in Israeli hands. In the crucial Jordan Valley, about 80 percent of the land is estimated by specialists to be owned by Israel, thus encircling the highlands still in Arab hands. . . .
>
> In the years that will come, with more of "no war and no peace," the Israeli government, using "security" to cover anything it does, will go on to create more new "facts" until this hopeful moment is past and the West Bank effectively is Israel. It may already be.

Then in the spring of 1981 I wrote an analysis of the passing of power from the Ashkenazim or European Jews who founded the state to the Sephardic, or Oriental, Jews who came later and who had totally different values. Now I wrote:

> . . . Congress is dealing with an Israel that no longer exists. The special American relationship with Israel is based on a moral premise of support for the people who suffered the Holocaust. Yet the Israel of Prime Minister Menachem Begin—and the negative twist he has brought to the original Zionist mission—is now a state with a majority of Sephardic, or Oriental, Jews who know neither Europe nor the values of Central and Eastern European Jewish culture.
>
> The Sephardim have no personal experience of the Holocaust, but do have a great deal of personal experience with Arabs. They like and support autocratic leaders such as Begin. Their hatred for Arabs is

legendary, and the most brutal treatment of Arabs and of Arab prisoners on the West Bank virtually always turns out to be from Sephardic soldiers or prison officials.

It is the Sephardim, too, who are the strongest supporters of Begin's "Greater Israel" policy, which would annex the Arab West Bank as part of Israel. There is virtually none of the moral questioning among them that there is among the original Ashkenazi founders of the state over these matters. Nor, at heart, is "security" really their major concern—expansion of the state and the use of power are.

In all of this I remained a staunch supporter of Israel. But I could simply not accept the fact that I could not criticize another country when I freely criticized my own, particularly when that country was not only totally dependent upon us but when our foreign policy and its were closely interwoven. But I soon discovered that to the Begin people and thus to the professional American Jewish community, which followed Jerusalem totally, I could not criticize anything about Israel. I could not criticize anything about policy or any government of Israel at any moment, or even anything that they did that impinged upon American policy, which was clearly expected to follow the Israeli lead.

The moment I wrote the slightest thing suggesting that Israel was not totally right, I began to get dozens and then hundreds of letters. Though I'd never so much as permitted an anti-Semitic (any more than an antiblack or an antifemale or an anti-Arab) remark to be made in my presence, these letters called me a "vulgar anti-Semite." Others, encouraged by American Jewish leaders who never budged overseas, wrote, "I hope you die of the most painful kind of syphilis." Though I tried in my reporting to work toward a real peace for everyone in the Middle East, I was told by American Jewish leaders, whose directions came straight from Jerusalem, that I was not writing in the "American" interest. There was no way that a person of conscience could not but grow more and more disturbed—and finally disgusted.

Then in 1978 I attended an "Arab-American Dialogue" conference in Tripoli, Libya, sponsored by an American Arab committee and the Libyan government. I gave a paper, which was a great deal of work, on the American press and the Arab world, in which I was extremely critical of the Arabs but in which I also tried to offer them ideas about how to open up more—legitimately—to the American media. For this I received two thousand dollars, about what I get for a speech in the U.S. I wrote two columns about Libya and in each one clearly and honorably specified that I was a "guest" of the government and a paid speaker. I was extremely critical of Qaddafi and carefully outlined his terrorist connections.

Different American Jewish lobby groups peppered my papers with letters saying I was a "Libyan agent." My publisher at the *Los Angeles Times* was embarrassed at a publishers' conference by papers circulating that implicated the *Times* with Libya. Even today, four years later, every few months I get a letter from some concerned person at one of my papers because some "nut" has again accused me of "taking money from Libya." When I spoke at Georgetown University, on something quite different, there was a vicious letter in the student paper. When a young woman student went through all the letters, from very different places, she found all of them included exactly the same points and phrasings.

Yet, unlike some self-styled friends of Israel, I was the one who really tried to help. In the spring of 1973, after spending weeks in Cairo and "listening" to what the Egyptians actually were saying, I had the instinctive and informed feeling that they were going to attack Israel. I wrote this and said this in an interview. When I was in Jerusalem, I told this to Moshe Sasson, the very intelligent Israeli diplomat who then headed the Foreign Ministry.

He roared with laughter. "My dear," he kept saying, "my dear girl, you just don't know our Arabs."

Later that year in October, when the Egyptians rushed across the Suez in one of the most startling attacks of military history—and, caught totally by surprise, the Israelis even brought out their atom bombs in desperation—I wondered how well they knew *their* Arabs, or who was really their friend.

In the ensuing years I also tried to tell them that Egypt's President Sadat was totally changing; that he wanted to make peace; that the Egyptian people themselves were pushing Sadat toward an end to all the fighting. Again all the Israeli officials I spoke to scoffed at this. Had they "listened" then, they would not have been so surprised when Sadat sprung his trip to Jerusalem upon them that fall of 1977 —and they would have been far better prepared to benefit from it.

To make the whole Israeli situation even more painful, my Jewish friends at home would not usually criticize me but I could see their hurt. Meanwhile, incongruously, friends in Israel, many of them leading Laborites, would openly urge me to criticize the Begin policies, which relied upon the original moral reputation of the Israeli state, while carrying out the most immoral policies. They couldn't criticize them, they said—and they didn't want to urge the American Jewish leaders to criticize them.

However, I continued hoping that, as the situation in the Middle East indeed was changing—Egypt had made peace, the PLO would accept a confederation with Jordan, Jordan would work with Arafat, even radical Iraq was changing—we could arrive at a true peace, with security for Israel and a just solution for the displaced Palestinians. And there was one man in Israel who I believed—and still believe —could carry this through.

I interviewed Shimon Peres, the leader of the Labor Party, on a sparklingly beautiful April day atop the Mount of Olives, in the spring of 1981, with the single most spectacular view of the Old City of Jerusalem spread before us. Golden domes glowed in the spring sun, as this eloquent and rational man gave precisely the opposite viewpoint from Menachem Begin. Where Begin used the historic suffering of his people in the most evil of ways, not to transcend but to impose suffering on others, and to create a new, fortified ghetto that would lash out at everyone, Peres wanted to return Israel to its original transcendent and superbly decent dreams.

"I think there is an opening in the Middle East," Peres told me, speaking thoughtfully yet forcefully. "And we have to try our hand to take part." Then in words that echoed those spoken by Egyptian

President Sadat three years ago, he said, "There is always a psychological dimension. Perhaps, today, the Arab world exists more in psychological terms than in political terms. We have to break the logjam of suspicion and hostility. What has happened is we've grown used to the jargon of belligerency and not the reality of peace.

"On local issues, we'd be willing to negotiate straight with the Palestinians on the West Bank—and with the Jordanians also, if they like. After all, these Palestinians were the legitimate leaders there." He wanted to bring Jordan into the negotiating process with the eventual idea of a West Bank Palestinian entity confederated with Jordan (which was what any rational person looked to as the solution to the decades of misery and slaughter). "If Saudi Arabia came in [to the peace process], Jordan would," he went on. "We even see a change in the traditional, hard Iraqi position. The Iraqis are unhappy with Russia and they blame Russian technology for their problems in the war. This is a change, and a vacuum."

About the Israeli settlements on the West Bank, which now include upward of twenty thousand persons and which were the dishonorable tool for the annexation, Peres said, "They would remain, as would Arab settlers under Israel and Israeli settlers under Arab sovereignty. The main problem is not the settlers but settlement." He would "enlarge our relations with Egypt, which is the key: conclude the autonomy talks [for the Palestinians in the occupied territories] and start autonomy in a specific place and in good faith. I'd say the Gaza Strip would be a good place to begin."

Finally he outlined a fascinating new vision of the area, taking in the entire rift and sea area from the Dead Sea to the Red Sea to make it an "area of peace without threats and armaments." Peres's ideas, worked out over the previous four years, were not to create more hatred in this area of the great religions of the world, as Begin and his people are doing, but to build in this area the "infrastructure of goodwill from which we could begin" and to concentrate Israel's new policies on working in the Middle East itself instead of in Europe and in the rest of the world. In effect he believed in the "normalization" of the Jewish people that was the very crux of the

240

dream of the original Zionists, while all of Begin's policies and all of his impulses were precisely and psychologically designed to keep the Jewish people forever in a ghetto, alone and despised and under attack from everyone without.

I left Peres that day feeling that I had seen and heard a man of perception and vision not seen since the halcyon days of Ben-Gurion. While Begin's unsavory coalition looked constantly backward, Peres was looking forward. But when the election came that June of 1981, Begin won over Peres by a hair's breadth. In the last days of the uniquely bitter and dishonest campaign waged by Begin, as his bully boys broke up Labor meetings and burned down Labor offices, Peres and other Labor leaders had desperately warned of "Jewish fascism." They could see what was happening to the state they had founded and loved.

In short, the coverage of Israel, with its pulls toward the very best in man and its tugs from the very worst, with its undertones of guilt and its overtones of rage, tormented me, as it has many journalists and diplomats and others who have covered it and worked with it. Yet it helped no one, certainly not Israel itself, not to tell the truth about it, as many Labor friends urged. The others, those who did not want the truth out, were leading Israel to a new holocaust and slaughter—there was not the slightest question about it—and they were following blindly a mad leader who wanted, not Jewish right, but Jewish conquest. You cannot have both.

I suppose the Middle East was the most tormenting area for many journalists because there always was so much hope. Somewhere underneath, in deep-flowing currents never lost in history, we always really believed something could be done. On the parts of both Jews and Palestinians there was often a yearning for the other. They would remind you that, after all, they had historically lived together —and it was completely true that the Moslems had always treated the Jews much better than the Christians had.

Then, suddenly, in the fall of 1977 the entire "hope" became palpable. Indeed, it was right there before our eyes. Anwar Sadat went to Jerusalem, and it looked for a moment as though the whole

241

world teetered on the brink of real change: only this time real, deep, lasting change. And suddenly I saw this change, before my eyes, in the Cairo Conference where the Israelis went to Cairo for the first time to meet with the Egyptians.

The mood was euphoric, contagious, unbelieving. My friend Zeev Schiff, the brilliant military analyst of the Israeli newspaper *Ha'aretz,* stood in Cairo one of those golden days in the shadow of the pyramids shaking his head. "All these years, I've been studying this area in terms of military maps from the air," he said, a distinct sense of wonder in his voice. "Even the pyramids I saw from up there. Now, being down here, I can't quite absorb it all."

Quite unintentionally I came to cause the only "stir" of the entire Cairo Conference, which was noted for its remarkable harmony. Most of the press was staying at a jolly little motel, appropriately called the "Jolie Ville," right across from the historic Mena House Hotel, where the diplomats were housed. We had been warned to look for any "trouble," for it was believed that the Palestinian Left or other forces might try to disrupt the conference. There were Egyptian security men standing at the end of every arm of little cottages, and . . . it was raining! It never rained in Cairo, never. Yet it was raining, giving an additional eerie turn to the mood.

The second night I returned from a pleasant dinner downtown and repaired in an appropriately jolly mood to my little room. I was lying in bed when I heard this "tick . . . tick . . . tick. . . ." It was exact, and it was exactly like a clock. Only there was no clock in the room. I dismissed it for a moment—and then remembered all the warnings. When I called the security, they ran to the room, heard the ominous tick, and immediately evacuated me. I was lucky, because they just moved me to another room, where I immediately went to sleep.

In the morning when I was walking calmly across the lobby to breakfast, I heard this sort of muted hiss come up from some of my colleagues seated around the lobby. Then they started in unison to go "Tick . . . tick . . . tick. . . ."

What it appears happened, for I ignored their taunts and did not ask, was that as I was settled peacefully into my new room, the rest of the motel was evacuated from their rooms. The security men thought my *ticks* were a bomb, as I had myself feared. As my friends stood out in the rain, the security men discovered it was only the certain way the rain was falling upon my roof which caused the terrifying *tick*. My colleagues never forgave me this contribution to the Cairo Conference.

The Cairo Conference and its mood, its transcendence, its beauty, did indeed show what *could* come in the Middle East. I went from there to Jerusalem, where I wrote with a deep hope and belief that history has seldom allowed me to express:

> What has really happened here in the Middle East this last month is Christmas Wonder updated, if you will. The transformation of the spirit that is at the core of Christmas has just, to filch from the Bible, been made flesh. . . .
>
> We have tended to think that the transformations they created were magical or mystical things. Lightning bolts from heaven. Signs given because of grace or whim but not because of worth or virtue. Proper and even edifying to observe but not, if we are to be honest about it, really for us or for our time.
>
> Well, maybe these few weeks in the Middle East have got me a little lightheaded, but they have led me to wonder why we cannot or do not think of updated wonder and, God forgive me, even updated miracles for our time. With this stroke of the typewriter, I forever decry leaving the divine to the dead, and I declare myself for modernizing wonder, transforming love and redefining transformation. . . .
>
> So what, then, is left? Hard work, complicated work. People who work to heal not only people's bodies but their psyches. People who work to feed people and regulate the overpopulation that kills and maims. People who study the psychology of nations and work doggedly in the diplomatic realm to bring an Egypt and an Israel together because they saw that, despite all the apparent hatred, there was a deep longing for transformation. People like President Sadat who have the courage that Churchill called the most important virtue because it "guarantees" all the rest.
>
> Here you have real transformation in our time. Here you have the

243

sense of wonder acted out before you in modern ballet and the prophetic tradition democratized by modern communications that include everyone, not just the waysiders that Paul met on the road to Damascus. Here you have my friend Zeev seeing the universally horrible bombing maps transformed into the soul-quenching beauty and mystery of the pyramids and Sphinx, once he can touch them.

In the spring of 1973, I got to know Kemal Nasser, then the spokesman of the PLO. Kemal was a square-shouldered man, husky, with a good face whose eyes gave him away. Though working for the PLO, his eyes and his smile were the eyes and smile of the poet, which is what he was. He was a good one. He never fought, never carried a gun. At night, by candlelight, he still wrote.

One afternoon the Lebanese diplomat Clovis Maksuud and his wife-to-be, Hallah, and Abdul Karim Aboul Nasser, the columnist for the respected paper *an-Nahar,* and I had a memorable lunch. It went on for six hours at an exquisite blue and white fish restaurant that hung off the rocks over the sea.

Kemal was in absolutely top form, telling stories about his old friend Yasser Arafat and about himself. Though they were the same age, Kemal joked that "I told him that I was a babe in arms when he was in Jerusalem." Kemal lived in the downtown Hamra district, and Arafat wanted him to move to the Sabra refugee camp for his own protection. "I told the Old Man [the nickname for Arafat], 'Better to die in Hamra than to live in Sabra.' "

How telling.

Later, as we walked down the street, the Mediterranean Sea spreading out before us toward Spain and Italy and then the New World, he said to me, a sudden sadness overtaking him, "We must protect this city, we must. It is all we have left."

Looking at his face then, I saw a terrible vulnerability behind all the tough pronouncements he made so confidently. He had been talking a lot about dying recently; all his friends noticed it. Yet the next night, when he took me to visit his aunts who were visiting from the West Bank, he was again the happy, debonair man of the world.

Through the next weeks in Beirut I was struck and at times overcome by a strange, haunting sense of things ending. I thought it must be the unusually early hot weather, because that early, cloying part of spring has always depressed me. It promises too much, and we are driven to dream of impossible heights and perfect emotions that we never can reach.

I went from Beirut to Baghdad. One day I was walking into the archaeological museum with a young Italian diplomat when he suddenly spoke. "Oh, I meant to tell you," he said. "You did hear about the killings in Beirut, didn't you?"

I stared at him. I had the consciousness of my heart stopping as the question hung there in the air.

"The Israelis . . ." he stuttered. "They sent commandos right into the center of Beirut. They killed three Palestinian leaders. Abu Youssef and Kemal Nasser and . . ."

So Kemal was dead—one more statistic in the slaughterhouse.

From then on, as I continued to travel about the Middle East, I felt somehow driven to know more about the Kemal Nasser whom I had known so little. So I talked with his friends and family, and a picture of him began to emerge. He was often playful, always romantic. He loved to sit up all night in coffeehouses, arguing poetry, love, revolution, in his dramatic, ultra-British accent. "He was such a presence," Abdul Karim said. Yet in his last months his hulking, graying, forty-seven-year-old body seemed to tire as though the growing brutality of the Middle East conflict was wearing it out. He talked of having a fifty-fifty chance, perhaps of retiring and "leaving things for the young people."

After his death Kemal did not return to the stern and stony hills of the West Bank, where he had been born and nurtured. He was buried in Beirut in the commandos' cool, dark "martyrs' cemetery," under black cedar trees. But when I was on the West Bank later that spring and drove up to Bir Zeit College, which had been founded by his family, they were still mourning him.

There in the exquisite stone Turkish-style buildings of the Nasser family's college, I found Hanna Nasser, the young director of the college in this rocky land with the golden glow. He spoke softly, a faraway look in his eyes. "I last saw Kemal two nights before he was killed," he began. "I had gone to Beirut to see him, and when he came up to my hotel room he was pleased that the concierge downstairs recognized him." Nasser, a tall, lanky, American-educated Palestinian, shook his head. "I always told him that a revolutionary is not supposed to be recognized. Then he told me, 'We'll meet next time in Bir Zeit!' . . . and that was it.

"Everybody wanted to make a demonstration for Kemal here, a silent march to his house. But when it was written that there would be a service for Kemal at four P.M., the Israeli military governor came here—there were jeeps all over our college. The military governor said, 'We hear you are having something on at four P.M.' 'We bury and respect our dead,' I said. He said, 'Oh, I didn't know it was a funeral service.' "

Hanna Nasser smiled a bitter smile. "What really surprised them was that so many of the Arab 'notables' who cooperate with them came—that was what they couldn't stand. There were more than five thousand persons here in the Bir Zeit alone to mourn for Kemal."

The Israelis, of course, thought otherwise. "I was very surprised that the West Bank identified with these terrorist leaders," Israeli Chief of Staff David Elazar said in a press conference two weeks after the raid. "All we can learn from the fact is that there are still many Arabs who regard these terrorists as their leaders."

Hanna Nasser's wife commented softly on this surprise: "The Israelis blind themselves. They think that only Israel is permissible. Therefore, anything they do is permissible. We wonder how long we can endure it. Yet, as much as we suffer, we think we are less nervous and upset than they are. When you know you are right, you can fight for it."

As I traveled about the West Bank, I kept hearing more about Kemal—there, in those barren hills, studded with jagged rocks and lit by that strange golden light. His relatives were going through a period of thinking and rethinking, evaluating the life of their fallen loved one. And they spoke of him always in the present tense.

"Kemal is a humanist socialist revolutionary," said Mrs. Nasser, her large, sensitive eyes brooding. "That is why everybody always trusts him. He is far from being a bloodthirsty revolutionary." Then the tense shifted.

"He was always terribly romantic," she went on, leaning forward eagerly. "He always felt something mysterious about himself. 'But I really feel it,' he would say. In his poetry, he was prophetic. He was about himself, too." She paused. "There must have been something in him that didn't want to fight anymore. He always had a sixth sense—he always escaped before."

The time they remembered best, since it was the last time he was really home in Bir Zeit, was the six months after the 1967 war. "It was a rare occasion when he could spend time with the family," she recalled. "We used to go walking and pick mulberries. . . . He went to Jerusalem, and I remember he came back and said that, despite the occupation, 'We must never be responsible for killing those Jewish children.' "

Hanna Nasser interjected, "The Israelis at that time used to ask him to speak all over, and he would try to tell them that Jews and Arabs should live together. He would come home so frustrated and say, 'Those bastards have a golden opportunity to live with us—they won't do it.' "

After seven months Kemal, with about one hundred other West Bank leaders, was deported by the Israeli occupation authorities. He had been trying to organize passive resistance movements. It was then that he went to Jordan and joined the Palestinian resistance. However, he never joined any of the commando groups, he never fought, and he knew nothing about guns. He was called the "conscience" of the movement, and not even the Israelis accused him personally of being a member of Black September or an active terrorist. Some said in Israel that he was killed simply because he happened to live in the same building as the other two, who were the real leaders. But unquestionably, though he constantly publicly decried the Black September terrorism, he had come to a point himself, because of the growing Palestinian desperation, where he thought some forms of terrorism were necessary and even justified. And in those days fewer and fewer distinctions were being made on both sides.

"He must have enjoyed his funeral," Mrs. Nasser was musing. "All those women throwing flowers on his grave. At the same time, he must have been asking, 'Why all this fuss about me?' " Three hundred thousand persons came to his funeral in Beirut.

But then in Bir Zeit reality introduced upon the growing legend of Kemal. As the Nassers were speaking, Kemal's aged mother, a bulky little woman all in black, walked down the street outside, helped by an aging sister. And the young Mrs. Nasser was saying in a soft voice inside the room, "Kemal never wanted to kill Jews. He wanted to live with them in a Palestinian state. All he thought was that we Palestinians have a right to live, too, and that nobody can take it from us.

"Now, because of Kemal's death, my son says he wants to kill. I tell him that even Uncle Kemal did not want to kill. It's an awful thing to bring up a whole generation like this."

Two months after Kemal's death, I found myself in Israel. The talk had died down on the "Raid into Beirut," but there was still excitement about it in people's minds. Then, one day, Clifton Forster, a particularly good American information officer, suddenly said to me: "A lady in the office knows the Chur family. What would you think of going down to their kibbutz in the Negev and interviewing them?"

Avida Chur, twenty-two, was one of the three Israeli commandos killed in the raid on Beirut. Had he himself killed Kemal? What was *he* like? I had been looking at both sides for a long time, but this was a breathtaking opportunity.

I said that, yes, I would definitely like to go to see the Churs, and Clifton arranged it. And so we drove south, across the "desert" now dotted with attractive kibbutzes and farms, with the Bedouins still close by.

248

I have always hated stories like this—how can one, if one is human at all, invade or impinge upon others' grief?—and yet one had to do them. Often afterward, I reassured myself, the family was grateful. Years before in Chicago, for instance, I had been the first to tell Charles Evers that his famous civil rights leader brother, Medgar Evers, had been killed; we had sat on their big porch on the South Side as I imposed my dark knowledge, and I had mourned with him, but somehow this was worse.

The Churs were a lovely family: sensitive, intelligent, dedicated people. Ironically they were people of the Mapam, the far leftist party which had always wanted to live with the Palestinians—indeed, Mapam even wanted a binational state. But bullets do not stop to pose ideological questions.

As soon as we sat down in their simple but comfortable modern apartment, I realized that there had been a grave misunderstanding. They had not understood, clearly, that I wanted to interview them about Avida, and I was smitten with guilt and with sorrow. We decided to forget the idea . . . the grief for their son was so intense that both it—and he—seemed present in physical form. His loving and sorrowing kibbutznik parents had kept him alive with a deep and, as it transpired, sometimes strange search into the life, conscience, and character of their dead son.

At first they looked at me, from their dark, haunted eyes, as an intruder. But, please, they said, sit down and have something to eat. I did, intending to leave soon, and then something very strange occurred. As if the voices were coming out of nowhere or some chamber far away and long ago, they began to talk of Avida. Spontaneously, hauntingly. The words just seemed to push out, and I became the vehicle for their search.

It soon became clear that they were obsessed with this dark contradiction, troublesome to so many conscionable Jews today, between the Jew as idealist and the Jew as warrior.

As we sat there, they began to talk about his last days, how he had even seen the angel of death approaching shortly before he died. "My starting point for everything is from a humanistic basis," the doomed young man had told his lovely, dark-haired wife-to-be as they had driven late at night from Tel Aviv to this green kibbutz where he was born. They described his voice as tormented as he poured out his feelings in a kind of midnight confessional that became his ideological last will and testament. "I believe in solving the refugee problem. We should do everything for peace. But as far as the terrorists go, we should do everything against them."

The Churs—he from Poland, she from South Africa—had come to this desert as Mapamists to build the now thriving farm and dairy. Believing that, as Chaim still insisted, Israel is the "common home-land of both Jews and Arabs," they made friends with the Bedouins across the road. When water was piped in by the kibbutzniks, it was brought for the Bedouins, too, and they sang a song that proclaimed: "Some say that generals make history, some say that presidents make history, but here we say that plumbers make history."

And now—in one of the great quirks of history—it was the sons of these kibbutzniks, and in particular the tolerant, liberal Mapam kibbutzniks, who formed the majority of the elite Israeli commandos assigned to the most dangerous and lethal special raids against what had become the "enemy."

"From my son's class, ten out of the twelve went into the special commando units," Chaim Chur, a graying, honest man who worked as a journalist for the Mapam newspaper, went on relating, "and the others were not accepted only because of physical disqualifications. All ten became officers. The way they were raised on the kibbutz, they didn't want to be professional soldiers. But the atmosphere created the idea that if a person goes to the army, he must go to the best unit or he is shirking his duty to prove himself."

He paused, and a hesitant note entered his voice. "I think it is because of their humanistic motives that they are so good," he added, with a strange wistfulness. "They have an integrity of purpose.

"I later heard from the other commandos on the raid in Beirut that they found families living in the one house they had planned to explode in connection with blowing up the Popular Front building. So as not to hurt these families, they used a different house, even though it wasn't as effective. I know my son, as the commander, was in favor of this, and that his point of view prevailed. He said, 'All right, maybe we won't blow it up this way, but they'll know we could have done it."

Avida was killed when Popular Front commandos began shooting back as soon as the building exploded. "I know for a fact that my son did not like the army," said Chaim Chur. "But he knew he had to do it. He had completed his three-year service in February, but because they needed him as a commander, they asked him to sign for a half-year more. He signed because it was his duty. If he had not signed . . ." At this he looked like a man whom grief might overwhelm at any moment.

Others told me, as we strolled quietly about the neatly manicured kibbutz, what had happened. Chaim Chur was in his newspaper office when he got the news. When he saw the two military officers coming in the door—heralds of death, just as Avida had seen some herald that dark night's ride across the Negev—he gave out a blood-curdling cry and fell to the floor. After that friends poured in to see and try to comfort them—army commanders, friends of Avida, even the Bedouin sheikh's family across the road, whose son wrote a touching letter saying, "Among our tribe, Avida will be remembered as a hero of heroes." But what came through over and over in the flow of conversation that entire afternoon was the family's obsession with moral conflict.

"It's not such a simple thing to take a youngster who couldn't kill a fly and turn him into someone who kills face to face," Chur continued. "Something has to work inside him."

"They told us he was such a tough leader," Avida's pretty, dark-haired mother said thoughtfully. "That was not connected with our image of Avida at all. We interviewed a lot of his friends, and we learned much we didn't know. What we finally understood was that he always aimed for perfection—the soldiers he trained had to do the best. He knew that if he taught them to do things properly, he would save lives in the time of war. If one thing was not done right,

251

he made them do it over and over. Then he felt they were the best. . . ."

After his death they found a sheaf of peace poems among his things. "Does the soldier see above the rifle sights the gray image of all the widows?" read one. And, "You mothers, teach your infants the word 'peace' before the word 'mother'!"

His father recalled that Avida was moving away from his more dovelike beliefs. "Before, he was quite extreme in his political views," he said. "He was for giving everything back to the Arabs, even Jerusalem. When he was in the army, he retained his convictions, but he was more mature. He didn't criticize the government so much. He definitely changed his views on giving the occupied territories back. I don't see any real contradictions. He was for fighting the terrorists but for living with the Arab people."

Some believed that the young kibbutzniks, having emerged from the womblike security of the kibbutz, found comparable security in the tightly structured commando units. This may help explain why, though the kibbutzim comprise only 4 percent of the population, they suffer 26 percent of the casualties. In the 1967 war they tended always to serve in the most dangerous units. And despite what the parents liked to believe, their sons were not always perfectly humane in such situations. Kemal Nasser, the Palestinian poet and spokesman—a man whom the Churs would have recognized as a kindred soul had they met him under different circumstances—was first killed by shots across the shoulders; then he was shot around the mouth.

But then, what I was seeing, day after day and week after week and month after month, was less and less room for the "humanists" and no room at all for distinctions.

Finally it was time to leave. We had been there seven hours: seven hours of this wondrous and terrible outpouring of grief and memory. Before I left, I ask Chaim Chur, softly, whether he could think of the Kemal Nassers or the other Arabs who also died that fated day.

This good—this quintessentially decent—man could only whisper, "I just can't go that deep."

When I wrote about these two men of the Middle East, I ended with what I really believed:

> It would be naive to suggest that peace would descend on the Middle East if such men as Avida Chur could come to know such men as Kemal Nasser. Good men both, as are many of those caught up in this new holocaust, they were, nonetheless, driven by memories and circumstances that surpassed their powers of rational and humane reflection. But the hard fact is that, sooner or later, such men as these *must* come to know each other.
>
> Perhaps, even after this most recent war, there is still some hope because there are such men as these. Perhaps, as a result of this conflict, the Arabs will lose some of their self-contempt and the Israelis will lose some of their over-assurance. Perhaps, then, the Israelis and the Arabs—the Churs and the Nassers—can look upon each other with awareness that they must live together, like the mountain and the sea. Perhaps, then, for the first time, they will see hope.

XIV.

You Are Not in Our Plans

"Mystery alone is at the root of fear."
—ANTOINE DE SAINT-EXUPÉRY

In retrospect it seems ironic that I should have been so pleased that spring day in 1976 when I was notified from Luanda that the new "revolutionary" government of Angola had awarded me a visa. Since the revolution in 1975, when the MPLA or Popular Movement for the Liberation of Angola had caught in its Marxist hands an exhausted Portuguese colony that was virtually abandoned by the Portuguese colonialists, the country had been harder for a journalist to get into than the White House bedroom at three in the morning.

My delight was only slightly cut short by the knowledge, which came by the way, that the "new Angolans" were allowing in a large group of journalists so they would cover the trials of the British and (a few) American mercenaries who had come in, paid by the CIA and others, to fight against them.

That night in early April when I arrived in the war-wracked city of Luanda on the luxuriant coasts of the South Atlantic, I perhaps should have been aware of many indicators of trouble ahead, but in fact everything went almost too smoothly.

"Ah, yes, Miss Geyer," the dour young woman sitting at the table to "welcome" the foreign journalists said, "you are the correspondent of the *Los Angeles Times.* Welcome to Angola." But she didn't smile.

"No," I remonstrated hastily, "actually, I am not the 'correspondent' of the *Times,* I am a syndicated columnist with the Los Angeles Times Syndicate." This was a very delicate thing, because the correspondents belonged to the paper, and thus certainly deserved more direct attention in countries like this than I did. Belonging to the syndicate, one of the corporate bodies of the Times Mirror Company, meant only that I was an "independent contractor" and on my own, for I had left the *Daily News* in 1975 to become a columnist.

She stared at me in an odd way. It was clear that she wanted me to be the correspondent of the *Times,* so I let it drop.

The next morning when I phoned Dial Torgerson, the top-notch journalist who really was the *Times* correspondent, this always gracious man was gracious but a little restrained. And when we met for coffee in his room, I understood why.

"It was interesting to come in the other day," Dial, a wiry Nordic soul who in another era would have skippered a great sailing ship to the New World, "and tell them I was the *Times* correspondent. They said, 'No, Miss Geyer is the *Times* correspondent.' Then they got very suspicious. . . ."

It turned out that since Miss Geyer was the *Times* correspondent, they held Dial at the airport for *eight hours* before allowing him to enter the empty city of Luanda. It is really quite a wonder—and credit to his good humor and wonderful spirit—that we became such close friends.

Luanda in those days (and still in these days, six years later, as I write this) was a ghost city. The beautiful pastel-colored colonial buildings that the Portuguese had built were still there, but they stood now as eerie fronts for the new emptiness of the society. Cobblestone streets wound up the hillsides to the glorious old pink, yellow, and blue buildings of the once luxuriant Portuguese overseas empire. But behind these lovely facades there was only the omnipresent emptiness. The poor black Angolans, who were supposed to gain from the revolution they were told they had "won," had pru-

255

dently run away to the edges of the city. There they paused, collectively and hesitantly, in the thrown-together camps and shantytowns that spring up around all revolutions as palpable expressions of people's new freedom, and fragmentation, and fear.

It is difficult to explain how a journalist operates and lives and continues as a (more or less) normal human being in such a gruesome place as Luanda was that peculiar spring. During the day Dial and Lee Griggs of *Time* and I would walk down the graceful hill to the Old Opera House, where the trials of the mercenaries were being held. There in the steamy, crowded upper balcony we sat for as long as we could bear it, watching the poor fools of mercenaries who had risked their lives for cash or adrenaline, some to see the world and some to kill their kings, being tried with all the pomp and circumstance of a simulated European court.

The new Angolans of the MPLA "government" wanted to impress everybody with their power and with their efficiency, and so they brought handpicked, ideologically approved observers from all over the Third and socialist world and they would have been very angry indeed had these observers not supported them on every single move.

On the way down to the trials we would often peer into a most wonderful and magical shop where one "Dr. Sambo" had his wares. Most unfortunately, it was closed at the moment. It seemed that Dr. Sambo, a black Angolan resplendent in his pictures in a black top hat and tails, had his herbs for any need, whim, or particular disability. I still have one box, which Dial was able to procure for me on the rare day Dr. Sambo opened up to the revolutionary air, which reads:

SPECIAL TEA FROM CABINDA, ANGOLAN PLANTS NO. 5, FOR
SEXUAL MASCULINE WEAKNESS AND INDIFFERENCE
OR FEMININE FRIGIDITY.

It then told you to take three spoonfuls in three liters of water and to abstain from eating alfalfa, fried meats, fruits, grapes, tapioca, chocolate, ginger, and any alcoholic drinks. Clearly a complicated solution to complicated problems.

There were pathetic little dramas day after day. The second afternoon it was duly announced by the "government" that there would be *demonstração grande* by all the good folks crazed by the revolution. Naturally we did not intend to miss something like that, so Dial and I got to the square early and eager. It soon became clear that they were busing into the center of the city all the poor black Angolans who had been hovering out there on the dark borderlands of the city, waiting to see what the revolution would bring them.

Dial and I climbed up the littered, broken back stairs of a once elegant apartment building in order to get to the roof. The scene was so sad it made me want to cry. Here were all these poor, good, black people, like those of my youth, now having had "the revolution," and now being massed and managed by the new rulers. They held giant signs saying DOWN WITH MERCENARYDOM (Mercenarydom?). They were against—yea, united against—"imperialism." They shouted when they were told to shout and sloganed when they were told to slogan and sang when they were told to sing. (Prince Sihanouk had once said wryly to me, "When I tell them to dance, they dance.") Then the black marchers—the new revolutionary breed—would withdraw inside themselves, just as the peasants had in Vietnam. They would be standing there, still carrying the signs, having sung and chanted, but now with their eyes covered as by a film, with their eyes now looking inward at themselves again.

Then there were the times that Dial and I would set out in the morning (with one of the exactly six taxis still extant and working in Luanda) to find "the government." It is always a mistake to assume there is a government in these situations, but we always kept diligently trying. We went from ministry to ministry, from building to building, from hope to disappointment. No one was ever there. Where were they? Who knows? It was a ghost city with a ghost government.

At night we sat on the roof of the Hotel Trópico, still then a pleasant place, and looked over the darkening city that once had

257

been the pearl of the southern Atlantic. We drank up, systematically and happily, a good deal of Portuguese wine that was left behind. The nights didn't touch us—yet—but we knew enough to know that "out there" at night there were roving gangs of bandits and lots and lots of trouble. It was a little like the Raffles Hotel in Singapore, when the Japanese were invading and everyone sat at the bar daring the world by drinking to life.

We often complained about the toughness of the meat, and Dial later found that the revolutionary Angolans, so resourceful in everything, had raided the protected animal refuge and that we were eating the poor wildebeest!

There were early indicators of trouble, but in truth they did not loom very large on our busy horizons. I kept having small run-ins with Luis da Almeida, the "press secretary" of "the government," who was the only person we were permitted to see. And despite my Spanish and reasonably good Portuguese he kept misunderstanding me.

I kept saying, in Spanish, when he would ask me what I was, *"Yo soy columnista"* ("I am a columnist").

For some reason da Almeida, who talked to me in a normal human manner only once—and that because he had just stepped on my foot —kept thinking I was saying, *"Yo soy economista"* ("I am an economist"). And he would answer, his eyes wary and clouded, "It is a strange time for an economist to come to Angola." And indeed it was, there being no economy!

Nevertheless we forged ahead, covering the trials and gazing with hope ever sprung anew into Dr. Sambo's closed shop. I filed a story on the trial:

> They brought in scads of the world's press and a strange international commission of 44 people from 27 countries (whom they also peevishly won't let the press see). They even got 10,000 of the Angolans who remain in this beautiful, empty stage setting of a city to march with a marked display of lack of anger with perfectly lettered

signs (all of which came out of the prosecutor's office) saying growly things like "Death to the Mercenaries." And then, oh my, and then you see the mercenaries, and you have to know the West is declining.

Remember the days of William Morgan, the handsome, gentle American who fought with Fidel Castro, only to be finally executed by him? Remember Rolf Steiner, the Brit who led black armies in the south of the Sudan and who finally was sentenced to jail for dispensing medicine without a license and being in the country without a visa? Remember mad Mike Hoare from South Africa?

Well, they may not all have been very nice, but at least they had a certain class. Errol Flynn and Clark Gable would not have delicately excused themselves to throw up when they saw them.

What, on the contrary, do we have here? Since the world is growing more and more ethnocentric, we will bypass the 10 Brits on trial and focus on the Americans.

This leaves us with Daniel Francis Gearheart of Kensington, Md., a dropout Vietnam veteran, and Gary Martin Acker of Sacramento. He flunked out of the Marine Corps and on his last job, which was getting paid piecework for putting up gutters, he ruined so many gutters he owed the contractor money. . . .

Certainly nobody in the press corps at the Hotel Trópico is drinking any toasts to these poor saps. But neither are most of them drinking any toasts to the Angolan Marxist regime here, which is charging them for crimes in February under a law written the first of May.

After the parade the other day, in which the happy marchers demanded death to the mercenaries, Information Minister Luis da Almeida held a press conference accusing the foreign press of pre-judging the trial. Maybe da Almeida and the government are correct in saying that imperialism itself is on trial, but if this was imperialism, one has to ask, "How did imperialism ever manage to function?" . . .

Mercenaries. Soldiers of fortune. Dogs of war have never been exactly the kind of clean-cut boys you'd want your daughter to marry. But there was at least a time in history when there were Janissaries and Mamelukes and Morgans and Steiners. And today we have a world where a great mercenary extravaganza is being waged on behalf of the Gearharts and Ackers. The losers. The dropout marines. The poor half-baked machos of an ever-more-tasteless world.

I don't know whether to cry for the poor Angolans or for us.

After five days in "revolutionary Angola," I was ready to leave: ready and more than eager. Travel in Africa was awful, and in order to go south to South Africa and on to Rhodesia I had to go through Mozambique—otherwise I would have to travel all the way back to Europe and all the way south again. But Mozambique, which is also in the post–Portuguese colonial period clutches of a "new Marxist" government, had not even responded to my visa request. When they did, months later, their message read, "You are not in our plans." By then how glad I was!

I was getting itchy. I wanted to leave. Now "the government" told me they had "lost" my passport. I was growing downright mad. Then that Monday, da Almeida eyed me sidewise in a strange manner and, after making the usual ritual observations about what an odd time it was to have an "economist" in Angola, said, "I think you are going to leave tonight."

We were all seated in our regular places on the roof at 11:00 P.M., having our usual good-natured and laughing evening, when the manager of the hotel himself came up to the table. "Miss Geyer, your passport is in my office," was all he said.

I was jubilant, and Lee insisted upon accompanying me to the lobby. "Mr. Griggs, why don't you stay here," the manager told him, and so Lee, always very much the gentleman, remained behind. Once in the manager's small office at the back of the lobby, I suddenly heard the door shut behind me, and I half-turned. Then I saw that I was trapped. Three very young, very ugly-looking black thugs stood in front of me. I immediately saw that one had my passport. I wasn't exactly frightened—at that moment—because I was so very surprised at all of this.

"The government has issued an order for your deportation," one of the thugs announced grimly. I remember feeling rather pleased and thinking to myself, "Well, now I'll be able to leave, at least."

260

But then they started to push me out the back door and it didn't all seem such a good idea after all.

At this all my Teutonic upbringing raced to the fore. "I have to pay my bill," I said, absurdly. This angered them—perhaps they thought I was making fun of them—and they growled and started to push me again. I did, however, in that moment, not miss noticing the flicker of a smile of hope pass over the manager's lips.

Once in the car, flanked on both sides by these thugs, it all seemed even less of a good idea. "Where are we going?" I asked, hearing my voice come across in Portuguese with an anxious ring. "*Al aeroporto,*" one answered. But we didn't go toward the airport at all, we went ninety miles an hour through the empty and hostile streets to the old Portuguese *cuartel* or prison on the sea. We crashed through the gate and slid to a halt in the courtyard amidst the ominous cluster of scabrous, 1876 buildings.

It was then that I lost my taste for the whole adventure, because they opened the trunk and there were my bags. So they had gone through the room while we were at dinner! That was ominous. And then I remembered that just before going to dinner, the door to my room had suddenly opened. A young black man had started to come in but had stopped, very surprised to see me there, and backed away. I had thought at the time that he had just been a room man.

Once inside the peeling old room, for some reason I gained heart. Once we were talking—once I could engage in the process and the exchange, even though I was under arrest—most of the fear left me. Fear, they tell me, is connected intimately with the unknown and once you know where you are, it takes its hesitant leave. That is to a great extent true. At least for me the truth of the matter was that I became very "interested" in the whole exchange.

The interrogator was a young mulatto man, very Portuguese looking and obviously well educated, and he kept honing in on only one subject. "We want you to tell us whom you have spoken to in Luanda," he kept repeating. "And you are not going to leave until you do."

Here, all of your journalistic and personal ethics—or lack of them

—come in: that and just common sense and decency, which is of course what ethics is. So there was no way in hell or heaven that *I* was going to tell them the names of the people I had spoken to. That is probably the first area of a journalist's responsibility. But as he kept hammering in at me, I found myself basically wondering only one thing: "Why?" Why did he care? Who was he? What did he represent? Why were they doing this? Actually it was much like watching myself in a suspense movie.

Gradually, from the tone and tenor of his questions, the reality began to dawn on me. Revolutionary Angola was in the hands of the MPLA, whose president was Agostinho Neto. But within his "government" there was also a man named Nito Alves, the minister of the interior, and Alves was known to be on the severe "outs" with Neto. It was an obvious supposition, at first, to think that they had picked me up because I had been interviewing their Cuban visitors, but that wasn't it at all. These were Nito Alves's men, and they wanted to know whom I had interviewed because I had written— and filed it from Luanda by public telex—that Alves was increasingly against Neto.

They thought someone in Luanda had given me the priceless information that they were in effect conspiring against Neto, which they were. The situation was even more dangerous than I thought. For I was not even in the hands of "the government," but in the hands of the Alves satellite group—and that group was indeed conspiring against the government. It was a ready-made "She-died-while-trying-to-escape" type of situation, or a "But-we-never-saw-her" type of situation. A few drops of sweat ran down my brow and I tried to brush them away. I didn't want my epitaph to read, "Shot By Mistake."

I had read about the Neto-Alves feud in *The Washington Post*, but my Chicago street sense told me absolutely not to say this to them. They would think I was making fun of them. So what to do? I don't recall thinking about this consciously, but suddenly I saw myself, as from afar, carrying out a little drama.

Gee Gee was hanging her head appropriately and saying, in Span-

ish and Portuguese, "I am truly very embarrassed to tell you this.
. . . I really don't quite know how to tell you this . . . This is very
embarrassing to me, but . . ." They were looking suddenly interested,
and Gee Gee, another person, was saying, "You know I live in
Washington and . . . well, you know how my government is . . . and,
before I left, the State Department took me aside and completely
brainwashed me . . . and they told me exactly what to say and
. . . I am truly embarrassed, but I didn't really see anyone in Luanda
as you know because you've been following me and all the information and everything I wrote came straight from the State Department."

And Gee Gee hung her head, so appropriately, so humbly, so
convincingly.

They hadn't been watching me, of course. And the State Department does not brainwash people. But subconsciously I knew quite
enough to feed their prejudices. Here were Marxists who blamed
everything on the United States and they were easily taken in by
anything that supported their prejudiced conclusions. In fact they
were delighted!

And as I continued to hang my head in, oh, such embarrassment,
the interrogator primly used me as an ideological example for the
young Angolan troops who were sitting around the little room on the
floor.

"You see," he said with barely concealed glee, "here you have,
right here before you, exactly an example of what we have been
telling you about. They say they are objective journalists and then
they come here, after having been brainwashed by the . . ." On and
on he went, with such pleasure, while Gee Gee hung her head—and
thus got safely out of Angola without compromising anyone except
"the State Department," confirming a myth that existed already in
their minds.

Kate Webb, the wonderful Aussie who was United Press's star
reporter in Vietnam and was captured herself for two weeks with the
Viet Cong, later told me that I had indulged in a little bit of Marxist
"self-criticism," thus utterly delighting and even soothing them.

Whatever, after his little ideological speech to the young soldiers the interrogator began (how insulting!) to lose interest in me and even in the names he had so fervently wanted. I could see his attention becoming frayed and moving elsewhere. He sighed heavily. "When we can get a car, I guess we can take you to the airport." He looked at his watch. It was 2:00 A.M. by then. "You can get the seven A.M. flight to Paris." Then he left—and the interesting part began.

For the first time in the week that I had been in Angola, I was able to talk to some of the real revolutionary soldiers. I sat there in that dank, Humphrey Bogart–style little room in the old Portuguese prison and talked for more than two hours with the little black soldiers, most of them only thirteen or fourteen years old. Their voices hung in the still night air as they told me, in their simple and true way that was so different from the ideologues', what the war in the jungle had been like. And I felt wonderfully like a journalist again, instead of a prisoner.

By 4:00 A.M. they came to get me and take me to the airport to be "deported," and I had one fleeting, admittedly unworthy and petty thought—a wave of resentment washed over me that I had already bought a ticket to Paris on my own, because had I not, they would have had to buy me one. On the other hand, I had bought it with black-market Angolan money and so the entire trip from Luanda to Paris and back down to South Africa cost me only three hundred dollars!

On the way to the airport, through the oppressive dankness of the dark early morning, the interrogator made one more try. In one column I had referred to a woman by the made-up name of "Marcella" and he insisted upon knowing who Marcella was. Actually she was a young Angolan housewife who worked at one of the embassies, but now a reckless mood came over me.

"All right," I said, now feigning a willingness to work with him, "I'll tell you." He looked around in the car, and even in the semi-darkness I could see his eyes light up. "You go out the front of the Presidente Hotel," I began, making up the apocryphal story as I went along, "and you walk around the park. At the first corner you go to the right for three blocks. There are a bunch of shacks there and you turn and walk about half a block. . . . On the left, in a little white house, you'll find Marcella. She's a Portuguese woman, about sixty years old, and she has six children. Her husband has gone back to Lisbon and she's very bitter about being left here. . . ."

It was all made up—and it was only after I was in Paris and mentioned it to a friend that he reminded me of a certain story by Albert Camus, in which a prisoner tells a similar story and the jailers go to the place—and find exactly the person. It sent a terrible chill up my spine.

At the airport they deposited me in a room with several young Angolans who were directing the few planes in and out. It was early morning still, and the air was cloying in the Angolan heat. Rats were scurrying about the floor, so I secured my feet on a chair. And all the while, as we sat there snoozing, from an old, high radio from the 1930s came the music of "Radio Cabo Verde," singing its way suddenly out of my childhood and into this strange African night with "You Belong to My Heart," which had been one of my mother's early favorites. At that moment I grasped the reality of the existentialist moment.

So, yes, I got to Paris, and I wrote in the lead of my long piece which was printed all over the world:

> PARIS—Most travelers do not come to Paris by way of Angola. I had not planned on it myself. But the new Angolan government decided I should see Paris in the spring—and I didn't see any realistic way to refuse them.

But "incidents" like these, having intruded into your life, do not just then leave you alone. They remain to haunt you and taunt you. What remained with me, I guess, was the kind of fear that comes from the fact that each time I was arrested or held, it happened so unexpectedly that it seemed to come out of nowhere. If you know you are being watched, or stalked, or sought out, then at least you can plan for it—it is another kind of "knowing." This incident in Angola, as well as the ordeal in Soviet Georgia, left me with the terrible feeling that anything can happen at any time and that anyone can turn without any warning into some kind of monster. It is something I have not got over and something I doubt I ever will quite get over.

Fear and courage are the web of our work and in our lives, yet ironically correspondents seldom talked about them. When they had taken me into that prison that night in Luanda, I took God aside with an arrogant little promise. "If I get out of here alive," I told Him confidingly, "I will never complain about anything again." It was a foolish promise (what can one expect when one tries to bribe God?), mostly because I assiduously kept trying to observe it long after it was at all appropriate to real life.

"Mystery alone is at the root of fear," Antoine de Saint-Exupéry said, and, as in many things, he was right. "Once a man has faced the unknown, the terror becomes the known." Dial one day read me the part where he says that in our strange business you become deeply close to your colleagues, and when you hear that one has died "out there," while performing your shared chores of life, often you cannot really believe that he is gone. "They land alone at scattered and remote airports, isolated from each other in the manner of sentinels between whom no words can be spoken," he wrote. "It needs the accident of journeyings to bring together here or there the dispersed members of this great professional family. Life may scatter us and keep us apart . . . but we know that our comrades are somewhere 'out there'—where, one can hardly say—silent, forgotten, but deeply faithful. And when our path crosses theirs, they greet us with such manifest joy, shake us so gaily by the shoulders! Then, bit by bit, nevertheless, it comes over us that we shall never again hear the laughter of our friend, that this one garden is forever locked against us. And at that moment begins our true mourning. . . ."

I saw great, and often quiet, heroism on the part of many of my friends: the ones, like the wonderful Joe Alex Morris of the *Los*

Angeles Times, and so many others who died on duty. When I saw *The New York Times's* Henry Tanner in Cairo just after he had been ambushed in Beirut and the others in the car killed, I remonstrated with him not to go back. His answer was simple and undramatic: "It's when you most want not to go that you most have to go." And he went.

There was another odd quirk to the whole conception of heroism, which was implicit in so many of the correspondents and which Freud called in effect "the overcoming of death": the correspondents got damned angry and enraged with the world, but they didn't get depressed, they didn't get pessimistic, they didn't in general feel it was all for nothing and that mankind was no good. Given the things they had to witness and live through, this always struck me as very strange indeed.

I finally came to the conclusion that it was mainly because the correspondents were "there." They were experiencing things firsthand. Life and history were not abstractions to them, and somehow nothing is so bad when experienced as it becomes when lived secondhand—and thus not experienced at all. Vietnam, in a strange sense, was much worse to people watching it on a distant and abstract TV screen than it was for those of us who were there. The solution to despair is "being there," in whatever work and profession; being in the intense and passionate center of things instead of on the dull, gray, alienated outskirts of life, experiencing things secondhand.

A footnote: I suppose that subconsciously in those days I sought out people who in themselves reflected this conflict—this chasm— this delineation—between thought and action, between observer and protagonist, between writer and actor—and I found a different courage on the two sides.

Perhaps the most dramatic person of this world—and the one that personally I found the most courageous and the most moving —was the famous Argentine writer, Jorge Luis Borges. I called him one day in Buenos Aires and to my delight he invited me for dinner. So it was that I found myself waiting at nine on the dot in the darkened hallway of his building in downtown Buenos Aires, and immediately the elevator door opened and he emerged. So frail. So old. So blind. He felt his way in his own darkness with his cane and spoke to me. It was as if his greeting were coming from quite another world, which it was. We walked around the corner to his restaurant, where he ate only rice and tea, he was so sick.

I felt as never before in my life that I was in the presence of true genius. As we sat for several hours at the table, what struck me was the way his soul shone through his frail body, as though it were a human lighthouse. The "beacon" was so clearly him, the body only an appendage, necessary, but so unendingly troublesome. But it was more than genius and greatness; it was, finally, that he was wholly and totally one; his personal decency and integrity perfectly matched his literary genius. I adored him.

He talked that night, as in so much of his writing, about the "macho" world he had been raised in (for he had been raised on the great estates of the Pampas, where *machismo* was the very essence of manly life). And yet he was so different, so very different.

"When I think of people in my family who had their throats cut or who were shot, I realize I'm leading a very tame kind of life," he said. "But really, I'm not, because after all they have just lived through these things and not felt them, whereas I'm living a very secluded life and am feeling them, which is another way of living them—and perhaps a deeper one, for all I know."

The other thing that impressed me so immensely was his utter lack of any feeling sorry for himself, although he had by then been blind for many years. This awful affliction that would have destroyed the powerful machos, a little man like Borges took with simple courage.

Indeed, the theme that shadow-boxes within and throughout Borges's life and work is this dialectic over types of courage. In his work you find men who become paralyzed but find unspeakable joy in it because now they are truly able to see the world, and there are men who fight to the death after some hoodlum's challenge only because a bartender recognizes them—once given a name, they exist and must take responsibility for that existence. There is his fantasy literature in which he describes in third person his own suicide, suicide being the means of moving from the inaction of the thinker to the action of the actor. Dreams, dreams, dreams. The only thing he was ever known to say publicly about his divorced wife was, "She did not dream."

The other thing that so impressed me about Borges was the extent to which his person was at one with his work and his work at one with his courage. For it was Borges, this little man, this nonfighter, and not the macho saloon fighters, who had become the symbol of resistance to tyranny against Perón, against Argentine Naziism, against communism. In him the literary quest became the moral quest, flesh first created the word and then the word was made flesh.

There was also a duality about Borges that on a more primitive scale I had felt in my own life: there was Borges, the private man, and "Borges," the literary character created by the former. It is to "Borges," the other man, that things happen, and Borges himself described the process in *The Aleph.* "Little by little," he wrote, "I have been surrendering everything to him, even though I have evidence of his stubborn habit of falsification. And so, my life is a running away, and I lose everything and everything is left to oblivion or to the other man. Which of us is writing this page, I don't know."

So by becoming "Borges," the literary creation, he had finally obliterated himself—which is what all great writers do. He made the most perfect marriage of art and life that I suspect we have in this generation. Art is—becomes—life. He is its breathtaking personification.

All the macho leaders with their power and women and wars— all the men that I had seen—controlled others, but they never could control themselves. Borges did. As his biographer, Emir Rodriguez Monegal, wrote of him:

> Borges lives forever inside a magic space, totally empty and gray in which time does not count. . . . Protected and isolated by his blindness, in the labyrinth built so solidly by his mother, Borges sits immo-

bile. He doesn't bother to turn on a light. Everything is quiet except his imagination. Inside his mind, the empty spaces are filled with stories of murder and wonder, with poems that encompass the whole world of cultures, with essays that subtly catalog the terrors and the painful delights of men. Old, blind, frail, Borges sits finally in the center of the labyrinth.

I still feel Borges's presence so deeply that I shall never forget him. "Borges," I wrote at the time," has realized the center we all seek, free and creating, while the macho saloon fighters who haunted his life turn out to be only fodder for his pen. He not only has overcome, he has won."

I suppose Borges fascinated me so because he personified and resolved the conflict between people who live things but do not know them, and those who know them and understand but do not live them. I was trying to do both, and in the very special way the first women journalists experienced—and knew—this world.

The Angolans were the predecessors of a new situation in the world—an ominous syndrome that I named the "Lebanon Syndrome"—which came to haunt us all. It came unnoticed at first, like an uninvited ghost that no one wanted to acknowledge, and finally it swept in like an overpowering wind of change.

I went back to Lebanon in the spring of 1977 for the first time since the fall of 1974. During those three years the country had been wracked by one of the most brutal civil wars in human history. Group against group, family against family, clan against clan, religion against religion. Lebanese against Palestinian, Moslem against Christian, Syrian against Lebanese . . . there seemed, after a short while, to be no more glue to put together the shattered pieces.

I wanted to know what the war had been like—really like, inside. "What is striking here," a member of the French architectural team that was then trying to redesign the city, said, standing in the midst of this perverse devastation and shaking his head, "is that it is as if there were a willful and deliberate effort to destroy." Professor

270

Umayam Yaktin, one of a group then studying the "Beirut phenomenon," told me, "Both sides wanted to kill innocent people. All the hospitals were hit—from all sides. I could go into Freud—that people are innately born with aggressive impulses—but I think it's more than that."

What we were really seeing was a totally new kind of war. Once the various sides saw that no group could win, at whatever cost, each side began to bomb its own people, to hit its own neighborhoods, with artillery, and to bomb theaters in which its own people were watching movies. I began to call it "pathological war"—military men like General Andrew Goodpaster told me he called it "irrational war."

Whichever title one wanted to give it, it was not really war, it was the breakdown of war. And it catapulted the foreign correspondent —as well as all the "in-between people" like diplomats, businessmen, missionaries, Red Cross people—into a new type of danger never before dreamed of in modern times. For in these dark new wars there were no borders. There were no recognized civilians—indeed the "civilians" became the deliberate targets. There were no respected neutrals, most definitely including journalists. Red Cross trucks and hospitals were deliberately hit instead of protected. Children fought and were killed, without second thoughts.

What had happened in the postcolonial period was the breakdown of the great powers' ability to keep peace in the world. With this had come total dismissal of the "rules of war" that had been built up over the centuries. "To die in Spain," I wrote, "was to be a hero to the generations. To die in Beirut was to die without benefit of clergy, embassy or even public note. To die in Beirut is, for a journalist, moreover, to die with your story on Page 13 and your death notice on Page 27."

What it meant for us foreign correspondents was that we had become the new targets. No longer did we have even psychological protection; indeed, we were sought out to be killed. Angola had only been a taste, a forewarning, the suggestion of a world changing before our eyes. What I started to see in the late seventies was a

271

world in which more and more pockets of the world were coming to be completely closed off to us for information and knowledge. And we, who used to see the world in bipolar terms of democracy or totalitarianism, are now faced with the new alternative and ultimate horror: permanent anarchy or permanent disintegration. For the modern journalist it was a new and particularly murderous development.

Meanwhile my own life was moving, developing, changing. In between my trips abroad, which now often extended to eight or nine months of the year, I would return to Chicago to lick my wounds in the bosom of my family. My dear mother, not really comprehending what I was doing but always loving and supporting me, of course wished I would get married and "settle down." So did the men I knew and cared for. It was difficult, for I felt at heart that I was disappointing everyone. My brother Glen was there, always supportive, always the wonderful rock for all of us, not to speak of our dear friend Bob Simpson, like a second brother to me, and all the rest of our Chicago friends.

My most serious love, among a good number in those years, was the famous *Chicago Daily News* Asia correspondent, Keyes Beech, and we came close to marrying. (Indeed, I met Keyes and fell in love with him just months before Paco escaped from Cuba. By then it was too late.) I even went for six months to Vietnam to be with him. But whenever I came close to "settling down," for that was what marriage meant to me, I fled; I couldn't give up what I had; perhaps marriage was too confining, too imprecise, too dangerous at some deep level. Whatever, I never resolved my conflict over my love of my work and my love of the potential of marriage and children.

And that was certainly not surprising! How hard it must be for younger women today to understand our generation, raised in the assurance that sex was dirty, that evil was incarnate in us but also (somewhere) purity; that men must be envied but also controlled and used. If we "fell," there was, believe me, no way to rise again. To tempt, to tantalize, to flirt, to seduce with our eyes, to coquette

—all of that was all right, but it must be within bounds of chastity. For once you "gave yourself," you had lost control of the situation and irrevocably so. There is no going back on a deflowering, no matter what the French and Japanese say. You were suspended then between being the victim and being evil. Everything was over. You had made your first slip and your last slip. Relations between men and women, therefore, were those of constant tension, and constant friction, as relations between two enemies, for that is what we were; men were the robbers who would steal not only our virginity but, because of the absolute sovereignty of that virginity, our very futures and our very souls.

On the other hand, there was one advantage to the setup: everything was very clear.

In my curious lifetime I went from that beginning, when men were insecure because women could turn them down, to a point where women were supposed to advance toward men and take the consequences; from a point where sleeping with someone was something you committed suicide over (if he would not marry you or left you pregnant) to a point where you were not even expected to expect a phone call afterwards; from the point where women like me were so considered misfits and freaks (and everyone kept wondering when we were "ever going to settle down" or who would have us) to a point where we became extremely fashionable and were ironically and incongruously called "role models"; to the third point which is where we are now, where women are trying desperately to have everything. It is quite a wonder that we were not all more daffy than we clearly are.

Indeed, to carry it to another plane, it is typified in the words of my dear friend, Ernie Weatherall, a fine foreign correspondent, who was confronted by some little snake in the grass who insisted that, because of my work, I was probably "not good in bed."

Ernie rose to the occasion as the man he is and defended me soundly. "She is *too* good in bed," he said. Then later he asked me in bewilderment, "Before, I was supposed to say you were a virgin. Where are we?"

But if my generation—my often tormented generation—was anything, we were also rather special. For we were the women in between, haunted by the old devils, by the "evil" of sexuality within ourselves, lured by men and determined not to betray our intellects. So it was that we saw more, knew more, felt more, suffered more, had greater joys and greater tribulations and darker disappointments. We had old morality and new female ethics.

But my generation had also an obstinate pride in being "new women." A dear friend became pregnant by a European in a love affair. She knew that if she told him she was pregnant, he would marry her. But she could not. Unlike the women who came before us, we were too proud and too honorable to trick men or, more, to trick ourselves by using our bodies in this time-hallowed manner. We were the women who, in our very selves, as though we were the laboratory of our times, represented the great drama of the changes in women's lives. We were trying to raise ourselves above the "realm of necessity" of children and caring for home and hearth and onto the "realm of freedom," in which the independent will and intellect and soul could operate. It was very, very difficult, and what it took out of us—and of me—is more than I can measure. But at least we were no longer women dominated totally by the rolls of the dice. We suffered the pains and the glories, but our heroism is that no other generation will know it exactly the way we did.

Why, then, did I never marry? You see, all the first part of my life I fooled myself. I pretended, oh, with great ability and agility— over and over that, yes, I certainly did want to get married. I usually put it in the future tense, which should have been a clue. And then I wanted, yes, to have children, so long as they looked just like me and wanted to be foreign correspondents. I usually put that in the future tense, too, which should have been another clue. And then . . . each time I went through agonies until the situation was finally resolved with my going "free" and taking off for points East of Suez.

In part, to be fair to myself, it was because of the inequalities of the basic independent/dependent setup between men and women.

This is certainly no fantasy and this exists full-blown and not really very much changed, to this very day. I saw every love relationship in terms of my being totally absorbed and even destroyed by the relationship. I would cease to exist; it was really that simple. And what had been utterly crucial to me in the entirety and scope of my life—the exercise of sovereignty and spirit—would be exactly what I could never again enjoy. I had seen no women, tied, who did; and I still see very few. But there were always a lot of men in my life, and I related to them on many levels. I could never treat men one-dimensionally, any more than I expected or wanted them to treat me in that way. My deep relationships had to be primarily emotional: passionately so. Confounding all my mother's generation's warnings, I have more interesting and loving men in my life now than when I was twenty-three—the cutoff age after which they solemnly assured me no man would ever again want me! And, living your own life as a woman and not the life others set out and contoured for you, you find you have men who are sometimes lover-colleague, or colleague-mentor, or lover-student, or, well, many things that were not "supposed to happen." But one thing was absolutely crucial for me: I had to care about them deeply, on many levels. No relationships were superficial or exploitative.

I was also trying to figure out how to live on other levels, and the enormous tragedies and setbacks in the world sometimes drove me to despair. Once when I was confused about where we were going and how ideologically to stand, my old friend, Father Roger Vekemans, the Jesuit priest from Chile, wrote to me. "Ethically, I confess not even to see the problem. No fight against the Right has driven me to the Left and no fight against the Left will drive me to the Right. Once and for all I have chosen the extreme center and whatever storm is coming, I shall stand fast at any price. It is not a matter of balance; it's a matter of conviction. The battle against both extremes at the same time may be hopeless. I am aware that the center is not holding. Still I will keep on fighting. I am responsible for my fight, not for the outcome!" That is exactly the way I felt —"I am responsible for *my* fight. . . ."

*   *   *

Vietnam was the one area I never felt I mastered—but, then, nobody else really did. But I did uncover some interesting changes and trends. I did a series on the U.S. army called "The GI Who Wants to Know Why," which really came far before others understood the changes in the U.S. soldier, who was becoming a far more autonomous individual. And occasionally I would take short trips around Asia. My very favorite place was Phnom Penh, when Cambodia was still beautiful, that graceful city of water festivals and French culture. Indeed, at the end of 1967, I was able to get in at a time when Prince Sihanouk had thrown all the Western correspondents out. Being new and unknown in Southeast Asia, I was not on his "list."

I started making the rounds: everyone from Wilfred Burchett, an Australian communist journalist who could get you into Hanoi if he wanted, to our embassy, to Charles Meyer, a French economist who had been very close to Sihanouk.

I met Meyer (pronounced Mey-YEAH) in his graceful old French mansion in Phnom Penh and we chatted for a long time about the economy. Then I asked him how I could get to the Prince.

His eyes opened theatrically wide. "But, mademoiselle," he said, "you know he will not see any American journalists. If he sees you, he will surely throw you out."

"I know," I said calmly. It was an enticing idea.

What I did not know at the time was the fact that Meyer was on the outs with Sihanouk. Meyer was a Maoist, and Sihanouk was, despite our shabby American intelligence, violently anti-Communist. Meyer wanted to get even with the Prince by playing a small joke on him and if the joke was me, well, so be it!

"He is up at Angkor Wat," Meyer told me dryly, "making another movie." I knew already that the Prince, with his beautiful wife, Princess Monica, made his own movies. Being a confident man, Sihanouk starred in them, directed them, produced them, and wrote the music for them. "He likes very much American tourists, and if you go up and tell him you are an American tourist, he will surely

276

see you." When I left him, Meyer had the touch of an amused smile on his lips.

That night at the Hotel Royale, now a hotel of ghosts but then one of the most luxuriantly lovely hotels in Asia, I met (I think by accident) a fascinating man, Kurt Fuerrer, now known throughout Asia and a man whose sagacity is respected by spy author Le Carré. Kurt, a husky, utterly charming man, was a Swiss ship's captain, as unlikely as that may seem. To this day I do not know exactly what Kurt was doing, but he knew more about Cambodia than practically anyone I knew. Over dinner, when I told him I was going up to Angkor to pique the Prince, he asked if he might go with me. I immediately said yes.

The next morning Kurt and I took off for Angkor Wat and its gorgeous Khmer ruins and checked into one of those lovely motels that Sihanouk had built in the jungles. Soon we were riding through a sun-stroked jungle in one of those open carts that used to grace this land. We ran into some of the Prince's soldiers near a river where His Highness was bathing, and Kurt helped immensely by talking to them in French. Yes, Sihanouk would see us the next morning at nine o'clock. I was delighted.

Knowing what has happened to Cambodia today, I find it odd to think back on those days. Kurt and I sat that evening in the exquisite bar and restaurant of the motel, talking, laughing, lingering into the most mellow of evenings. The lost Cambodia of another age.

And, indeed, the next morning, we were duly ushered into the Prince's royal presence. I will never forget the scene. Sihanouk, a medium-sized, pudgy man with large, quizzical eyes, was standing as regally as a short pudgy man could stand in front of the great, whispering trees of the enchanted forest of Angkor Wat. He was the grace of Southeast Asia incarnate. And as we talked for twenty-five minutes, he revealed to me many things he had never said before. He admitted to me, for instance, that there were indeed thirty-five thousand Viet Cong troops in Cambodia but that Cambodia was a small country with a small army and "What am I to do?"

But back in Saigon it was never forgiven that Sihanouk did not try to expel the Viet Cong. And when we did try, we brought on the horrible Khmer Rouge communist regime that wreaked the terrors of the grave upon that quiet, that perfect land. These were the sins of Keyes's generation.

Kurt and I drove back to Phnom Penh by car, observing the beautiful, quiet, incredibly prosperous Cambodian countryside. Once the terror started I was always to think of that perfect land and how unnecessary "revolution" was there. But Sihanouk always knew it would come. When I left Cambodia that time I thought he would never permit me to return, since I had lied to him. On the contrary. He liked the article so much that within two weeks he sent me a cable. "Permit me to congratulate you for your objectivity and to compliment you for your talent. With my respectful sentiments, Norodom Sihanouk, chief of state, Cambodia." I always felt he had known who I was.

But Sihanouk knew very well what was coming to his doomed land. Once, when a group of us met him later during a festival in the north at Battambang, he was showing us through the kind of motel he had learned to love and emulate in the States and he suddenly put his champagne glass down and said without emotion, "But soon we all will die."

Another time on that trip Sihanouk was reviewing a cadre of blue-uniformed young people from a factory. He was sitting—we of the press corps behind him—on a palatial stand, with Oriental carpets under him and a fluted tent of many colors over him. With his special, wry, bemused charm, every once in a while he would turn around and say something humorous to us.

At one point he gave some command in Khmer ostentatiously to the young workers and they immediately broke out into a joyous dance.

Sihanouk turned around and said to me with a wink, "I told them to dance."

How could this joyful, happy, rich kingdom go down into the savagery of the Khmer Rouge? How could this kindly people be brought down by a brutal regime that killed four million of its seven million people, mostly with axes? It is a question I have pondered many times in my darkest moments; it is a question that still has only a few answers.

Certainly the refusal of the U.S. to support Sihanouk—indeed, our officials in Saigon were always trying to think up ways to bring him down because he was so independent—contributed to the unspeakable tragedy. Certainly the mixture of French Marxist training and Khmer tradition was lethal to the minds of the Khmer Rouge: something, interestingly enough, that Sihanouk foresaw when he (too late) stopped Cambodian students from going to Paris. And, certainly, we had underestimated the sheer cruelty within the Khmer history and tradition. We had not yet learned how a new heretical movement, like the Khmer Rouge and others, takes on these particularly bestial qualities.

What we saw with them are elements we should watch elsewhere. Among the warning signals were the fact that after the Khmer Rouge took over, they did not use names. Anonymity in revolutionary movements is always extremely dangerous, for it designates a special madness and unwillingness to take responsibility for your deeds. These were movements which wanted to obliterate the past, to destroy identities, to build new classes, *to destroy* culture. We must, in the world now and in the world to come, watch for their deadly signs, because they are everywhere.

The world moved on. My involvement with Keyes moved on. I began to write books, *The New Latins, The New 100 Years War, The Young Russians*, but I did them like I had done everything: by myself, with no one to advise me or tell me how to write a book. There were not only no role models for women, there was precious little advice from anybody. Perhaps it gave us a freshness. We were cracking the world anew with each step. I also began to speak publicly, and it took a long, long time before I could do it without the most abject terror. People perhaps find odd or even unbelievable this contradiction: courage overseas, persistence in interviewing world leaders for instance, and shyness approaching breakdown at

279

home. Certainly I found some special freedom, as a woman and as a human being, in cultures other than my own beloved one.

And as I was changing and developing, so was the world of journalism changing and developing. In Vietnam particularly, we journalists stopped being simply the conveyors of the announcements from the institutions of society that we had been in my early days working in Chicago—and we became what I have called the "arbiters of truth." So many official Americans lied that it was left to *us* to decide what was true and what was not. We became moralists—and many of us mistook our relative judgment for absolute moralism. "New Journalism" reporters began to judge and criticize, to take it upon themselves to reform, if not the world, at least their own evil country. These same saw goodness everywhere, except in the United States.

Not surprisingly, people within the institutions of our society—in particular, the military, but also the politicians and the more conservative citizens—came to feel these particular journalists were against them.

I had never really been a moralist about Vietnam. Keyes truly believed that Vietnam was a kind of moral crusade, and he wholly ignored the intrinsic quality of the country, the government, the politics, the fighting. I, on the other hand, had great concern about all those intrinsic qualities, seeing that without them there could be no workable denouement. At the same time, I saw Vietnam as a strategic absurdity—and when you do things that are unpragmatic, unwinnable, unstrategic, then really evil consequences follow. Strangely enough, self-interest is always and everywhere the most accurate and even moral measure to use.

But now the next generation of journalists came to feel that they had the duty and the right to make every most astonishing judgment, to change society through their writings, not merely to report it or reflect it but to redeem it. They became very dangerous—and I am barely exaggerating when I say that they nearly destroyed the truth in journalism in the United States.

After I returned from my short stays in Vietnam, I was often

280

invited to the war colleges—Army, Navy, and Air Force—to day-long seminars and conferences on the media-military confrontations brought on by the Vietnam War. And they were confrontations indeed. One I recall particularly. It was in the spring of 1977, up at the Navy War College at Newport, Rhode Island, a lovely spot swept by the cool Atlantic waters.

Seymour Hersh, the hotshot investigative reporter in the States at the time, got up and said some interesting things. "National security secrets?" he said. "That's where it is. In all my stories I violate national security—I'm not worried about it. I don't care. I'm a 'bad news' guy. The only qualification to this is common sense. We're entitled to publicize any secret we can get—and keep. The right to call it—without any qualifications whatsoever—that's ours."

He went on. "My definition of national security has changed a lot," he said, here so perfectly mirroring the sixties reporter's feelings and morality. "I'm not sure it doesn't have a lot more to do with better air and water and ethics for corporate executives than military problems." Then: "I did hate the Vietnam War; it was an evil." And: "We're such a big country, we can afford the diversity." And: "I publish something and—surprise!—the next day the Russians still haven't taken San Francisco."

And then the military, some quite rational and some not at all rational and some really quite crazy, put to him the classic question that for them determines loyalty to country: Would he print the metaphorical story about his country's troopship sailing in time of war?

Hersh had not the slightest hesitation. He hesitated not a whit.

"Would I write the story about the troopship sailing?" he repeated. "Yes, I would. Let it sail some other day. Does that make me less of an American? I'd worry more about my opposition—about what *The Washington Post* would have—than national security."

I was horrified by Hersh's speech. Since I was on the ensuing panel, I commented on it. "What Mr. Hersh is doing," I said, "is exactly what he criticized the U.S. military for doing during Vietnam. He is 'punching his own ticket.' " I went on to say that the

281

American press could not consider itself an amoral force, outside of society, with no responsibility or loyalty to the rest of society—or that society would eventually exclude it. I said that we cannot be a surrogate for society and an adversary to it.

What was surprising was the reaction of the officers that night. We all met at a lively little party at the admiral's house, and I was now further stunned. The military were not at all angry with Hersh, but they were completely miffed at *me*. At first I could not understand what was going on. Then it hit me: Hersh they could understand. Hersh fulfilled all their angry expectations of us in the press. My sense of complexity and ambiguity confused and angered them because I made them think something else about journalists!

The new challenges to the foreign correspondent did not end there. What to me, when I started in 1964, had seemed such an exciting and romantic life—dangerous, yes, but dangerous in a way that was comprehensible and predictable—now had become something of immense complexities. Not only were there the new-type dangers of an Angola and a Beirut but there were countries that virtually wanted to close down the world to us.

In the mid-seventies, for instance, some Third World countries, backed strenuously by the Soviet bloc, started the formation of a New Information Order under UNESCO. It began simply enough, with some Third World countries feeling genuinely and strongly that the Western press, in particular the news agencies like Associated Press and Reuter's, which saturated the news world, were not giving enough attention to Third World problems and development. To some degree this was true, and in the beginning Western publishers responded positively with offers to back up, even financially, the formation of Third World news networks.

Then as the Soviets got their hands deeper into it, it became a real down-the-line fight over the free press in the world. Now, in this new alliance of the Soviets and the Third World dictators, foreign correspondents could even be "licensed" by UNESCO—and punished by them if they did not write the "right things." Soon all transmission of news and ideas was to be controlled, even computer information from companies to their home offices and military satellites. These developments were encouraged by the Soviet bloc, anxious to weaken the workings of the Western free press in the world, and by certain bloody dictatorships eager to keep out a press they did not want snooping around.

In the late seventies I began a new part of my career—speaking on American journalism for the U.S. government's International Communication Agency (the former U.S. Information Service), which sends journalists on trips to various countries to speak to the journalists there. It is a fine program, very straight and very sound —and since you are paid seventy-five dollars a day for marathon speeches, interviews, and meetings, no one can accuse you of being in it "for the money."

My first trip for ICA was in the fall of 1979, when I went to four countries in Africa, including two of the original New Information Order countries, and learned a great deal. In Nigeria, whose government had most pushed it, I sat every night for long talks with Nigerian journalists. I kept bringing up the New Information Order —only to blank stares. Indeed, I could not even get them to talk to me about it.

Finally one prominent editor told me, as the others nodded, "We are not interested in that. But can't you help us get more freedom, can't you help us pressure our government to give us visas for the States so we can cover other countries?"

An even more interesting lesson in the new attempts to control the international press on the behalf of the socialist bloc and the worst dictatorships came a few weeks later in Tanzania, another of the fosterers of the New Information Order.

Tanzania, which faces the dramatically azure Indian Ocean on the southeast coast of Africa, where the Arab slave-traders used to ply their doomed human wares between Zanzibar and the Sahara, gained its independence in 1961. But by the time I was there almost two decades later, it had only marched resolutely backward. Not only were the poor Tanzanians far worse off than they had been in 1961, but the mammoth amounts of international aid that had been poured into Tanzania from well-meaning folks like the Finns and the Swedes had only helped the country not to progress—because it made Tanzanians rely on outside help.

One day during my week there I was sitting with the editors of Shihata, the official government news agency, and they were as usual berating me for excesses, real and imagined, in the American press. I was actually only half-listening—listlessness can serve many purposes—as they squabbled on, when suddenly for no reason I decided to change the dull subject and asked:

"Tell me about your coverage of Uganda."

Since the Tanzanian government had just sent thirty thousand Tanzanian troops into Uganda to overthrow the murderous Idi Amin (an event I heartily applauded), it seemed an obvious question to ask. But to my surprise and then to my curiosity, the five men sat there without speaking.

"But you did cover the Ugandan war, didn't you?" I asked, in total innocence.

"You know, the military nowhere in the world likes journalists," the director of Shihata finally answered, with all the indirection of a cobra in heat.

"That's very true," I replied agreeably. "It was the same in Vietnam."

"Well, we did send reporters in," the editor went on, brightening suddenly, perhaps because I had mentioned Vietnam. "But the generals didn't like them and they made scouts of the reporters."

"Scouts! Of the reporters!" I was aghast. "Did they survive?"

"Oh, yes, yes, they did," he went on. "And finally we did cover it."

"When?"

"About five weeks after it started," he answered.

"Five weeks? For five weeks there was nothing?" They all nodded, a bit chagrined. "But why?"

Now the editor drew himself up. "Why, we might have lost," he said. I nodded.

284

"That was what our generals told us in Vietnam," I said with a dryness that escaped their notice.

Then I added, "But didn't your readers notice that you weren't, ummm, covering the war?"

He smiled. "Oh, yes, they would come to us and say, 'There are thirty thousand Tanzanians in Uganda. You journalists must be the only people in the country who do not know they are there.' "

Right there you had the problem—the problem that all of us everywhere were trying to come to grips with—and the operative truth. You had to have press freedom, not for some esoteric reason but because it was the only way to keep the compact between the people and the government, the only way to keep the basic agreements of society, relatively truthful. It was the new challenges to this compact and to this faith that we were beginning to see across the developing world.

XV.

Covering the Khomeinis and Their Dark Worlds

"Saints should always be judged guilty until
they are proved innocent."
—GEORGE ORWELL

When a friend suggested in December 1978 that I try to interview the Ayatollah Khomeini as I was going through Paris, my prescient answer was, "I don't think he'll really turn out to be anybody."

Still, I did telephone, first Reuter's News Agency in Paris to get Khomeini's phone number in Neauphle le Château. Then I called there and talked for about five minutes to Ibrahim Yazdi, later to become foreign minister. Yes, Khomeini would see me that Thursday at 11:00 A.M.—but I must telephone in my questions the next day. When I did, I got my first taste of the strange mixture of modern and ancient elements, and sheer cunning that was Khomeini. I read the questions, all very general, to Yazdi and he said, "Fine, we have them recorded and we'll have them translated by the time you get here." Nobody had said anything beforehand about "recording"—funny, I thought.

When I arrived that cold and snowy day, tired and fretful from the overnight plane ride, I was conservatively dressed. I had a long loose dress on, high black boots, and a long fur coat. Nevertheless a young Persian, smiling, came toward me with an ugly scarf which he dutifully wrapped around my head so that only my eyes were showing. Like all women, I was far too enticing to be allowed to run about uncovered.

On the walls was one message repeated over and over: THE AYATOLLAH HAS NO SPOKESMAN. They did not want the members of the press, who were pouring out here to see the ayatollah, to accept the word of anybody else. In actuality what he was saying day by day and hour by hour was so confusing and so contradictory that it was questionable whether they needed this additional protection.

Soon Yazdi led me across the road, lined with Persians of every possible religious gown and hat *and* filled with French police watching the dark gowns and hats, which always seemed to be marching in proclamatory processions, to a small, wooden French worker's summer cottage. There lived the ayatollah: in a tiny room emptied of furniture whose walls were covered still with the frowsy, flowered wallpaper of the limpid French bourgeoisie. Yazdi and I sat quietly, crouched in what must be the outer limits of discomfort on the floor.

After a few minutes "in" swept the Ayatollah Khomeini—actually he floated in. He was a massive presence then, a huge black moth of a man, and when he sat down, he floated to the ground like a specter. His round white ayatollah's hat hovered precariously atop his head like an obstinate halo, but the thing that I will always remember were the eyes. For the hour and a half that we spent with him, his eyes never rested on either of us—not on Yazdi and certainly not on me, the dangerous female. Utterly black and sinister, those eyes stared between and beyond us. If we existed at all to him, it was surely as lower creatures who could never understand the vision he alone could see.

I had deliberately, as usual, made the questions quite general. Did he consider this a "holy war"?

"Yes," the answer came back through the Persian interpreter, "we consider this a holy war—and by that we mean for the sake of Islam and for the sake of God and for the liberation of our own people."

How strange, I thought to myself, an ancient cry for a "holy war" going out from this snowy little French town, with its mewing cows outside and its faded wallpaper!

287

And the Marxists in the revolution? "Our aims and goals are different from those of Communists and Marxists," he said. "Our movement is based on Islam and monotheism, and they are against both of them. Thus there is no cooperation and compatibility between our movement and theirs." And all the while the strange, dark, expressionless eyes stared between us—and far, far beyond us.

He talked of an Islamic state that is a republic which "relies on the general vote of the public, neither capitalist nor socialist." He believed there were enough Iranian "experts" in exile to run a modern, industrialized state "in an Islamic way." When I mentioned Saudi Arabia or Libya, even in his impassive manner he was able to show an utter disdain.

And so it went on, for more than an hour, while I sat there covered over like some armchair during spring house painting. And when the time came, Khomeini just rose, his eyes still showing no emotion whatsoever, and . . . floated out.

Interviews with Khomeini were certainly interesting, but hardly conclusive. The very next week after this call for a Moslem "holy war," he told Marvin Zonis, the fine Iranian specialist at the University of Chicago, that "No Moslem would kill another Moslem. The people doing the shooting in Iran are one thousand Israelis imported by the shah." So it went; every interview totally contradicted the other, something the Persians cleverly call "dissimulation."

Afterward we wandered back across the road, and while Yazdi translated the answers from Persian for me, I strolled (my enticing limbs and raging beauty still covered up) about the house. I was flabbergasted. Every room looked as though it had been set up for a moon shot. Electronic gear of every conceivable sort lined the walls. When I returned to Yazdi, I asked him what it was all about.

"This is the way we operate," he told me. "When the ayatollah wants to send a message to Iran, we make twelve recordings of it. Then we put those on the telephones to different parts of Iran. There they are rerecorded onto cassettes and boys on Hondas carry them all over the country."

It was staggering. I had seen, I thought, every kind of revolution

—but never had I seen this very new, very modern phenomenon of using the modern technology at the service of such an ancient faith. It was a long time and a long way from the original countryside guerrillas in the mountains of Guatemala: one of many strange voyages I was to see and make in my lifetime of observing revolutions and revolutionaries without, while all the time going through my own woman's revolution within.

I had to ask myself, as honestly as I could, whether being a woman —and being all bundled up by them, for my own protection, bothered me. I didn't like it, but it really didn't upset me unduly; after all *I* had the power to interpret *them* to the world, didn't I? What was an old rag compared to that? Had I been one of *their* women, a woman forced to live out her life under a black veil, I would have either rebelled totally or gone stark raving mad. But then, I asked myself, how to explain the Iranian women who, first as a mark of support for the revolution, and later for other reasons, themselves *adopted* the chador?

(Actually, as odd as that was, it was at that time also understandable. The women were taking up the sanctuary of the black robe as a defense of their personality, in the same—yet apparently contrary —manner as Western women were disrobing in defense of their personality. It is strange, but true.)

My position as an outsider—as a Western woman—was intensely clear to me. And yet I knew that men would talk to me, even (or perhaps more so) in places like the Middle East; I would remain "woman," the listener, the absorber, the understander, the unifier of elements. How lucky to be able, through journalism and writing, precisely to use those elements that are disadvantages for other women as an advantage in my work.

Indeed the first time I visited Saudi Arabia, in 1973, I ran head-on into Moslem attitudes toward women in a classically dramatic way. I had a fine guide, a good man who was both smart and trying very, very hard to be honorable and fair. I knew I was somewhat of a problem for him, because they simply were not used to foreign women journalists. However, he was very tolerant and took me

289

anyplace I asked, and the only time he allowed himself to show a distinct displeasure was when I insisted upon buying some Bedouin silver—he waited outside the little shop, his back turned to me, because he could not sustain the idea that a Western "lady" would buy cheap country silver—instead of "ladies' " gold.

Then, since the Friday holiday was coming, he invited me to go with him, his wife, and their little daughter out to "the creek," which is a great, meandering arm of the Red Sea that forms a nice "swimming hole" for Jedda. I was delighted—it was a most unusual invitation.

Their house was a small one, protected by large fences, where no one could see us. So we—he and I, for his wife was pregnant—changed into swimsuits and walked out to the pier. The moment we emerged from changing clothes, I felt the most terrible shame sweeping over me. Ahmed himself had turned several shades of red. He did not—could not—look at me. I stared straight ahead, feeling that I was indeed (as I, too, had been raised to believe, though more subtly) the very incarnation of evil. Eve's supposed grave is in a wild field in downtown Jedda, so one might argue obscurely that it was the propinquity of the past evil that also was affecting me.

We both got quickly into the water, where I swam eagerly up and down, but I shall never forget those feelings. The shame that society cast on my body and thus soul had overtaken both of us, a man of goodwill and a woman of goodwill—but it had not destroyed our innocent attempt to ignore it. All my professional life I have deeply appreciated and revered people—men and women—who are trying honorably and sensitively to live out in their own brief existences, and despite the deep conflicts imposed by their pasts, the great epic changes of our times.

What we are talking about—in all of this—is a basic way of looking at societies, and then of analyzing them, and finally of writing about them. It is a process that proceeds on several levels, until it goes from your usual surface "reporting" of a society to a deep and mysterious and totally penetrating psychological portraying of it. It is a new kind of "reporting" and, to my mind and soul, an absolutely crucial one. But let me put it into practical form, with practical questions. Let me start again with Iran, because it became such a crucial example of the madnesses of nations in our time.

Was Iran difficult to cover and understand? No. When I started to cover Iran in 1968, basically I asked the same questions you would ask in Chicago: Who are his enemies? Would they kill him? The mullahs, you say? What do they want? What would they pay for it? Where do they get the money? Only . . . I wasn't talking about Richard J. Daley, I was talking about the shahanshah of Iran—and Ruhollah Khomeini.

Iran is in Central Asia, and for centuries before our beautiful little democratic experiment ever was dreamed of, Mongols, Tatars, Chinese, Persians, Medes, Assyrians, and all those other Central Asian folk had been overrunning whatever and whenever the slightest spirit moved them. Genocide there was not a fun word for intermissions at rock festivals—this is where it really happened, as whole peoples disappeared from the face of the earth, leaving skeletal cities as mute reminders of whole civilizations that once were. This has been the single most brutal and convulsive part of the world throughout history, and it seemed clear to me that they weren't going to change just because some Rousseauian Americans thought people were basically good.

By reading Persian history you could know that because of all the invasions, the Persians were paranoically afraid of strangers—and hostile toward them. You would see that taking hostages was their idea of a release of national tensions: their *Oktoberfest,* only they did it in November, without alcohol. You would have been able easily to predict that bringing eighty thousand Persian students to the United States, where they felt miserably inferior and alone and out of place, would only bring about, at the right time, a disastrous countereffect. And you would have known that all throughout modern Persian history, the Shi'ite clergy took the lead again and again against all and any outside invaders.

But on top of all that there was something even more curious that

291

was generally missed. R. K. Ramazani, the fine Iranian-born scholar at the University of Virginia, pointed it out to me after the hostages were taken, when I was interviewing him on *Meet the Press.* "What they have done is so very odd," he told me. "They are pretending to be against us because we have not supported their democracy. But there is absolutely no tradition of democracy in Persia. They got this precisely from the United States. They are rebelling against us for not supporting there what *we* believe in."

And even beyond this bizarre reasoning, you had to see what I had seen that December-cold, snowy morning in Neauphle le Château: the eerie juxtaposition of these ancient beliefs and modern technology. Yes, indeed, the ancient imam, Khomeini, learned one might say overnight—as fast as the overnights of the Parisian playboys—to use "Satan's Sonys," not to speak of the French telephone system, to try to carry his people back fourteen hundred years.

But it also seemed to me that what we were seeing in Iran was also something we were seeing in one form or another all over. I tried to analyze in a column as early as 1977 the roots of these seemingly incongruous new forces:

WE STILL CAN'T GO HOME AGAIN

LONDON—With very few people noticing it, key groups of people in important countries are psychologically and culturally trying to "go home."

It now seems devilishly clear that one of the political problems of today (and of the next 10 years) is how to deal with these masses of people who are determined to return to old cultural, political and religious forms.

In Israel, for instance, I was confused for a long time about the Gush Emunim, the ultra-orthodox who are determinedly settling on Arab lands they consider theirs because of ancient boundaries.

It seemed incredible that the government would allow a small and unrepresentative group to poison peace possibilities. A well-off businessman with very liberal views who had been raised on a kibbutz explained it to me.

"They remind us of what we were, so even we liberals rather yearn for them," he said. "Clean, wholesome, sure."

Much the same thing has been going on in Egypt, where, in frustration over the failures of both socialism and capitalism, young people in masses have been returning to traditional Islam. The key to the movement, which was one element behind the recent anti-Sadat riots, is a return to unity—in this case, the ancient unity of Islam.

In Africa, it is a renascent tribalism, and the retreat to tribalism is not, interestingly enough, occurring only among African blacks.

Leroy Phillips, a young Jamaican-born black social worker in the London ghetto, told me recently that black power and "soul" had been superseded on a large scale by a "back to the roots" movement that has young black people meeting in basement study groups to reconstitute their tribal heritage.

The numbers of similar, emotionally irredentist situations are endless, ethnicity in the United States, the American Indian movement, Slavicism in the Soviet Union, the Palestinians' passion for "The Return."

But what does all of this really mean? Does it have any great importance?

Importance it certainly does have. The Palestinians could start a world war: the Gush Emunim could stop Israel from making peace: tribalism could cause untold suffering: ethnicity in the United States or in Russia could enormously weaken the countries' unity.

But, does it make any sense? Clearly, it does not. The transcendental experience, the "kick," is basically the same in all of them—frustrated or psychically wounded by the demands of the modern world, all would like to "go home again," to go back to a time when life was sure and simple and encompassable.

Science and technology and ideologies are without soul. None of them turns out to be ultimately satisfying for everybody. If, in addition, as in Egypt and Africa, they don't even bring material well-being, then why bear them? . . .

[But] the world has not stood still, even if . . . imaginations and memories have. What [these people] are suffering and struggling for is something that no longer exists—they can only come back to the future.

293

This is typical of the situation everywhere. What is needed is not impossible attempts to "go home," but attempts to develop post–"Era of Certainty" goals and reasons for living. What is needed is a combination of inner moral certainty and an outer sense of the relativism of an interdependent world.

What I am saying is that these new situations—these Irans and the Jonestowns and the Cambodias and the brainwashing and the national psychoses—pose levels of deep questioning for everyone, but particularly for the journalist. How do we journalists deal with these questions that are basically questions of national psychology, of pathology, of neurotic leadership? How can we interpret them in normal language, when they do not respond to normal language? How in the most practical terms can we apply a knowledge of cultural differences and relativeness within our work, incorporating that into our writings? First of all, we prepare our internal selves to understand.

One particular story I did prepared me, in a very basic and very different way, for reporting and understanding the depths and breadths of the new pathologies of the world that we were being asked to report.

All through the sixties, when I was in and out of Latin America regularly, the Galapagos Islands off Ecuador beckoned to me with a strange siren spell. These were the islands—barren, volcanic, with trees with limbs like gray specters against the stark, blue, equatorial sky—that a Spanish buccaneer spoke of three centuries ago. "We will never arrive there," he said, as the ship twisted in the strange sea. "They are enchanted islands, mere shadows and not real islands." Later Charles Darwin himself, when he arrived there aboard the H.M.S. *Beagle* in 1853, said (ingrate!) of the isles that were to ensure his place in history that they were "what we might imagine the cultivated parts of the infernal regions to be."

Why, when I finally was able to go to the Galapagos in 1970, when they first opened up to two small ships, was I so enchanted

294

with these islands? Well, it was simple, I suppose—they represented to me the very inner mystery of the species, the most basic saga of how human life develops.

The animals were still unspoiled. Since most had never known "man," they did not fear him. They lived in a general harmony together because there were so few predators and because they had over the centuries implicitly divided up the feeding grounds. It was a strange, lost world, but one of a unique balance among creatures.

Fear: there was virtually no fear on the part of the animals. I felt a sense of awe . . . and bewitchment. Baby sea lions, totally unafraid of the "man" they have never known, swam playfully with you in the shining sea, while their grandmothers rode the waves in like surfers. Prehistoric black and red iguanas curled langourously up in the sun on the lava rock while the ancient turtles, which disappeared elsewhere in the world seventy thousand years ago, lumbered so slowly they seemed aching with historic exhaustion. Isolated for more than a million years from the great continents, the Galapagos became a safe harbor for the reptilian animals of prehistoric times. In this glorious isolation—and here alone—they were preserved from the evolved mammals that would have destroyed them on the great land masses.

Then one day on the lava rocks of James Island I was taught a most dramatic lesson. Everywhere the animals were friendly. But here when we approached a group of furred sea lions on the rocks, they suddenly fled in terror. I was bereft. What was wrong?

Later I asked the scientist why this had happened. He paused, as if he did not want to answer. "You may not believe this," he said slowly, "but this is the only island where the animals were hunted."

I stared at him. "You don't mean . . ." I started. Then, "When?"

"Two hundred years ago."

Now I truly gaped. "You are not trying to tell me that they have passed that knowledge down within them through the centuries. . . ."

He nodded. "Yes," he said, "I am."

*   *   *

So it was that seeing this world developing around me from Guatemala to Iran—a world of guerrilla warfare, and pathological warfare, and leaders like Khomeini who lived in a world much like the eerie but very real world of the Galapagos—I immediately began to seek out the small but fascinating coterie of people around the country, mostly psychiatrists with a political sense, who could interpret these things for me on the deeper level the times called for.

There was Dr. Steve Pieczenik, the leading terrorist negotiator at the State Department, who looked at countries and societies in much the same way as one might look at human beings. When Congressman Leo Ryan was going to Jonestown, for instance, Pieczenik advised him not to go. Why? Because Jonestown was a paranoid society. Just as individuals can be paranoid, so can societies or cults be paranoid.

When you start thinking in this way, you could see that the Carter administration had piled mistake upon mistake in dealing with Iran: giving up its long-formed terrorist policy of not negotiating or paying blackmail, trying to woo the American hostages' captors, negotiation from a point of apparent weakness. Certain psychoanalysts saw just what was happening. One of my columns, on a top-level psychohistory conference sponsored by my late friend and mentor, the analyst Heinz Kohut, showed the direction of this thinking:

PSYCHOANALYSTS PROBE THE "MESSIANIC" POWER OF LEADERS LIKE KHOMEINI AND QADDAFI

CHICAGO—"How do you deal with an Ayatollah Khomeini in the future?" is beginning to be asked—with deadly seriousness—in many quarters. And at a watershed conference, on "Psychohistory—the Meaning of Leadership," here, the answers amazingly all turned out the same. . . .

At the meeting at Michael Reese Hospital here, the first conference where so many analysts and historians met in such seriousness and felicity, the Khomeini question kept rising.

Dr. Heinz Kohut, the psychiatrist of the Chicago Institute for Psychoanalysis, who many feel is the preeminent man in his field today, said of the Iranian situation, "Through the hostages, Khomeini is trying to prove to his people that he can win against the Great Powers . . . but without bloodshed."

Then he spoke of the Iranian people "making an enormous change from their old selves to their reshuffled selves." The West imposed "a new self that they did not feel was really their self instead of letting them gradually absorb the changes."

And still another thought which came up regarding the extremist leaders so seemingly prevalent in the world (not only Khomeini but Libya's Qaddafi, for instance): "Each group lets the extremists within it take over when in crisis situations because it feels that they best express the past and sense of the group. During the crisis, the doves, who rule much better in non-crisis situations, represent only a weak commitment to the group self."

But the conference—and more, the times—dictate deeper questions. The psychoanalysts may come to an agreement on how to deal with such "messianic" leaders (or, leaders who in effect think they are God), but how could you sell the injured country, in this case, the U.S., on doing "nothing"? How do you translate their perceptions into politics? How do you begin to imbue our political leaders and diplomats with the tools to carry this out—and the original knowledge to explain it? How do you explain it to a Ramsey Clark who has more than a few "messianic" feelings about himself?

All of these questions are difficult to apply to everyday life, and all too often the people who espouse them have couched them in such arcane terminology that they are barely understandable. They are changing, as shown here, but the other side is not.

And, finally, we must ask ourselves, what is "everyday life," these troubled days? Well, it is Khomeini and his raging mobs and Jonestown and its zombies and Cambodia and its piles of bones—events so earthshaking that we simply must come to an understanding of the real explanations for them.

There is a new breed in the psychohistory area—not the old half-baked charlatans who used to use the name—and they are developing their disciplines side by side. We need them: in training our diplomatic corps, inserting their knowledge into policy, in alerting our politicians in this new-old world.

The problem is that, when the dust does settle over Iran, our thought will doubtless be directed, again, to the fruitless question of, "Who was guilty?" Rather, we might save ourselves the next time by asking, not in its political sense, but in its deepest sense, "Why?"

If our policy had been thinking along these lines earlier—and I mean thinking about the intrinsic problems of countries instead of thinking in terms of our ideological preference of the moment—we would have come out far, far better in virtually every part of the world. Take, since it has so come to bedevil us, Central America, where for me it really all started.

Almost two generations after my trip to the mountains with the Guatemalan guerrillas, the entire isthmus was in flames. In Guatemala my guerrilla "friends" had come back in force and were even doing something quite extraordinary: organizing and inspiring the historically passive Indians to take part. El Salvador was in one of the most bitter civil wars of all times, with thirty thousand dead in only two years of fighting. Nicaragua had been all but taken over by the hard-line Marxist wing of the Sandinistas who fought against the dictator Anastasio "Tachito" Somoza. And all of this could have been and should have been avoided had the United States only analyzed these societies, right on our borders, the way we journalists analyzed them at best: with respect for their intrinsic political and psychological needs.

As it happened, I returned to Nicaragua the week after the Sandinista *triunfo* or triumph in August of 1979, and it was one of those most fascinating of times: when the curtain opens and you see the change actually taking place before your eyes.

I had known Somoza and had interviewed him last only a year and a half before his disgraceful exit from the country he had plundered for decades and then bombed to dust in the last desperate months. He was a recycled dictator then, sixty pounds lighter, hair and mustache mysteriously darker, talking tough. He also did not go out of his famous "bunker," which was just that, a bunker in the National Guard camp downtown. When he spoke, it was from behind

298

a bulletproof glass enclosure. "It's gone, the control," I wrote, "it's gone, the mystique that the Somozas cannot afford to lose. He is a leader imprisoned by his own people."

There was one amusing moment during the interview, in which he excoriated the United States for allowing communism to come to the country he had raped for years. We had just begun talking when he looked at me with an odd focus and then said, "Wait a minute, didn't you write a book on Latin America?"

I said I had, and I almost prepared to back toward the door, for I had certainly not been kind to him in *The New Latins.*

"You got me into a lot of trouble," said this man who was half American cowboy and half brutish banana republic dictator. He shook his head, then went on, "You said I had a mistress and my wife read it there. She had quite a fit."

"Well, *Señor Presidente,*" I said, with deliberate irony, "she must have been the only person in Managua who didn't know it."

He looked up brightly. "She was," he replied.

When I went back just after the Sandinista takeover, I was willing to give the new forces the benefit of the doubt, despite the prevalence of hard-core Marxists in the top command. Part of the reason for this was that I had been so harsh on Marxist Cuba over the years that I wanted to be especially fair, trying to believe there could indeed be a "new" kind of revolution here. In retrospect, I was too fair, but that is the question of another of those balances that we journalists have constantly to arrive at within ourselves—and the only thing finally to draw on is our own ethics and our own skeptical intellect.

Anyway, one evening I was returning from the pool about 10:00 P.M. and walking, very wet indeed, through the lobby, when I saw the hardest of the hard line, Tomas Borge, in a clutch with Latin American diplomats. Borge was the powerful minister of the interior, a small gnomelike man who had suffered unspeakably under Somoza and become a total Marxist, so I was fascinated by the chance to listen.

As I stood there dripping, unnoticed by the group, Borge actually outlined their entire plans for Latin America. "The fewer problems we have, the more Latin America will be attracted to us," he was saying in a low, conspiratorial voice. "The more problems we have, the less." He went on to say that the Nicaraguan revolution would be less sanguinary in its aftermath than the Cuban, when Castro executed eight thousand men in one day, but he made it clear that this was only tactical. "Me," he said, "I would shoot the Somozistas. But we won't because we do not want to turn the rest of the Latin American revolution against us."

One day I got Comandante Daniel Ortega, later to become the first president of the regime, out of Somoza's old "bunker," which the Sandinistas now inherited. A slim, dark-haired man with a sort of perpetual pained expression and deep-set eyes that gave him a kind of cocker spaniel look, Ortega emphasized over and over the *compromiso* or agreement that the Sandinistas had with all the forces of the country, for the simple reason that it was all the forces of the country that drove out Somoza. "This revolution has a *compromiso* with the entire country," he told me that day, as we sat at a table in the lobby of the Intercontinental Hotel. "That is about the national reconstruction and we're going to comply with it. The most radical measures already have been taken—agrarian reform, nationalization of the banks, takeover of the Somoza properties, and the evolution of the National Guard."

"The final power?" I asked.

"The final power lies in the participation of all the forces," he insisted.

By the time I had returned in the winter of 1982, that *compromiso* was basically finished. The hard line was the hard line, and it had taken over the ruling directorate, even against the warnings of Fidel Castro not to go his way because of the economic consequences. I arrived at the Managua airport as a bomb went off, destroying much of the central part of the airport and bringing me as close to death as I had come, bar Vietnam, Beirut, and Guatemala.

Yet I was never without hope. The world had come to a point where I could, after all my searchings, see clearly two major developments: (1) Marxism, which I had studied and suffered over firsthand, had worked nowhere, and (2) democracy was the only workable system, and never had it been more attractive to the peoples of the world. And this despite our often woeful policies!

Moreover, Marxism, it was now utterly clear to me, was simply another way of oppressing man: but totally, in the soul as well as over the body. Its mind-controlling elements, which had fascinated and confused and frightened me in the beginning, I could now see as part of a history that stemmed from ancient Persia to the trances of Khomeini's Iran today . . . and continued later in the hysteria of an Argentina over the Falkland Islands. On the other hand, I had come to see that the democracy and democratic ideals I had always loved were more than just a system, more than just a balance of passions and forces; they were in themselves an ideology, for the basic compromise inherent in democracy was at heart an abiding respect for the uniqueness and for the individuality of our fellow man.

People were always asking me why, after having seen so many horrible things, most of us foreign correspondents did not become hardened, or deeply depressed, or even suicidal, and I think there are psychological explanations for that too. Like fear, depression usually comes out of alienation, out of a feeling of being out of control of things. The correspondent, even while often seeing horrendous things, is seeing them for what they are; they are not abstract, and thus not so frightening (something that argues for as direct an experience as possible, on every level of life). Moreover, we also saw such wonderful things. . . .

Out of my "little countries" had arisen tragedy but also true saintliness, things that stay forever locked in my soul. Probably the single man I most admired—and was privileged to know, if briefly—was the great Archbishop Oscar Romero of El Salvador. Here was this simple man of Indian descent plunged into the archbishopric. Nonconfrontational before, once in power he spoke with simple magnificence of the sufferings and needs of his people.

When I interviewed him that same Sandinista summer of 1979,

I felt for the only time that I was truly in the presence of a great human being. He was a beautiful man. His skin, which came from his Indian ancestors, was a rich cocoa brown and, in his white priest's robes, he was a figure of eloquent colors. A radiance seemed to flow from him as though he were infected with so much good that his body could not hold it all.

At the end of the interview, which came just six months before he was assassinated—as he said mass in his chapel—by rightist gunmen of the same sort that had tried to kill me in Guatemala, I asked him, "Your Eminence, wouldn't it have been easier to have taken another road?"

He smiled that radiant smile, pausing and speaking slowly. "Perhaps it would have been easier not to have mixed myself in politics," he answered. "I could have just stayed quietly in the archbishop's palace." Then he smiled that radiant smile again. "But that would not have been very easy either, would it? I did what my conscience asked." He paused. "I feel a great freedom," he said finally.

What was so special about Archbishop Romero—truly one of the three or four most impressive men I have ever met—was that his anger sprung from no ideology. He was a simple priest. He just couldn't bear killings and injustice. It wasn't a self-conscious or even conscious thing; it was a response as normal and uncomplicated in some people as hunger or thirst—or the need for God. That was why "it would not have been very easy" for him to take any other road.

That's a funny thing—it never is.

XVI.

Buying the Night Flight

"There is no buying the night flight, with its hundred thousand stars, its serenity and its moment of sovereignty."
—ANTOINE DE SAINT-EXUPÉRY

It was late November of 1980, a gloomily dark Friday afternoon, and I was standing in a melancholy mood looking out at the sparkling lights of downtown Chicago. John Fischetti, the magnificent political cartoonist, the big, glowing man with the big, booming voice, was gone. John had been a power in all of our lives with his wanton generosity and boundless spirits; he was one of those rare human beings on whom all the others lean for protection and for renewal. Another of the great "band of brothers" of the *Chicago Daily News* was gone. Life was passing, too rapidly.

One of the speakers at John's simple but impressive service at the Fourth Presbyterian Church praised John's "childlike" nature, how he was able to see things anew every day and, despite everything, never lose his great sustaining human power. It was so true. Like all the really great journalists, he was not childish but he was childlike, which only meant that he kept the ability always to see things new, and to respond with genuineness and spontaneity.

Watching the glimmering, blinking lights of my city that afternoon—lights that go on again and again, regardless of which one of us passes into human darkness—I felt wave after wave of intense emotion. Then I began to think, as John would have wanted me to,

303

of what I was just about to do. There swept over me the strangest mixture of feelings of inner excitement, and fear, and satisfaction too, for the next day I was going to Iraq—I was going to Baghdad to try to get the first firsthand story of why they had started the war with the Ayatollah Khomeini's diabolical Iran. And the stakes were higher than any I have previously rolled for.

There had been enough madness the last year for any civilization to absorb—American hostages held by chanting, maddened mobs in Teheran; the Arab world in ferment with desert-haunted tribesmen under a "messiah" holding the great mosque at Mecca; threat after threat of the oil flow stopping underneath our eyes—and now there was more: Khomeini was sending Shi'ite agents across the Arab borders from Persia, just as the early Moslems had sent their legions across North Africa, into Spain, and to their final, fateful battle at Tours. Borders would fall (that was his mad and destructive dream) and regimes would perish under the religious dream of spiritual and political conquest driven by a half-sane old man sitting cross-legged and scowling in Qum. And the West was faced with dual fears of ancient holy wars destroying the already fragile borders and of the oil supplies already burning from Abadan to Kirkuk.

Under the harsh Arab Ba'athist government of President Saddam Hussein, Iraq had then attacked, not in religious hordes but in harsh military formation, across the Iraqi-Iranian borders. I was going into the heart of modern political darkness.

The questions to which I wanted answers were as clear as their answers were then obscure: Why had the Iraqis started the war? What did they hope to gain? Would they take the Iranian oil fields? Did they want to destroy Khomeini? The western industrialized world? What, now, did this leftist government, until now virtually allied with the Soviet Union, want from the United States? Was there any change in its always bitterly hard-line position on the Arab-Israeli conflict?

The answers to these questions were critical to the United States —and yet, having no direct diplomatic representation in Baghdad, we had no answers. Once again we journalists—now also become the new "diplomats"—were the ones who stepped in.

This time, however, I was not going blind or on chance, the way I used to go, hoping for luck or fortune or rain. Now I had prepared the situation as carefully as a Chinese cook prepares the Szechuan duck, or a Russian cook the fine pelmeny. I had woven a fine web, using and calling upon every contact and pressure that I could bring to bear to influence the Iraqi leadership to talk to me. (Men in the field, incidentally, use the word *grid* where I used *web*, an interesting male-female distinction.)

Looking out over the city that evening, I felt an odd sense of destiny. How many years ago had I been only, as Mike Royko and the people I knew put it, just a "goofy kid" dreaming improbable dreams? Yet now everything I had ever dreamed of had been more than fulfilled. And in a very real sense everything I had ever done seemed to lead directly to this assignment.

First, once I got the idea, I had contacted an American of Lebanese birth who knew the Iraqis well. He contacted them, explaining my plan. The fact that I had been the first Westerner to interview the Iraqi strongman, Saddam Hussein, in 1973 was an extremely helpful card. Next I called the Jordanians. Since they were strongly backing the Iraqis in the war, I asked if they could put in good words for me with the Iraqis; they would. Last I contacted a prominent Palestinian of Christian birth and asked him to intercede with his good friend, Tareq Aziz, the Christian thinker who was the spokesman for the regime and close to Saddam.

All the years of experience, all the lines I had thrown out over the years, the nights I had pored over history books, the friends I had made—suddenly all of it was pulling together. Abadan was then blazing, sending the industrialized world into spasms. Much of the future, East and West, could rightly be said to depend upon the outcome of this war.

Had the romantic "little girl" from the South Side of Chicago finally grown up? Well, let's not carry things too far.

*   *   *

The plane landing in Jordan carried me again to a friendly world I knew well. But now it was only a dropping-off spot. I was moving on as quickly as possible to the hostile world of Baghdad.

But the first night in the Intercontinental Hotel in Amman, where I had stayed so many times, I immediately ran into my "pals" in the hotel and we began to indulge in our usual crazy exchange of ideas.

Could we really be considered "serious" people? One advanced very soberly the knowledge that you could always get a seat alone, with space to stretch out and sleep, on Air India in the following hallowed manner: You choose the smoking area, naturally, to avoid the families with children. Then you ask for the second seat in one of the four-seat rows in the center. This means that very probably no one else will come and it's all yours, particularly on weekdays. Good sound advice for people for whom a great deal of one's time is involved in getting around the world with as little hassle as possible.

That night, for some reason, I also realized in what a very special way this life freed me. Even at forty-five, when one should have long ago exorcised one's demons, the restraints for me fell away when I got overseas. It wasn't that I acted differently, it was that I felt differently about my actions.

Hesitations, shyness, guilt—all fell away like a snake's skin in molting season. Suddenly I had been doing this so long and so concertedly that I had come to the precious point where I simply *knew* things. And yet the work was only the more exciting for being effortless. No longer did I consciously have to think about every single element of every single case. Now certain things were simply given; they fell into place naturally. There was no shortcut about it because it was only the years of experience that made it happen.

That night we stood around the bar, and Youssef Ibrahim of *The New York Times* and Bill Claiborne of *The Washington Post* and I pondered aloud our odd profession. "What could be better," Youssef asked, "than to work all day in some fascinating country at

306

some world event nobody else sees, to have access to everyone and then, in the evening, to sit around with your friends and be further amused."

We left for Baghdad by old and dirty taxi one day later, traveling down from the hills around Amman to the long, 750-mile gray, rocky "desert"—a very poor man's desert when one compares it to the glorious reds and purples of Jordan's Wadi Rum or Egypt's delicate sands by the Nile—and the trip was long and always the same.

While traveling with Bill and Youssef, two remarkably fine companions, I noticed some of the subtle changes in the correspondent nowadays. First of all, Bill soon brought out his "ears," the two electronic earphones that allowed him to listen, privately, to rock and roll all the way to Baghdad. Youssef kept the "ears" on while punching the telex. It was a way of shutting out the unpleasant parts and living your own life, even in the midst of all of this.

Such great early explorers and writers as the wonderful Englishwoman, Freya Stark, had taken this road. In 1937 she opened her book *Baghdad Sketches* with the line: "In a very short time a railway will link Baghdad with Europe." So much for predictions.

When we finally hit the Jordanian-Iraqi border, it was dark and cold. Winds howled now across the great plain here that separated antiquity's old land of Mesopotamia, to which we were going, from King Hussein's modern, rational kingdom. Egyptian-born Youssef strolled out of the immigration shacks shaking his head. "They want to keep our typewriters," he said. Then, dryly, "I told them we were journalists, and they said they had never seen journalists with typewriters before."

He got us through, forbidden typewriters and all, but it was another reminder to me of the closed and suspicious part of this world. In Iraq, as in many other countries, typewriters must be licensed and registered; they are looked upon as propaganda devices and are thus dangerous. Later, when I told a Jordanian minister, with some irony, about our scene at the border, he narrowed his eyes and said with sad mischief, "The Iraqi was probably telling the truth. In their country they probably never *had* seen a journalist with a type-writer before."

Baghdad. Legendary, shabby, magnificent, cruel. One day it was the Empty Quarter swirling with dust in a windstorm; the next its mosques' gold and blue domes glimmering in the sun. A world so ruthless that its symbol has been men hanging in the square: in Nebuchadnezzar's time the king banqueted while his enemies' bodies swung silently in the wind in the corners of the vast and pagan banquet halls.

I liked Iraq, but I knew it for what it was. Yet, I immensely preferred it to Iran; the Iraqis might stab you in the back, but they won't tell you you made them do it. Also there was little problem with writing about them. You could say they were ruthless, killers, assassins, and they didn't really mind because basically people know what they are. Here, as elsewhere, they didn't like the gratuitous insult, like, for some reason, being called "secretive."

But I was thankful I was not Iraqi. One night a Kurd told me how he had been in jail and tortured for three years. He had not been at all involved in politics. "All that, missy," he cried out to me, "all that . . . just to stay honest." That was the bitter world of Iraq.

Our first call was to the Ministry of Information, an organization formed for the express purpose of keeping journalists from other countries from making any contact whatsoever with Iraqi officials or people. My interview with Tareq Aziz? Oh, yes, of course, they knew about it. And day after day after day, nothing got done.

Several of us made the rounds of the embassies to talk to the diplomats. In closed societies the foreign diplomats are always the major "other" source of information, as skimpy and spare as that sometimes is. Actually they could give us interpretation but precious little actual information because Iraqis are forbidden even to mix or to visit the homes of foreigners.

Meanwhile the hotel had taken on the contours of a world in itself. Most of the scores of journalists were stationed there for weeks in order to cover the war. Usually they could not leave the hotel until the ministry arranged some vague and rare trip to the front. One could easily get cabin fever . . . or go a little crazy.

But the very first morning there I was amazed—and initially delighted!—to find all the others up early, bustling about as though covering the war itself. At first I thought, "How industrious they are!" Instead what they were doing was typical of the spirit and ingenuity of the correspondent corps. They were making a movie! About themselves! They wrote the script and organized the hotel staff to take part and they spent intensely busy days filming it with their video cameras.

The script was about a young reporter from the *Kalamazoo Gazette* who wanders, green as the young spring grass, into "legendary, ancient Baghdad." The screen pans first from the Lebanese "fixer," one of that world of Levantine procurers of anything and everything anyone might need in this world or the next, as he counts his money in the lobby, to the disco (which the hotel opened for the journalists' film), to the photographer Eddie Adams in an Arab headdress playing a slimy minister of information (a little scene they kept secret from the ministry).

In the end everyone has left. One of the best and unrehearsed moments was when one of the little Iraqi cuties at the front desk says spontaneously to the young reporter: "All the journalists is gone. So sorry." Our film ends with Mr. *Kalamazoo Gazette* having become "the fixer." The last shot has him, his eyes now having taken on that slitted, special Levantine glint, sitting in the lobby counting his money and watching for the next green gringo to arrive.

What struck me again, watching this, was the wonderful égalité of the foreign correspondent corps. There is no other profession with so many able to go across often forbidden borders in such a privileged and yet equal way. Among us there were only a few rules for acceptance, but they were certain. You had to be honest; you never undercut a friend; and you paid your part of the drinks. Particularly either of these last—not helping a colleague and not paying your part —would get you ostracized forever. They are not really a bad set of rules for life, when you think about it.

In the isolation our little group was making up its own games, like children caught indoors during an interminable summer squall. While we waited for the Big Guys, we were penetrating the society from our position of isolation, strength, and weakness. Yet without us, without this crazy little band of brothers and sisters, the world would be without its couriers, not carrying Saint-Exupéry's mail but conveying messages through the night that at best allowed people to know one another.

I had pretty much gotten over the old questioning, like why did I need all of this? The terrible intensity, the scattered loves, the fever, the dark and isolated nights, the gray sky, the great desert around you, the skeletal new Sheratons and Intercontinentals so incongruous with the war a few miles away, the palm trees blowing, the ominous sounds, the chicken-in-the-basket every night for dinner—they now spoke for themselves, or didn't.

I have a Uruguayan print by an artist named Ojeda of which I am inordinately fond. It is called *Homage to the Poet,* and it has a stylized little man leaping squarely toward a radiant orange sun, carrying inside himself his houses, all his needs. In his hand is a single flower for the sun, on which his eyes are firmly fixed, and above him the word *Libre,* or *Free.* That was very much my life.

Baghdad—and in particular one of that splendid race of men who were Lebanese drivers, Tony—reminded me of this. Tony, a graying and sweet man, invited me up to his room one night for a drink. And there, in him, was the little man of my print. Tony carried his world with him. He had enough pills for anyone in the entire press corps that ever got sick. He had marijuana cigarettes, flashlights for everyone, Lebanese bread sufficient for his stay there, an oven to warm it in, liquor. . . .

When the afternoons drew down late upon us, suddenly, however, the hotel became quieter. The winter sun began to go down at four thirty, and a long night awaited us. There were constant blackouts (because the Persians struck a power plant in Basra, because Kirkuk had been sabotaged, because always of vague and unsubstantiable rumors as untraceable as the wind). Often we sat with candles in the bar and in the restaurant, and often we walked up the darkened stairs with candles to our sixth-floor rooms. And we repeated *Newsweek's* Nick Proffitt's typical correspondent's crack: "The final indignity is that there is no final indignity."

But the fact was that the days were passing too quickly. And I was not getting my interview. In fact I was not getting any interviews, which is precisely what the Ministry of Information was working night and day to assure. I, meanwhile, was growing more and more anxious. How would it look if I had to leave without anything? Fifteen years later it was the Guatemalan syndrome all over again. To make it worse, I had left the Los Angeles Times Syndicate and gone with Universal Press Syndicate. It was a dream. I loved the new people and I was now in *The Washington Star*, something I had always dreamed of. Why, in God's name, had I made my first assignment with them such a virtually impossible one? It would all make one despondent, if one were a normal human being.

It had been twelve days. Now my time was really running out. Every day Selim, my contact at the ministry, assured me they were in contact with Tareq Aziz—and every day there was "no answer" or "no answer yet, but surely tomorrow." It was a Thursday, and we were even thinking of leaving Friday for Amman. I hated to give up. So I decided to take things into my own hands.

All along I had thought that as a last resort I would simply get a cab and try to go to the Revolutionary Command Council, where Tareq Aziz's office was, and at least try to get a note to him. But that was a long, long shot. The RCC was guarded like the Kremlin. Virtually nobody there, I knew, spoke English. Any foreigner even approaching might well be arrested or even shot. Yet I had to try *something* before leaving. Then one of the diplomats suggested I try phoning—and somehow he dug up the top-secret number of the RCC. If appearing on the doorstep of the RCC seemed like a one-hundred-to-one shot, this seemed like a thousand-to-one shot.

I dialed. A man answered in Arabic. I just kept repeating, "Tareq Aziz, Tareq Aziz, Tareq Aziz," over and over and over. Different

311

men speaking in Arabic in different voices kept coming on the line. Then suddenly something utterly astonishing happened. A man speaking perfect British English was there on the line saying, "May I do something for you?"

"I am Georgie Anne Geyer, the columnist from Washington from *The Washington Star*," I was saying, my voice indignant. "And I want to speak to Tareq Aziz."

"This is Mr. Fawaz," the nice voice responded. "I am Tareq Aziz's assistant. We have been expecting you. Did you just arrive?"

"I've been here two weeks," I said indignantly. "Waiting. And I have to leave very, very soon." I wanted to say: "I can't wait forever," but with difficulty restrained myself.

"Oh, my," he was saying. "We did not know you were here. But let me talk to Tareq Aziz and call you back."

To my further amazement, in half an hour I was leaving the hotel when I heard the girl at the front desk speaking my name. It was a call from Mr. Fawaz, saying that Tareq Aziz would be happy to see me, but on the third day hence. I said I would stay.

It was six thirty Sunday night. What had now become every day's blackout was fully upon us. The mysterious city along the sprawling Tigris, a bloated gray elephant of a river, in this strange darkness became frightening indeed. The military man, grim as are so many Iraqis, marched across the lobby. He was taking me to see Tareq Aziz, and everybody knew it. The Egyptian bellboys, "foreign workers" uprooted from their poor homeland to find work in a faraway and alien place like so many in this part of the world, were delighted. They all smiled knowingly at me. And I had the strangest feeling at that moment. I felt, in a very real sense, that I was doing it for them —that I had in effect broken through, in this and other closed and harsh societies, for those good and decent and uprooted and sad people.

I could not see the Revolutionary Command Council buildings— certainly one of the world's most mysterious and closed places—but in the darkness we passed through several guard posts and soon I was being rapidly ushered into simple modern buildings. Within mo-

312

ments, for now I had entered the inner sanctums of Ba'athist efficiency, I was sitting in a commodious armchair in an office sprinkled with silver trays and decorative pieces across from Tareq Aziz, one of the hardest men in the world to see.

He was a small man, of lean build with cold dark eyes that bespoke systematic thinking and a world in which the strong survive and the weak die very young. His dark, curly hair was flecked with gray and his pin-striped suit was perfectly tailored. He turned out to have a good sense of humor, but even when he laughed at what he said— or intimated—it was a very cautious laugh. Even laughing at yourself in Baghdad could be dangerous.

One Iraqi journalist, whose feelings can be easily ascertained, called him the Goebbels of the regime. Maybe. As a Christian in this land of Moslems and Armenians and Kurds and Zoroastrians and power-worshipers in general, Aziz had overcome everything with his systematic mind and finely tuned intelligence. And there was something else: no Christian could threaten Saddam Hussein in this Moslem sea. So Aziz was not only smart, he was safe.

"You must remember," Aziz started out, unsmiling, "that our grandfathers died on horseback." And then he proceeded to tell, for the first time, the entire Iraqi story of the world's newest and most dangerous war—one not over horses and conquest but over the oil that fuels the industrialized world and over missiles and atom plants. A long way from Guatemala and the simplicity of that sierra.

Why had they started the war? For one reason only, he said. Because Khomeini was trying to put the entire region in flames, to destroy the borders and reignite the struggles of the sixth and seventh centuries, when Islam swept from Arabia to Spain.

"They must have sent a lot of agents," I volunteered at one point.

"The Iranians sent hundreds of religious agents," Aziz said, in what must be one of the greatest quotes it has been my pleasure to hear, "most were hanged. Iraq is a very well-organized society."

I wanted to know exactly how the decision to go to war came. And he told me: "We had this meeting, I remember, and we received news that they intended to close our airspace over Iranian territory and the passages to the Shatt-al-Arab. We analyzed that that was a step toward war. They were shelling our ships. That meant they wanted to close our waterways. Later we also found out that they had transferred their transportation planes to Pakistan. This meant they were preparing an air strike. By September, with all the news before our leadership, the analysis was that the Iranians were preparing for war."

And what about the Russian support—or, more important, non-support—of the Iraqi war? This was utterly crucial to the entire Middle East equation because Iraq had long been *the* Soviet "friend" in the Middle East, and this had affected everything in the region from the Arab-Israeli conflict to the oil question. What he answered was staggering in its implications:

"I made two visits to Moscow in the last two months," he told me. "In these two visits the Soviets stressed their care for and relations with Iraq. They said that their friendship had not changed, but that while Iraq is a friendly country, Iran is a neighboring one. They did not want to spoil relations with Iran. They wanted the war to stop as soon as possible. They have stopped giving us arms. They are very strict on that point. We understand the situation."

"But," I persisted, "they must have given you what was in the pipeline?"

Aziz shook his head soberly and deliberately. "They stopped completely. They have given us nothing . . . nothing . . . nothing."

Was it possible that Iraq, the "best friend" of the Soviets, was breaking with them? The next words confirmed that they were, for they constituted an obvious opener to Washington.

"The major reason for our nonrelations remains the Arab-Israeli conflict," he said. "We do not ask the U.S. not to take sides. We are a realistic people. We only ask for a balanced attitude. Consider the French. They have strong relations with the Israelis. They have even built up their military apparatus. They care about the security of Israel, but they do not support the invasion by Israel. The U.S. is still patronizing Israel—and all of its policies. Americans are not only supporting Israel, they are guarding the Israeli invasion politically, economically, and militarily—and that is an anti-Arab attitude.

"What we'd like to see is for the American attitude to get closer to a balanced attitude toward the conflict. Then Iraq would not have objections toward resuming diplomatic relations. We are not permanent enemies of the United States."

The surprises did not end there. He then went on to say that while they still took a hard position on Israel, they would "accept what our Arab brothers wanted." In effect they would accept a separate Palestinian state, which is what King Hussein and even Yasser Arafat had told me and some others.

He went on. For years the Iraqis had been the most brutal of the brutal, the assassins of the assassins. They had sent assassination squads out all over Europe, killing anyone who tried to escape, murdering the moderate Palestinian leaders. But in the last year that had stopped. They had also stopped supporting radical Palestinians, like George Habbash's Popular Front for the Liberation of Palestine.

"After 1973," he told me, "Iraq was active in the rejection front [i.e., the radical Palestinian groups]. They were radical but nationalist. Because of ideological weakness of the leadership, many of these groups lost their ideology and political independence step by step. Now they are totally communist. We support only groups that are patriotic, independent, and progressive."

We went from the serious things—which could quite literally affect the future of the world—to the humorous. A slight smile played across his face when he talked, contemptuously, of the disorganization of his Iranian neighbors.

"In every spot along the border, there is a struggle on the Iranian side," he said. "It is up to the officer. If a religious man is in charge, it is total confusion. If a military man and a religious man are in charge together, the men will fit well if the religious man is in Teheran."

When I asked him whether they had indeed intended to overthrow Khomeini himself, Aziz smiled enigmatically, but with just a touch of devilishness. "You know, we had some experience in our party with trying to change regimes," he said. And then he went,

315

year by year, down the Ba'aths' coup-ridden history until it got very funny indeed, and we both were laughing heartily. He ended up with, "We now have a conviction that a regime cannot be toppled from behind frontiers. We cannot topple Khomeini . . . but maybe the war could be an assisting element."

He smiled.

Within a year and a half, of course, that formulation had rather dramatically changed. By then, the Iranians, driven by their ongoing internal frenzy, threw wave after human wave against the Iraqis, defeating them. But that was not my problem and not my business: my business was to report and capture moments of history—and that was what I had done in Iraq that strange December.

By the next night I was growing strangely disquieted. I had decided to wait until very early the next morning but, now that I had what I had come for, I simply wanted to fly away: across the poor man's desert, over the cruel border posts, and back up the friendly golden hills to Amman. At the last moment I got a young NBC Jordanian driver and we decided to leave at 10:00 P.M., even through it meant doing the whole long drive at night.

The boy, they had told me, was a good driver—and completely safe and responsible for a woman traveling alone. This, as it happened, did not turn out to be the problem. As we approached the large traffic circles outside of Baghdad, where each spoke emanating from the circles flung you into a totally different—and fixed—direction, he suddenly went kind of crazy. He swerved here and there, seemingly unable to decide where to go, or why.

Finally he was actually in the lane turning off toward Kerbala, clearly marked in both Arabic and English, when I started to scream: "No, no, no . . . !" After all this all we needed was to be in Kerbala, the closed and holy city of the Shi'ites at midnight! A Christian Western woman during a Moslem holy war! When I finally got him out of that lane and onto the right road, marked RUTBA, I suddenly realized what was the matter: the poor boy could not read. For the rest of the trip he was wonderful. And for most of it, through the bitter cold of this winter night, through the unrelieved bleakness, I slept well under a blanket, swigging an occasional drink of Scotch from the little miniatures I had purchased in preparation for the trip at the foreign money shop and watching the darkness rush by outside while thoughts of my life rushed over me in waves.

At 1:00 A.M. we swept by Rutba, a town asleep and in darkness. The streets were empty and still; the cement villas had their shades drawn down like eyes closed to a harsh world. I noticed an oddly picturesque little hotel where I thought would have been fun to have lunch.

At 2:00 A.M. we stopped at a shabby little place for coffee. I sat up and watched the young man. He was fine. Now he was in his element, and he knew exactly what he was doing. I was pleased that he was so serious.

By 3:00 A.M. we were sweeping across the great red-brown plain, with its rocks and volcanic markings, and the sky was totally black. Every minute that brought me closer to Amman made me happy. From time to time we were stopped by guards along the road, and always they had those tough, leathery, harsh faces of the Iraqi tribesmen in this endlessly harsh land. They looked long and hard at my passport and at me, but each time they let us go through.

I thought about a lot of things in those strange and prescient hours. I thought about what I had given up for this life, about the joys and comforts of the other life of home and family and predictable love. I thought about how those things weren't so predictable anymore, either. I thought, without rancor but with sadness, about how the women of my generation who had taken this other—this night—flight had had to do it all alone: without really any close support from the men we loved and without even in our souls knowing whether what we were doing was fully right for women. I thought about how, despite that, we had done what we had to do with honor and dignity. And then I thought about the other joys and rewards.

The night flight: the hundred thousand stars, the serenity, the moment of sovereignty. After my interview with Tareq Aziz and his

317

story of the war, it was as though I were holding within me a totem, a magic amulet. Only those who care about information—unique or first information—can understand this. It was a kind of protection for me. I hoarded it. I protected it. The next day I would begin giving up the thing I had discovered. But it would really be no loss, because then began the next stage, the stage of being the courier, and the pleasure of seeing the information one has gathered dispersed throughout the world.

The "night plane" was only an all-night taxi ride through a bleak part of the world? The hundred thousand stars only blackness? No. The sense of serenity and of sovereignty and of completeness was there, and Saint-Exupéry is right that there is no buying it, no matter how you try. It is something you can only earn, something you find only for yourself, create only for yourself, and ultimately interpret only for yourself. It goes only to those willing to risk their comfort and their lives and their sacred honor for it. In this, as in so many aspects, it is like a very great love—and everyone has some of the night flight inside herself.

We came, through the bitter cold of Rutba and Ramadi and all those shabby towns of desperate dreams, finally to reach the border about 4:00 A.M. An old bus, scabrous and shaky, had stopped and its poor denizens were lined up with their odd bags and old sacks tied together with rope and placed pathetically in front of them. They were freezing in the bitter cold. It was as if they had been told to put their whole lives in front of them and that was all they could find. I was reminded again that this is a brutal world for the people who must truly live in it and are not privileged voyeurs, like me.

The old Lebanese woman, whom cruel turns of fate had made a searcher of women crossing this bleak border, was asleep in her small hut as the guard took me there. The winter winds were howling now like wolves across the endless desert plain. Outside, at four o'clock in the morning, it was total darkness. When the Jordanian customs man switched on the light, the woman shot up in bed. She was old and plump, wearing the traditional Palestinian robe-upon-robe, and she was to search my purse—my symbol of being in another world

—before I crossed the border and returned to what was in effect the Western world.

Suddenly, without warning or apparent reason, her broad, brown face shriveled with pain. "Lebanon," she said to me, and it was like an animal's cry of pain. She put her hands on her ample breasts. "From Lebanon," she said. Then she imitated planes dropping bombs. "All family killed," she went on. "I . . . I now here." Her arms motioned to the bleak outside, and it looked even more like a hell.

I had tried to give the poor woman some money, but she wouldn't take it. It had just been another of those moments—and there are far, far too many of them in this part of the world—when a single human being, driven beyond any capacity to bear, suddenly cried out to all of us.

And as we sped now toward Amman, this lost lone woman seemed very much a metaphor for the Iraqi-Iranian war—and for a lot of the people I had known in my life, and what I had given my life to. For just as she was one more tragic victim of the continuing saga of borders and refugees and too many people without homes from Lebanon to Ethiopia to Somalia to the Yemens, so was this war and all my stories at heart a war and a story about borders—and about her.

Everything in my curious life seemed to flash across my mind as we sped through the night, in flight from the most dangerous and unknown parts of the world and toward the light and the known. For as morning began to come upon the winter desert, as it happened we were just then reaching the friendly, low, and golden hills that lead to Amman. We stopped for a few minutes at a funny little café for coffee. The two Jordanian men who ran it, both friendly and pleasant, nevertheless looked at me—stared, really—as if I were a creature from another planet. They were not, of course, wrong, but I believed, as I always have, that I belonged as much there as anywhere.

Then, almost as if it were an omen, we started climbing the

319

beckoning hills just as the sun began shedding its golden morning light about us. Now, in place of the cold darkness, a kind of shimmering mist lay over everything. It was like coming out of a cave into a new dawn. The night flight had ended, with its serenity and also its fears, but the moment of sovereignty somehow remained—and still remains—with me, the final mark of transcendence and human control over the mundanities and cruelties of the world.

EPILOGUE

On Becoming a Columnist

"I don't have any ideas that are more than
seven hundred words long."
—A columnist

I recall exactly the moment I decided to come home again.
It was November of 1974, and I was sitting quite squashed and
exhausted against the window in a large jet plane en route from
Dubai to Bahrein to Dhahran to Riyadh to Jedda. Two enormous
and blubbery Gulf sheikhs in their flowing white robes had jammed
themselves in the seats next to me. I was perspiring in the endless
heat and dreading the endless stops and starts ahead of me, not to
speak of arriving in the steamy Red Sea port of Jedda without a hotel
room at midnight. Then, for some reason I turned around.

There on the three seats just behind us sat three falcons. Yes,
falcons. Their razor-sharp talons were tethered to a long plank of
wood which lay squarely across the three seats, but their hoods were
off and the jet black, beady, threatening eyes all focused oddly upon
me. Their keeper, a Bedouin in long robes, stood at the edge of the
seat calling each by name: "Ahmed . . . Zakki. . . ."

I turned my head back. Perhaps it was time to give up this strange
life. After all, I had been overseas, usually traveling constantly, for
nine months of each of the previous eleven years. It had been
extraordinary—a wondrous life—but could it not be time to move
on? I had had at least one fiancé tell me (and not sweetly) that my

321

favorite three words were not "I love you," but "Room service, please." As I sat that darkening evening on the plane, crowded by sheikhs and falcons, it suddenly occurred to me that when I died it would be just "going to the last transit lounge."

Even then the words *foreign correspondent,* voiced to some stranger on a plane, still filled me with a deep sense of excitement and yearning. But little by little, as the years passed and I saw "one more war" and one more country that I had loved fall to some squalid self-righteous totalitarianism, and as eighteen-hour flights every three days and eighteen-hour days began to take their toll, I began to see the need for some sort of change.

As much as I hated to admit it, I needed a home, perhaps just a city apartment but still a home. I wasn't going as far as marriage or children, but maybe a pet. A first step. I needed an address of my own, like the Palestinians. I needed a few—not too many but a few —full nights' sleep a month. I needed to be in a place where I could come back to people I knew and had known for years: the comfort of easy congeniality as opposed to the growing strains of meeting different people every day, of charming them (at best), of offending them (at worst), of convincing them. I needed some effortlessness in life.

I would become a columnist. And it would all be easy.

After all, I had been with the *Chicago Daily News* for fifteen years and Marshall Field, the publisher, had one of the biggest syndicates in the country. I was doing a column once a week for them already, which they admitted was doing splendidly on the wire. It never really occurred to me that my own "family" would not syndicate me— which shows how very naive we can be!

When I had lunch that winter with Dick Sherry, a lanky, laconic man who was then the top salesman for the Field Syndicate, things could not have gone more wrong.

Dick coughed. He turned different colors. I took a bite of my broiled fish while looking deliberately at him.

"I don't want you to be disappointed," he began, not looking at me. It was a bad time for syndication, he said, because papers were cutting back on everything. I wasn't well enough known nationally, not a celebrity item. The world was changing and columns didn't catch on so well anymore.

"But don't give up," he said in one of those voices that drive reasonable women to kill. "All this might change in two or three years. Meanwhile, do something to get yourself *known* as a journalist —and then maybe we can syndicate you!"

I had covered everything in the world; interviewed everybody; covered every war and met every guerrilla; and after all that I was told I should do something to make myself *known?*

"What . . ." I asked with just a touch of archness, "do you suggest I doooo?"

He warmed at once, actually thinking I was looking to him for advice. "Why, I have a friend who's publisher of Avon Books in New York," he said. "You could get a book out in six or seven weeks and get yourself known."

"Are you talking about a *sex* book?" I cooed.

"Naw, naw," he said, but as he said it, he brightened noticeably. "Not exactly." The possibility hung in the air between us while I cracked my fishbones noisily.

I was learning, the hard way, that papers were changing.

On the *Daily News* we had all been part of an epic time lag where a tight-knit, loving group of seekers and reformers worked together for the good of it and for the wonderful fun of it. But now the new newspaper style had taken over from our clan of bandits and night-flyers. As Dean Reed of the Gannett papers once put it, "Somewhere along the way, it became a business." Gone were the days when Malcolm Browne of *The New York Times* could say, "This is like a priesthood." Nicholas von Hoffman, another early friend, had said, "It was when I learned the ethics of journalism that I found my place in life."

The night the *Daily News* closed in March 1978—a little more than two years after I went to the Los Angeles Times Syndicate— was a night I will never forget. Although a lot of people's hearts were breaking, the final party at the old Sheraton Hotel in Chicago somehow also had elements of a victory. People came from all over the country. It was a celebration of something great that had existed in a moment in time—and then passed on. It was heartbreaking, but it was at the same time glorious because the fact that this paper— this joyful association of individuals, this spirited commitment of all to a common cause, this gallant undertaking—*had* existed. Bill (M.W.) Newman, one of the finest of the *Daily News* writers, wrote the final story:

> The *Chicago Daily News,* the writers' newspaper, ends as it began —a momentous Book of Life. It took 102 years to finish and these are the final pages.
>
> But the story isn't over—just the *Daily News'* part of it. A newspaper dies, but newspapering goes on. Life goes on. Tomorrow is the sequel, and all the tomorrows after that.

Bill's story had in it all the special Chicago newspaper-world gallantry that we had all so loved. So did the final banner headline: SO LONG, CHICAGO. Gallant, but not maudlin. For those of us who loved that paper and those people and that life, there would never come another time, another such moment.

When I went to the Los Angeles Times Syndicate in the fall of 1975 and moved to Washington, I knew little about syndication except that talent—columnists of all sorts, cartoonists, political cartoonists, etc.—was "syndicated" by syndicates usually, but not always, attached to big newspapers or newsmagazines. The merchandising and promotional staffs of these syndicates, which were in effect one of many corporate conglomerates like Field Enterprises or the Times Mirror Company, sold you to as many papers as they could, and you produced the "product." It was and is a tough business; the only business I know that is tougher is show biz, which writing a column rather resembles. Most columnists get a simple fifty-fifty cut on the amount taken in by the column. Since rates vary according to the circulation of the papers, a paper can get you for anything from five dollars a week to three hundred dollars. Then it gets still further confused because some large papers insist upon territorial rights, thus effectively acing out the smaller papers in the area.

I was lucky. I got an excellent five-year contract that provided the most unusual security of a guaranteed salary and even an expense account, which seems a lot until you take one six-week trip to the Middle East and see what you have left. I was an "independent contractor." I made all the decisions and decided what to write about and when, at least so long as the column was "working," which meant selling. I also had to figure out how to get columns into Los Angeles, to be sent out to the clients. When I was in Washington, this was easy; I just took them into the Times bureau and they went by Rapifax machine, which relayed one page every thirty seconds. When I was traveling about the country, I dictated into the Times's dictating machines by telephone. And when I was overseas, I had to plan to be somewhere close to a Reuter's News Agency office— or else file ahead. The wildest times were the last weeks before going overseas. I had to make all my own arrangements, make all the arrangements for interviews (either through the embassies in Washington or through my own contacts, now a network everywhere in the world). Then I usually had to file three columns ahead to protect me the first week, when I was often in some Reuter-less country. When I got on the plane, I collapsed happily—either it was done or it was not, but there was little else I could now do.

It would *seem* to be a profession without any controls. All that freedom! But that wasn't really true. The controls, in actuality, were awesome, both professionally and psychologically. Every editor on every paper that buys you has the control of life and death over you every day. Every reader's letter influences them. All you need to do is make one mistake—or give one really far-out interpretation—and you're finished. No, the controls were there, the classic controls of the free market, not to speak of your own inner moral and ethical controls, which must be fearsome.

I was not happy with the quality of the column the first six months. First of all I persisted in remaining a reporter: I ran around ceaselessly trying to "cover" things, only to find to my frustration that very little of what I got out of "covering" things actually was of much use to me in the column. Columns demand thought, meditation, judgment, original investigation: not so much running around.

Second, I began to realize how deeply difficult it was for me to reveal myself, which I had contracted to do for five years, three times a week, seven hundred words. It is one of those many paradoxes of life that there I was, a very private person who finds it painful to hurt anyone's feelings (particularly to do with beliefs) placed precisely in that position of hurting other people's feelings three times a week . . . in seven hundred words . . . for five years.

I was jumping from being a correspondent, where, after all, I basically did analysis and basic reporting, to being a columnist, where I did commentary and opinion: from objectivity to the strongest subjectivity. I felt at first almost a physical revulsion at making judgments on things. I felt I was being untrue to my journalist's calling and oaths; I felt a little intellectual-whorish. I suffered endlessly over hurting people. I had all sorts of metaphysical agonies. Clearly I was born to be a columnist!

And then there was something else: We all think we have well-thought-out opinions on everything. Well, let me tell you, when you are called upon actually to put down those opinions in seven hundred words, three times a week, you find that you don't. At first I was horrified that I could be found so wanting; later I became excited by the challenge.

And there was the new way of working. Now, instead of the city room at the *Daily News* or hotel rooms in strange countries, I was working at home. I turned the dining room of my Washington condominium into my office. I got two telephones, one with an answering service, so I could be on the first phone and at the same time take incoming calls on the second.

And I had a pet. Providentially, six weeks before I left Chicago in the summer of 1975, I went out one morning at an unusual time to mail some letters and there on the street, where I had never before ever seen a kitten, was this funny-looking white and black kitten. He was all legs and ears, with a tiny, almost mouselike white body and gnarled little head. He had rather artistic black spots down his back and the black fur on his head made him look as though he had a black toupee on. When I patted him, he purred—indeed, purring seems to be his major calling in life. The first morning he was curled up, his head on my pillow, in exactly the same curl as I. I named him Pasha, since I was and am convinced that he is a direct descendant of the Egyptian god-cats, and brought him to Washington, where he was the first cat to be allowed to stay in the cushy Fairfax Hotel. He also travels with me occasionally, usually between Washington and Chicago, where I often leave him with my brother Glen when I take lengthy trips overseas. He goes with me on the plane, of course, albeit under the seat, and he rides in a carrying case that has the stickers of elegant hotels from all over the world on it. He is a boon companion; at night, being an Egyptian god-cat with a great memory, he whispers me to sleep with stories of great caravans carrying myrrh and frankincense north from Oman and the Kingdom of Punt and of great sea battles off Alexandria. Some people do not understand that, but Borges would have all too well; he knew that people who dreamed were in truth closest to reality.

It took a while to iron out the problems of what kind of columns. At first the syndicate editor decreed, "No foreign-affairs columns—and no women." I was stunned, since that was all I had anything to say about. But soon Marian, my editor in New York, and I began slipping both in.

I got quite daring. I even wrote one on how Freud had been wrong about women and challenged the idea that any woman would want anything as unsightly as a penis. The last line particularly pleased me: "We must remain calm, and remember that there is nothing wrong with the penis. In its place."

Another time I wrote from Egypt after interviewing three women who as children had had clitoridectomies, the unspeakable operation in Africa and parts of the Middle East in which the nine-year-old

327

female's clitoris is ritually removed to "keep a woman chaste." It is quite a ceremony, in which the little girl clutches a tree while the little organ is cut out with a knife so she will never disgrace her family. Funny, but that column was never used anywhere. But I was not going to give up.

Gradually I realized the different qualities that being a correspondent or reporter, as opposed to being a columnist, called for. To oversimplify greatly, the qualities of being a reporter are accuracy, fairness, and an understanding of context. The qualities of being a foreign correspondent are accuracy, fairness, and a deep understanding of cultural differences plus a special gift in interpreting them. But the qualities of a columnist, while they stem from this, are sufficiently different to be bedeviling. They are accuracy of perception, an informed but opinionated perception, and an understanding of the effect your words can have on people and events. Once I saw the natural, though certainly not linear, progression, I was even a little overawed that I had been able to make the transition as naturally as I had.

As I came to this new work, however, the whole world of the columnist had changed drastically. Since columns began, the world of the columnist was a celebrity world. Columnists waged enormous power, papers made wars, as the New York papers did in 1898 in Cuba, and columnists were consulted by the powerful. Tempers got so short between columnists and "the powerful" that Harold Ickes called them "calumnists." Westbrook Pegler, who should have known, warned against the "deep-thinking, hair-trigger columnist or commentator who knows all the answers just off hand and can settle great affairs with absolute finality three days, or even six, days a week." And *New York Times* managing editor Turner Catledge once called them the "malignancy" of the news business.

So much for undeserved compliments.

But by the time I came to it, it was a different—a diverse and diffuse—world. Instead of a few, there were several hundred columnists, although probably only twenty-five were really of influence in the country and these mostly in the eastern papers. The all-purpose columnist, of which I was a modern version, was giving way to the highly specialized columnist—in science, in urban affairs, in lifestyle. Papers were experimenting with different ways of bringing the readership into the op-ed pages and also of bringing in individual specialists. Some insisted upon using their foreign correspondents or specialists as columnists.

Some of the effects were salubrious, because it did bring readership participation, and specialists did give depth to the pages. But something, too, was lost. The pages began to look like a hodgepodge of strangers to the regular reader. Who, after all, can pit himself and his ideas against a stranger identified only as "a housewife from Pasadena" or "a clerk from Winnetka"? As for the regular reporters doubling as columnists, to me it was disastrous. Once the reader knows, really knows, what you think about something, you are lost as a reporter. Your value is gone, your objectivity is finished. Most of the papers that were so enthusiastic about this soon gave it up.

Roy Fisher, the former editor of the *Daily News* and later dean of the Missouri School of Journalism, best characterized this sort of page as one with a "cacophony of voices that you cannot trace to their origins."

As I went along, I asked friends who are columnists what they do, and most do more or less the same. All think in seven hundred words and all laughed when I quoted my friend Deane Lord's dictum that, "Writing a column is like being married to a nymphomaniac, it's nice but . . ."

Sydney Harris, whose longevity in writing an excellent thought column is simply staggering, told me he had no system except perhaps a subconscious one. "I just write what wells up in me," he told me. He feels that the column must be consistently minimally good; that it would never be really poor. He tries to change pace from time to time because columns should not be too predictable. Remember, he told me rightly, people like personal things; they want to know about you.

329

Joseph Kraft told me that he (1) stays close to the front-page news, (2) balances his column between domestic and foreign news, and (3) only writes when he has something personal to say.

American column-writing, of course, is totally different from foreign column-writing. One day in Istanbul, Oktay Eksi, one of the great Turkish columnists, told me his style. "I go through the files, then consult with the editors." The difference—the big difference —there is that he would and could never write anything against the basic policy of the paper. In the U.S., on the contrary, columns often are taken precisely because they represent a different point of view from the editorial board.

But I must admit, in truth, that being so much on one's own— making all of one's decisions without benefit of really any institution or editor behind one—was often difficult. One felt very alone. I often recalled with wistful sentiment the old days on the *Daily News,* when we had our loving band. On the other hand, I was "free." When I remonstrated one day to a lady at one of my speeches that, yes, fine, I was "free" but I was free to work eighteen hours a day seven days a week, she said, with such truth, "Yes, but you are morally free."

On the best days—on the confident days—I reveled in that moral freedom and I reveled in my wonderful network. People called in from all over the world—and often the very damndest people. I had the Mujahadeen in Iran, the Palestinians in Beirut, Latin revolutionaries, very super-respectable people with the Jamaican government. . . . It was all quite wonderful. It was my world. I had created it and only I could pull the strings together. Most of all, I was proud that they all knew they could trust me. They could, indeed, although as a woman it had been at least three times as hard to build up that trust—that trust that so deeply coincided to both the old female morality and to public ethics.

Even as I settled into my blessed new life and even as I really began to know it, I still questioned, within myself, how I chose what to write—and how. Then one day Eric Rouleau, the fine correspondent of *Le Monde,* answered the question for me.

330

"How do you work?" he asked. (Journalists are always searching not only their own but one another's souls, for we are the world's consummate rummagers.)

When I answered, more than half apologetically, "Well, I tried planning, I made charts, I tried to balance everything and . . . well . . . I finally just decided to write on whatever I feel most strongly about that day . . ." Eric answered:

"But, of course! That is the *only* way to do it. One can only write what comes from deep inside oneself."

Index

GEORGIE ANNE GEYER

was with the *Chicago Daily News* for twelve years and is now a syndicated columnist for Universal Press Syndicate. She makes frequent television appearances on *Washington Week in Review, Meet the Press,* and *Firing Line* and is the author of several books, including *The New Latins, The New 100 Years War,* and *The Young Russians.* Georgie Anne Geyer has received many awards and honors, including the Maria Moors Cabot Award—the oldest international prize in journalism—and the Overseas Press Club Award. She grew up on the South Side of Chicago and lives in Washington with her Egyptian god-cat, Pasha, when not traveling around the world.